Identity and Ideology in the Haitian U.S. Diaspora

Identity and Ideology in the Haitian U.S. Diaspora

By

Paul C. Mocombe

Cambridge
Scholars
Publishing

Identity and Ideology in the Haitian U.S. Diaspora

By Paul C. Mocombe

This book first published 2020

Cambridge Scholars Publishing

Lady Stephenson Library, Newcastle upon Tyne, NE6 2PA, UK

British Library Cataloguing in Publication Data
A catalogue record for this book is available from the British Library

Copyright © 2020 by Paul C. Mocombe

ISBN (10): 1-5275-4571-7
ISBN (13): 978-1-5275-4571-7

This work, as with everything I pen, is done in the name of the ancestors, lwa-yo, manbo Erzulie, my grandparents (Saul and Eugenia Mocombe), my sons (Daniel and Isaiah), and my wife (Tiara Mocombe) ...

TABLE OF CONTENTS

LIST OF FIGURES

LIST OF TABLES

INTRODUCTION

This work puts forth the argument that in the Haitian Diaspora in the United States of America a new Haitian identity, "the my nigga Haitian," has emerged among Haitian youth, which is tied to the black practical consciousness of the black American underclass. The black American in the postindustrial capitalist world-system of America are no longer Africans. Instead, their practical consciousnesses are the product of two structurally determined dominant identities, the negro, i.e., black bourgeoisie, or African Americans, on the one hand, under the leadership of educated professionals and preachers; and the "my nigga," i.e., the black underclass, on the other hand, under the leadership of street and prison personalities, athletes, and entertainers vying for ideological and linguistic domination of black America. These two social class language games were historically constituted by their relations to the forces and relations of production and their different ideological apparatuses, the church and education on the one hand; and the streets, prisons, and the athletic and entertainment industries on the other, of the global capitalist racial-class structure of inequality under American hegemony, which replaced the African ideological apparatuses of Vodou, peristyles, lakous, and agricultural production as found in Haiti, for example. Among Haitian youth in the US diaspora, post-1986 following the topple of Jean-Claude "baby doc" Duvalier, the latter social class language game, black American underclass, would come to serve as the bearer of ideological and linguistic domination, forming the "my nigga Haitian" identity emerging today in the age of American postindustrial capitalism against the practical consciousnesses of the Haitian Bourgeoisie and Vodou Community.

The Constitution of Haitian Practical Consciousnesses

If the African and diasporic experience as encapsulated in slavery, colonization, abolitionism, and decolonization dialectically represents the intent of former slaves to be like their masters amidst racism, slavery, colonization, and their structural differentiation, the Africans of Haiti who met at Bois Caïman, August 14th, 1791, and other congresses to commence the Haitian Revolution attempted to do the contrary. That is, they, anti-dialectically, rejected not only their slave status, racism, and colonization, but the very practical consciousness of their former slavemasters for their own structuring structure or form of system and social integration, i.e., lakouism and the Vodou Ethic and the spirit of communism social class language game, which emerges out of their Haitian ontology and epistemology, Haitian/Vilokan idealism (Mocombe, 2016, 2017, 2018, 2019). Their discourse and discursive practices would eventually be supplanted by the practical consciousness or language game of the *Affranchis*, free (creole) blacks and mulattoes, *gens de couleur*, bourgeoisies, seeking, like their liberal bourgeois black counterparts in America and the diaspora (the black Atlantic), equality of opportunity, distribution, and recognition with their *blanc* counterparts within the capitalist world-system via the Haitian state and its ideological apparatuses. Prior to this usurpation, however, the Vodou and Kreyol ceremony or congress at Bois Caïman under the leadership of Dutty Boukman, Edaïse, Cecile Fatima, the Vodou manbo priestess, is a rejection of both slave status and European civilization, and cannot be, contrary to Susan Buck-Morss's (2009) work, *Hegel, Haiti, and Universal History*, and others, conceptualized within the framework of Hegel's master/slave dialectic, or within postmodern, post-structural, or postcolonial theories. Whereas the purposive-rationality of the two bourgeoisies, free landowning blacks and mulatto elites, can be conceptualized within a Hegelian dialectical, postmodern, post-structural, and postcolonial struggle, that of *oungan yo, manbo yo, gangan yo*, and *granmoun yo* of Bois Caiman, who would assume the leadership of the masses of the provinces and mountains, cannot. The purposive-rationality of the latter was not a structurally differentiated identity as found amongst the creole blacks and mulatto elites. Oungan yo, manbo yo, gangan yo, and granmoun yo of Bois Caiman offered an alternative structuring structure (form of system and social integration), social class language game, for organizing the material resource framework and the agential initiatives of social actors, and must not be enframed within the structurally differentiating dialectical, postmodern, post-structural, and postcolonial logic of the West and the Affranchis (today's Haitian mulatto, Arab oligarchy, and petit-bourgeois blacks) (Du Bois, 2012; Mocombe, 2016, 2018).

In fact, when the Haitian Revolution commences in 1791, there are three distinct groups vying for control of the island, the whites (*blancs*); free people of color and mulattoes (*Affranchis*), and the enslaved and escaped (maroon) Africans of the island. The latter, over sixty-seven percent of the population, were not a structurally differentiated other. They had their own practical consciousness, what Paul C. Mocombe (2016) calls the "Vodou Ethic and the spirit of communism," by which they went about recursively (re)organizing and reproducing the material resource framework. The former two, free blacks and *gens de couleur* (Affranchis), were interpellated, embourgeoised, and differentiated by the language, communicative discourse, mode of production, ideology, and ideological apparatuses of the West and shared the same European practical consciousness, the Catholic/Protestant Ethic and the spirit of capitalism social class language game, as the whites. The latter social class language game stood against the Vodou Ethic and the spirit of communism social class language game of the majority of the Africans who were interpellated and ounganified/manboified by the language, communicative discourse, mode of production, ideology, and ideological apparatuses of *oungan yo*, *manbo yo*, *gangan yo*, and *granmoun yo* (James, 1986; Fick, 1990; Du Bois, 2004, 2012; Ramsey, 2014; Mocombe, 2016, 2017, 2018).

The whites, were divided between large plantation owners, *grand blanc*, and *petit-blancs*, i.e., managers, slave drivers, artisans, merchants, and teachers. The former, *grand blanc*, were independent-minded, and like the American colonists wanted political and economic independence from their mother-country, France, where their rights and economic interests were not represented in the National Assembly. The *petit-blancs* were more racist and feared the alliance between the larger landowners and the Affranchis. The Affranchis were free people of color and mulatto, *gens de couleur*, property and slave owners on the island who shared the religion, culture, language, and ideology of their white counterparts and wanted then Saint-Domingue to remain a French colony. Although internal antagonism based on race (color) and class existed between the free (creole) blacks and *gens de couleur*, I group them together under the nomenclature, Affranchis, to highlight the fact that their interpellation and embourgeoisement via the ideology and ideological apparatuses of the West rendered their practical consciousnesses identical even though there were racial/color (based on phenotype, not ideology) tensions between them (racial tensions, which still plaques Haiti today). Unlike the majority of white large plantation owners, however, the Affranchis, like Vincent Ogé, André Rigaud, Alexandre Pétion, Pierre Pinchinat, Toussaint Louverture, for examples, did not want independence from France. In the case of the mulattoes, who after independence would come to be referred to as the children of Alexandre Pétion, the first mulatto president of the Haitian Republic, they simply wanted their social, political, and economic rights recognized by France within the colony, not an independent nation-state or the end to slavery. In regards, to the children of Dessalines/Toussaint, metaphorically here representing creole slave drivers and free blacks, they sought equality of opportunity, recognition, and distribution vis-à-vis the whites and mulattoes. The enslaved and escaped Africans, metaphorically speaking the children of Sans Souci (the Kongolese general of the Haitian Revolution who was assassinated by the Affranchis Henri Christophe), of the island were divided between field slaves, domestic slaves, and maroons. The domestic slaves, like their African-American counterparts, house slaves, more so identified with their slavemasters. However, for the most part, the field slaves and maroons, because of their relative isolation from whites, domestic slaves, *gens de couleur*, and free blacks, were interpellated and ounganified/manboified by the modes of production, language, ideology, ideological apparatuses, and communicative discourse of the Vodou Ethic and the spirit of communism, and many sought to reproduce their African ways of life in a national position of their own. In the end, the Revolution would come down to a struggle between the *Affranchis* and the enslaved and maroon Africans of the island, the latter of whom commenced the Haitian Revolution on August 14th, 1791 at Bois Caiman and other congresses (Genovese, 1979; James, 1986; Fick, 1990; Du Bois, 2004, 2012; Mocombe, 2016). Following the Revolution, between 1804 and 1806, the purposive-rationality of the enslaved and maroon Africans would become a part of the *modus operandi* of the Haitian nation-state until October 17, 1806 when Jean-Jacques Dessalines was assassinated by Alexandre Pétion and Henri Christophe. At which point, the purposive-rationality of the *Affranchis* with their emphasis on integration into the mercantilist and free-trade dialectic of the global capitalist world-system, capitalist wealth, French culture, religion, and language became dominant at the expense of the African linguistic system, Kreyol; Vodou ideology; its ideological apparatuses; and modes of production, subsistence agriculture, husbandry, and *komes*, of the African masses on the island who took to the mountains and provinces following the death of Dessalines (Fick, 1990; Nicholls, 1979; Du Bois, 2004, 2012).

Contemporarily, the continuous struggle between the mulatto-Arab merchant/professional class and the black landowning managerial (middle) classes for control of the state and its apparatuses, at the expense of the African masses in the provinces and mountains whose children they arm and use against each other as they migrate to Port-au-Prince amidst American neoliberal policies seeking to displace the masses off their land for tourism, agro and textile industries, and athletics (basketball and soccer), continues to be a hindrance for the constitution of a sovereign Haitian nation-state. The former two, interpellated and embourgeoised in Western ideological apparatuses, seek to constitute Haiti, with the aid of whites (France, Canada, and America), as an export-oriented periphery state within the neoliberal logic of the capitalist world-system under American hegemony against the desires of the masses of Africans in the provinces and mountains seeking to maintain their *komes*, subsistence agriculture, and husbandry, which are deemed informal. The *grandon* class, composed of educated professionals, former drug dealers, entertainers, and police officers attack the former Affranchis class, which is now a comprador bourgeoisie (composed of mulattoes, blacks, and Arab merchants) seeking to build, own, and manage hotels and assembly factories producing electronics and clothing for the US market, under the moniker the children of Dessalines against the children of Pétion in the name of the African masses of the island, the majority of whom are peasant farmers interpellated and ounganified by the Vodou Ethic and the spirit of communism social class language game (Mocombe, 2016, 2018). Instead of focusing on vertically integrating the lakou system and infrastructure (artificial lakes, potable water, food security, mache— modern market spaces for *komes*, universities, and state-owned companies for the peasant class to sell, etc.) to augment national agriculture and the productive forces of the latter group, who constitute eighty-five percent of the population as the socialist opposition attempted to do during the Boyer presidency of the nineteenth century, the mulatto-Arab elites and petit-bourgeois blacks emphasize the constitution of the Haitian nation-state via neoliberalism, i.e., individual freedoms, personal responsibility, job creation through foreign direct investment in tourism, agro and textile industries, privatization of public services, deregulation, austerity, infrastructure for an export-oriented economy similar to the one they had under slavery, and the constitution of a political bourgeoisie in control of the state apparatuses. However, their inabilities—given the voting power of the majority—to constitute two dominant rotating political parties to implement the neoliberal desires of their former colonial slavemasters, leaves Haiti in perpetual turmoil. As in slavery, the African masses continue to fight, against their interpellation, embourgeoisement, and differentiation as wage-earners (commodities) in the tourism trade and textile factories of the Catholic/Protestant Ethic and spirit of capitalism of these two power elites seeking to displace the masses off their lands and into urban centers of Haiti and elsewhere to facilitate capitalist development. This displacement and dislocation of the African masses of Haiti to urban centers at home and abroad have led to the emergence of new, structurally differentiated, identities amongst them as they scatter throughout the world in search of better opportunities in the face of neoliberal policies on the island. For example, Haitian immigration to the United States most recently has seen the rise of what is more appropriately labeled the "my nigga" Haitian identity, which is tied to the "my nigga" black American underclass consciousness of the inner-cities.

The Constitution of Black American Practical Consciousness

Black American practical consciousness and social agency were constituted by and within the dialectic of the American Protestant capitalist social structure of racial-class inequality. As such, black practical consciousness in America are a product of Protestant capitalist structural reproduction and differentiation. Unlike the African Haitians, the children of Sans Souci, no African ideological apparatuses were put in place to reorganize and reproduce (i.e., socially integrate) an African worldview on the American landscape. The African body, which embodied its initial African practical consciousnesses that were reified in Africa, were thrown in, interpellated by, and socialized (embourgeoised) in new "white" capitalist ideological apparatuses that they would subsequently adopt and reproduce, i.e., the black church, nuclear family, etc., in regards to the politics of their black bodies not an African worldview. That is, their social agency centered on their identification as members of the (Protestant capitalist) society who recursively reproduced its ideas and ideals as people with black skin not as Africans with a distinct worldview or social class language game (language, communicative discourse, ideology, ideological apparatuses, and modes of production) from that of their former slavemasters and colonizers. As such, American blacks, as interpellated (workers) and embourgeoised agents of the American dominated global (Protestant) capitalist social structure of inequality, represent the most modern (i.e. embourgeoised) people of color, in terms of their "practical consciousness," in this process of homogenizing social actors as agents of the protestant ethic or disciplined workers working for owners of production in order to obtain economic gain, status, and upward mobility in the larger American society and the world. Whereas, they once occupied the social space in relation to the forces of production as agricultural and industrial workers, the former less educated than the latter, which were much wealthier because of their education and industrial work and therefore made education and industry the means to economic gain and upward economic mobility during the period of industrial capitalism in America. Today, they continue to constitute the social space and their practical consciousness in terms of their relation to the means (forces) and relations of production (and their ideological apparatuses) in post-industrial capitalist America. This relation differentiates black America for the most part into two status groups, a dwindling middle and upper class (living in suburbia) that numbers about 25 percent of their population (13 percent) and obtain their status as preachers, doctors, athletes, entertainers, lawyers, teachers, and other high-end professional service occupations; and a growing segregated "black underclass" of criminals, unemployed, and under-employed wage-earners occupying poor inner-city communities and schools focused solely on technical skills, multicultural education, athletics, and test-taking for social promotion given the relocation of industrial and manufacturing jobs to poor periphery and semi-periphery countries and the introduction of low-end post-industrial service jobs and a growing informal economy in American urban-cities (Wilson, 1978, 1998; Sennett, 1998). Whereas street and prison personalities, rappers, athletes, and entertainers, many of whom refer to themselves and their compatriots as "my niggas," are the bearers of ideological and linguistic domination for the latter; the former, once called negroes, the black bourgeoisie (E. Franklin Frazier's term), and now African-Americans, is predominantly influenced by preachers and educated professionals as the bearers of ideological and linguistic domination. As structurally differentiated determined identities, both groups share the same ideals and goals, i.e., economic gain, status, and upward social mobility, within the class division and social relations of production of the Protestant capitalist world-system under American hegemony. Therefore, their practical consciousness is neither progressive, nor counter-hegemonic. It is reproductive and structurally differentiated.

However, America's transition to a postindustrial, financialized service, economy beginning in the 1970s, decentered the negro (black bourgeoisie/African American) practical consciousness, and reified and positioned black American "my nigga" underclass ideology and language, hip-hop culture, as a viable means for black American youth to identify with and achieve economic gain, status, and upward economic mobility in the society over education and succeeding academically as emphasized by black bourgeois discourse. Finance capital in the US beginning in the 1970s began investing in entertainment and other service industries where the inner-city language, street, prison, entertainment, and athletic youth culture of black America became both a commodity and the means to economic gain, status, and upward mobility (forces of production) for the black poor in America's postindustrial economy, which subsequently outsourced its industrial work to semi-periphery nations thereby blighting the inner-city communities. Blacks, many of whom migrated to the northern cities from the agricultural south looking for industrial work in the north following the Civil War (1861-1865), became concentrated in blighted communities where work began to disappear, schools were underfunded, and poverty increased. The black migrants, which migrated North with their Black/African-American English Vernacular (BEV/AAEV) from the agricultural South, became segregated sociolinguistic underclass communities, ghettoes, of unemployed laborers looking to illegal, athletic, and entertainment activities (running numbers, pimping, prostitution, drug dealing, robbing, participating in sports, music, etc.) for economic success, status, and upward mobility. Educated in the poorly funded schools of the urban ghettoes, given the process of deindustrialization and the flight of capital to the suburbs, with no work prospects, many black Americans became part of a permanent, BEV/AAEV speaking and poorly educated underclass looking to other activities for economic gain, status, and upward economic mobility. Those who were educated became a part of the social class language game of the Standard-English-speaking black middle class of professionals, i.e., preachers, teachers, doctors, lawyers, etc. (the black bourgeoisie), living in the suburbs, while the uneducated or poorly educated constituted the social class language game of the black underclass of the urban ghettoes where the streets, prisons, athletics, and the entertainment industries became the ideological apparatuses for their socialization. Beginning in the late 1980s, finance capital began commodifying and distributing (via the media industrial complex) the social class language game of the underclass black culture for entertainment in the emerging postindustrial (service) economy of the US over the ideology and language, social class language game, of the black bourgeoisie. Be that as it may, efforts to succeed academically among black Americans, which constituted the ideology and language of the black bourgeoisie, paled in comparison to their efforts to succeed as speakers of Black English, athletes, "gangstas", "playas", and entertainers, which became the ideology and language of the black underclass living in the inner-cities of America. Authentic black American identity became synonymous with black underclass hip-hop ideology and language represented by young athletes and entertainers, LeBron James, Derek Rose, Lil ' Wayne, Jay-Z, Kanye West, Tupac Shakur, Biggie Smalls, etc., over the social class language game of the educated black professional class under the ideological and linguistic domination of black preachers, TD Jakes, Creflo Dollar, Jamal Bryant, Juanita Bynum, etc., and other educated black professionals. In other words, in the postindustrial economy of the US black bourgeois traditional ideology and language with its emphasis on personal responsibility, individualism, economic gain as a sign of salvation and grace, and family values became juxtapose against the narcissistic exploration of self, sexuality, and identity of the black underclass for economic gain.

The black underclass in America's ghettoes has slowly become, since the 1980s, with the financialization of hip-hop culture as an art form and entertainment by record labels such as Sony and others, athletics, and the entertainment industry, the bearers of ideological and linguistic domination for the black youth community in America. Their language and worldview as constituted by and through ideological apparatuses such as the streets, prisons, hip-hop culture, athletics and the entertainment industry financed by finance capital, has become the means by which black youth (and youth throughout the world) attempt to recursively reorganize and reproduce their material resource framework against the purposive-rationality of educated black bourgeois or middle-class America. The upper-class of owners and high-level executives of the American dominated capitalist world-system have capitalized on this through the commodification of black "my nigga" underclass culture, which mainstreamed it. This is further supported by an American media and popular culture that glorifies the streets, athletes, entertainers, and the "Bling bling," wealth, diamonds, cars, jewelry, and money. Hence the aim of many young blacks in the society is no longer to seek status, economic gain, and upward mobility through a Protestant Ethic that stresses hard work, diligence, differed gratification, and education; on the contrary, the Protestant ethic in sports, music, instant gratification, illegal activities (drug dealing), and skimming are the dominant means portrayed for their efforts through the entertainment industry financed by post-industrial capital. Schools throughout urban inner cities are no longer seen as means to a professional end in order to obtain economic gain, status, and upward mobility, but obstacles to that end because it delays gratification and is not correlative with the means associated with economic success and upward mobility in black urban America. More black American youth (especially the black male) aspire to become, football and basketball players, rappers and entertainers, like many of their role models, LeBron James, Derek Rose, Lil ' Wayne, Jay-Z, Kanye West, Tupac Shakur, Biggie Smalls, etc., who were raised in their urban underclass environments and obtained economic gain and upward mobility that way, over doctors, lawyers, engineers, etc., the social functions associated with the status symbol of the black and white middle class (negroes) of the civil rights generation. Hence the end and social action of the larger society remains the same, economic success, status, and upward economic mobility, only the means (forces of production) to that end have shifted with the rise, financed by finance capital, of the black underclass as the bearers of ideological and linguistic domination in black America given the commodification of hip-hop culture and their high visibility in the media and charitable works through basketball and football camps and rap concerts, which reinforce the aforementioned activities as viable professions (means) to wealth and status in the society's postindustrial economy, which focuses on services and entertainment for the world's transnational bourgeois class as the mode of producing surplus-value.

This linguistic and ideological domination and the ends of the power elites (rappers, athletes, gangsters) of the black underclass are juxtaposed against the Protestant Ethic and spirit of capitalism of the educated black middle and upper middles classes represented in the discourse and discursive practices of black American prosperity preachers in the likes of TD Jakes, Creflo Dollar, Jamal Bryant, Juanita Bynum, Eddie Long, etc. who push forth, via the black American church, education, and professional jobs as the more viable means to economic gain, status, and upward economic mobility in the society over the street life of the urban ghettoes. Hence, whereas, for agents of the Protestant Ethic in the likes of Jakes, Dollar, Bryant, Bynum, and Long the means to "Bling bling," or the American Dream, is through education, obtaining a professional job, and material wealth as a sign of God's grace, salvation, and blessings. Rapping, hustling, sports, etc., for younger black Americans growing up in inner-cities throughout the US, where industrial work has disappeared, represent the means (not education) to the status position of "Bling bling."

Discussion and Conclusions: Haitian Integration into the American Capitalist Social Structure

Beginning in the late 1950s Haitians immigrated to the US differentiated within the racial-class socio-culture of Haiti previously highlighted, mulattoes, petit-bourgeois blacks of the Affranchis, and Africans of the Vodou Ethic and the spirit of communism. Post-independence, the first wave of Haitian immigrants to arrive in the US were predominantly your upper-class mulatto elites and members of the black grandon class escaping the Francois "papa-doc" Duvalier regime. They deemed the regime racist as it emphasized Duvalier's noirisme ideology, which highlighted Haiti as a black country that should be ruled by blacks (a black middle technoclass educated in the technical schools during the US occupation, 1915-1934) against the mulatto elites who for so long dominated the nation's politics via what is referred to as *politique de doublure* (the politics of having a dark-skinned Haitian as the face of the government while the mulatto elites directed its politics and their racial-class interest) (Du Bois, 2012). Highly educated, upon their arrival to the US, however, they became segregated from the larger mainstream society because of race, language, and culture, and the black American class structure because of language and embourgeoised French culture. Hence, Haitian practical consciousness early on evolved, segregated, by emphasizing the embourgeoised praxis of the mulatto elites and petit-bourgeois black grandon class of the island seeking to reproduce French culture, ideals, and ideas among their children. In public, they established small businesses catering to the segregated Haitian population, drove taxi-cabs, worked in factories and restaurants, and emphasized upward economic mobility, the French language, the Catholic religion, playing a musical instrument, i.e., the piano, and professional education, i.e., law, medicine, and engineering, over the Kreyol language and Vodou religion of the African masses on the island.

Following the fall of the Duvalier regime in 1986, more Haitian immigrants from the provinces and mountains began emigrating from the island to the US escaping the political repression of anti-Jean Bertrand Aristide forces and the American embargo, which sought to get the latter to adopt neoliberal policies. The push-pull forces (dictated by the US and international organizations such as the IMF, World Bank, United Nations, etc.) of neoliberal capitalist relations of production seeking to convert Haiti into an export-oriented periphery state within the global capitalist world-system forced many Haitians off of their lands in the mountains and provinces of the island and into the urban centers of the capital city, Port-au-Prince, and other countries seeking industrial and low-end postindustrial service work. Proselytized early-on by American Protestant missionary forces allowed on the island during the American occupation and under the Duvalier regime which used these missionaries to provide social welfare to the masses in place of government institutions as governed by the neoliberal logic of privatization, austerity, personal responsibility, etc., many of these recent immigrants to the US were darker-skinned, anti-Vodou (given their Protestant indoctrination), poorer, less educated, Protestant, and Kreyol speaking. Upon their arrival to the US they became segregated in poorer Haitian communities in proximity to the black inner-city communities of the black American underclass as wealthier Haitians had, following the black American bourgeoisie, relocated to the suburbs given the process of deindustrialization that had plagued US urban cities beginning in the 1970s. As late arrivals in the American post-industrial service economy, they obtained low-wage work as poor service workers, i.e., taxi drivers, hotel and restaurant workers, etc., while simultaneously facing the discriminatory effects of racism and classism in predominantly poor inner-city communities. In facing the discriminatory effects of the black underclass of these communities, the practical consciousness of their children became divided between the embourgeoised aspirations of their parents seeking to follow the practical consciousness of the previous immigrant generation and the shifting American postindustrial economy, which began to valorize the practical consciousness of the black underclass as enframed by the athletics industry and "Hip-Hop" culture as means to economic gain, status, and upward mobility in the larger society. As such with the rise of the Haitian rapper Wyclef Jean to prominence in the early 90s, the "my nigga" practical consciousness of the black underclass took hold among young Haitian immigrants who integrated and reproduced elements of it amongst themselves in their own segregated poor communities. Against the embourgeoisement of their parents, which took and takes place via Protestant churches, they sought economic gain, status, and upward mobility via athletics, hustling, and the entertainment industry. Becoming Haitian flag-waving, Jesus-loving, tattoo-wearing, Vodou-hating, and Ebonics-speaking Haitians whose only connections to Haiti were and are a broken form of Kreyol synthesized with English (Kreenglish), Wyclef, Kodak black (another rapper), zo pound (a Haitian gang that developed in the inner-cities of Miami to protect Haitians who were discriminated against by African Americans), soup joumou (the independence day pumpkin soup eaten by Haitians on January 1st), griot (fried pork prepared by Haitians), and the annual Haitian flag day festival in Miami, Florida held annually on May 18th.

Like many black Americans of the late 1980s and 90s who turned to roots and an Afrocentric culture to combat both the black capitalist pathologies of the black bourgeoisie and underclasses, in response to both the "my nigga" Haitian identity and the French embourgeoisement of earlier generations, the middle-age children of the first generation of Haitian immigrants have begun to return to their Vodou and Kreyol roots as constituted in the provinces and mountains of the island in search of an authentic Haitian/African identity by which to recursively reorganize and reproduce their being-in-the-world against both the "my nigga" Haitian practical consciousness and its bourgeois counterpart. For now, in the age of globalization and post-industrialism, "the my nigga" Haitian identity dominates in large urban centers in the US (Miami, Brooklyn, Boston, etc.) and is starting to take hold on the island over the latter two with the emergence of "rap" Kreyol and its accoutrements, which patterns the Hip-hop culture of the black American underclass, on the island. Concentrated in Haitian and US ghettoes, the "my nigga" Haitian identity in both Haiti and the US have reproduced and are reproducing the same practical consciousnesses that characterized the Hip-Hop cultural and violent (gang) practices of the urban ghettoes of the USA in the early 1980s and 90s to the detriment of any counter-hegemonic forces, which seeks to undermine the capitalist relations of production and its structures that is responsible for its constitution.

To begin this analysis, chapter one deconstructs contemporary postmodern/post-structural understandings regarding the nature and origins of black identity/practical consciousness. In the place of postmodern and post-structural thoughts on identity constitution I offer the structurationist theory and methodology Paul C. Mocombe (2019) calls phenomenological structuralism. Against postmodern/post-structural emphasis on the fragmentary or the decentered subject, this work, using the aforementioned Haitian idealist and structural Marxist perspective grounded in structuration theory, phenomenological structuralism, suggests that the constitution of black practical consciousness/identity must be understood predominantly as the struggle between two social class language games, a black bourgeoisie and underclass, of the Catholic/Protestant Ethic and capitalist racial-class divisions, social relations of production, and ideological apparatuses of the two bourgeoisies as constituted by the global capitalist world-system under American hegemony. Be that as it may, chapters three and four, respectively, highlight the nature and origins of globalization under American hegemony and the constitution of black American consciousness within a (phenomenological structural) structurationist framework. Chapter five explores the constitution of Haitian identity within the phenomenological structural approach. Concluding that in Haiti, unlike blacks elsewhere, Haitian practical consciousness became constituted within two forms of system and social integration, i.e., the Vodou Ethic and the spirit of communism of the African majority on the one hand, and the Catholic/Protestant Ethic and the spirit of capitalism of the Affranchis on the other. Chapter six concludes the work by highlighting how the dialectical response of the Affranchis class to reproduce the capitalist system of their former colonial masters on the island, consequently, gave rise to the "my nigga" identity in the US Haitian diaspora and subsequently Haiti. Concluding, in this structural approach to the constitution of Haitian practical consciousness, that in the historical denouement of the Vodou Ethic and the spirit of communism and the Protestant Ethic and the discursive practices of the spirit of capitalism from slavery to globalization under European and American Hegemony, Haitian practical consciousness emerged and became dominated for the most part by three social class language games, the *grandon* class, composed of Western educated professionals, middle managers, former drug dealers, entertainers, and police officers; the Affranchis class/comprador bourgeoisie of landowners and merchants, seeking to build, own, and manage hotels and assembly factories producing electronics and clothing for the US market; and the African masses of the island, the majority of whom are peasant farmers and *komesans*, whose practical consciousness, the Vodou Ethic and the spirit of communism and its lakou system, are marginalized and discriminated against by the two bourgeoisies who are interpellated and embourgeoised by the Protestant/Catholic Ethic and the spirit of capitalism of the West. Amidst these three identities, the chapter concludes, a new, structurally determined, Haitian identity, "the my nigga Haitian," which is influencing the Haitian youth on the island, has emerged as a result of the implementation of (neo) liberal policies in Haiti and the Haitian diaspora in the United States of America by the aforementioned Haitian bourgeoisie classes against the Vodou Ethic and spirit of communism and the Lakou system of the Vodou community.

CHAPTER I

BLACK CONSCIOUSNESSES AND IDENTITIES IN AMERICA AND THE DIASPORA

From slavery, to colonialism, to the present, race and class distinctions within black communities in the United States (US) and the black diaspora must be understood as being predominantly constituted within and by the two dominant structurally determined social class language games, a black bourgeoisie and underclass (a racial caste in class), created by the racial-class division and social relations of production of global capitalism or the Protestant capitalist world-system and its ideological apparatuses. This structural Marxist dialectical perspective, I am purporting, stands against contemporary postcolonial, postmodern, and post-structural theories, which focus on local formations, heterogeneity, the diverse, the subjective, the spontaneous, the relative, and the fragmentary as the basis for understanding the constitution of black identities and consciousnesses in the US and the diaspora in the age of globalization and neoliberalism. The latter positions, I argue here, are also the product of class division and social relations of production in late postindustrial capitalist development and organization. The concepts, i.e., ambivalence, double consciousness, hybridity, négritude, créolité, and intersectionality, coming from, or out of, these theories represent the concepts, psychological pathologies, and practical consciousnesses of the black bourgeoisies and other bourgeoisies of once discriminated against others in their dialectical quest to obtain equality of opportunity, recognition, and distribution with their former slavemasters and colonial administrators within capitalist relations of production. As a result, they fail to adequately address the issues regarding the origins and basis for the constitution of black identities and consciousnesses in America, the Metropoles, and the diaspora. Using a variant of structuration theory, what Paul C. Mocombe (2014, 2015, 2016, 2017, 2018, 2019) calls phenomenological structuralism, this work, against contemporary postcolonial, postmodern, and post-structural theories, seeks to offer a dialectical understanding of the constitution of black American and diasporic lives within the class division and social relations of production of the global capitalist world-system (and its ideological apparatuses), while accounting for black social agency. In the end, I utilize Mocombe's phenomenological structuralism to explore the emergence of the "my nigga" Haitian identity in America and Haiti in the age of neoliberal globalization or the contemporary capitalist world-system under American (Protestant) neoliberal hegemony.

Since the 1960s, there have been four similar schools of thought on understanding the origins and nature of black practical consciousnesses, the ideas blacks recursively reorganize and reproduce in their material practices, in the United States (US), the United Kingdom (UK), and the diaspora: the pathological-pathogenic and adaptive-vitality school in the US; and the anti-essentialist and anti-anti-essentialist schools in the UK and the diaspora. In the US, the pathological-pathogenic position suggests that in its divergences from white American norms and values black American practical consciousness is nothing more than a pathological form of, and reaction to, American consciousness rather than a dual (both African and American) hegemonic opposing "identity-in-differential" (the term is Gayatri Spivak's) to the American one (Elkins, 1959; Frazier, 1939,1957; Genovese, 1974; Murray, 1984; Moynihan, 1965; Myrdal, 1944; Wilson, 1978, 1987; Sowell, 1975, 1981; Stampp, 1956, 1971). Proponents of the adaptive-vitality school suggest that the divergences are not pathologies but African "institutional transformations" preserved on the American landscape (Allen, 2001; Asante, 1988, 1990; Billingsley, 1968, 1970, 1993; Blassingame, 1972; Early, 1993; Gilroy, 1993; Gutman, 1976; Herskovits, 1958 [1941]; Holloway, 1990a; Karenga, 1993; Levine, 1977; Lewis, 1993; Lincoln and Mamiya, 1990; Nobles, 1987; Staples, 1978; Stack, 1974; West, 1993). Just the same in the UK and the diaspora, the two main opposing schools of thought are the anti-essentialist and the anti-anti-essentialist (Smith, 1960; Vera, 1960; Gilroy, 1993; Mercer, 1994; Clifford, 1997; Mocombe and Tomlin, 2010, 2013; Mocombe et al, 2014). Anti-essentialists similar to the US pathological-pathogenic school argue against any ideas of a black innate cultural phenomenon that unites all black people. Proponents of this theory contend that diasporic identities and cultures cannot place African origin at the center of any attempt to understand the nature of black practical consciousnesses in the UK and the diaspora (Mercer, 1994, pg. 3). The anti-anti-essentialist position, in keeping with the logic of the adaptive-vitality school, posits, on the contrary, the idea that African memory retentions exist in diasporic cultures to some degree (Clifford, 1997, pg. 267-268). Contemporarily, all four positions have been criticized for either their structural determinism as in the case of the pathological-pathogenic and anti-essentialist approaches, or racial/cultural determinism as in the case of the adaptive-vitality and anti-anti-essentialist positions (Karenga, 1993; Mocombe et al, 2014).

In directly or indirectly refuting these four positions for their structural and racial/cultural determinism, contemporary post-sixties and post-segregation era black scholars in the United Kingdom (UK) and United States (US), especially, attempt to understand black consciousnesses and communities by using postcolonial, post-structural, and post-modern theories to either reinterpret W.E.B. Du Bois's (1903) double consciousness construct as an epistemological mode of critical inquiry that characterizes the nature or essence of black consciousness, a la Cornel West (1993) and Paul Gilroy (1993); or, building on the social constructivist work of Frantz Fanon, offer an intersectional approach to the constitution of black consciousnesses and communities, which emphasize the diverse and different levels of alienation, marginalization, and domination, class, race, gender, global location, age, and sexual identity, by which black consciousnesses and communities get constituted, a la bell hooks (1993) and Patricia Hill Collins (1990) (Reed, 1997; Gordon, 2000; Mocombe et al, 2014). In spite of their efforts, these two dominant contemporary critical race theory responses to the pathological-pathogenic, adaptive-vitality, anti-essentialist, and anti-anti-essentialist positions inadequately resolve the structural and racial determinism of the aforementioned approaches by neglecting the fact that their theories and the practical consciousness of the theorists themselves derive from the class division and social relations of production of global capitalism or the contemporary capitalist world-system (Fraser, 1994; Mocombe et al, 2014, 2017, 2018).

The former understanding, Du Boisian double consciousness, put forth by Paul Gilroy and Cornel West is not only problematic because it reiterates Du Bois's racial essentialism in constituting his notion of double consciousness (Reed, 1997; Mocombe, 2008). But the scholars are also mistaken because they assume their Cartesian, transcendental, intellectual activity, the epistemological mode of critical inquiry, in the academy as having ontological and epistemological status among the black masses in general in constituting their identity within and by the dialectical racial-class structure of global capitalist relations of production and its ideological apparatuses. In other words, they do this instead of viewing their interpretation of Du Boisian double consciousness, as an epistemological mode of critical inquiry, as being a by-product of a Cartesian transcendental vantage point afforded to them by their academic training and bourgeois class positions as black professors seeking to define black consciousness along the social class language game of the white bourgeois lifestyles of the upper-class of owners and high-level executives as it stands against and in relation to black underclass bodies, material conditions, language, and ideology. Gilroy and West assume their interpretation of double consciousness as an epistemological mode of critical inquiry, which is similar to the negative dialectics of the Frankfurt School, to be how ontologically and epistemologically black people, whether in the US or the diaspora ("the black Atlantic"), in general come to constitute their practical consciousnesses within the modern state and the dialectic of the capitalist social structure of class inequality and differentiation of the West. In doing so, however, they neglect the fact that their conception, as was the case in W.E.B. Du Bois's conceptualization of double consciousness following the American Civil War, derives from the racial-class divisions of the American industrial/postindustrial capitalist social relations of production and its ideological apparatuses, which created two social (racial) class language games, a racial-caste-in-class, a black bourgeois educated and professional class juxtaposed against the material conditions, practices, language, body, and ideology of a black underclass segregated in the ghettoes of Northern cities where industrial work was beginning to disappear to developing countries following the end of World War II. West and Gilroy, as Du Bois attempted to do for Southern agricultural black Americans following the Civil War, use double consciousness to highlight the contradictions of the society as encapsulated in, and revealed by, the material conditions of the black underclass of Northern cities in order to seek equality of opportunity, recognition, and distribution for them vis-à-vis whites and black bourgeois material conditions, bodies, language, status, etc. in a declining industrial social relations of production (Fraser, 1994; Reed, 1997; Mocombe, 2008, 2009).

Just the same, the latter predominantly feminist position, conversely, in refutation to the assumed hidden logic of heterosexual and patriarchal domination inherent in the theories of Du Bois, Gilroy, and West, attempts to offer an intersectional approach to the constitution of black consciousnesses, which emphasizes the different levels of domination or serial identities, class, race, gender, global location, age, and sexual identity, by which black communities and consciousnesses get alienated, marginalized, and constituted. This postcolonial, postmodern, post-structural, and black feminist theorizing of bell hooks and Patricia Hill Collins, especially, epistemologically dismisses the dominant ontological status of the capitalist system/social structure by which the masses of blacks attempt to practically live out their lives for the theoretical assumptions of the indeterminacy of meaning and decentered subject of postcolonial, post-structural, and post-modern theorizing. They attempt to read back into the historical constitution of black identity and community life within and by the dialectic of a global capitalist social structure of racial class inequality the indeterminacy of meaning and decentered subject of postcolonial, post-structural, and post-modern theorizing to highlight the variety of intersecting ways, i.e., standpoints, race, class, age, sexual identity, etc., individual black subjects were and are alienated, marginalized, and dominated. As such, they commit the same bourgeois Cartesian transcendental intellectual fallacy that Gilroy and West do. Both hooks and Collins, from their transcendental vantage points, put the ontological status of the capitalist world-system, or "matrix of domination" to quote Collins, as reflected in the practices of the majority of blacks under erasure for the ontological and epistemological assumptions of postcolonial, post-modern, and post-structural theorizing. As though their bourgeois epistemological assumptions within a contemporary postindustrial capitalist social structure that attempts to decenter the bourgeois subject in order to reify and commodify individual identities around their class positions for finance capital accumulation, is how all blacks, historically, initially encountered the matrix of domination and came to constitute their being-in-the-world within and by the global capitalist social structure of racial class inequality and differentiation. They fail to realize that intersectionality is a socio-political by-product of a postindustrial (finance) capitalist landscape or social structure seeking to decenter the bourgeois subject and allow a diversity of identities to emerge (around their class positions) within the class division and social relations of postindustrial capitalist production so as to accumulate surplus-value (diversified consumerism) by catering to the entertainment, financial, and service needs of these new and once discriminated-against identities and their constructed "fictitious" class-based communities.

Essentially, the theorists overlook their "double hermeneutic" (Anthony Giddens' term). Whereas Giddens' term refers to how a social scientist's "understanding of the social world may have an impact on the understandings of the actors being studied, with the result that social researchers can alter the world they are studying and thus lead to distorted findings and conclusions" (Ritzer, 2007, pg. 169). In this case, in my usage of it, the theorists overlook the impact that the capitalist social relations of production have on their understandings of the social world being studied, with the result that the social relations of production alters the world and the viewpoint of the theorists and thus lead to distorted findings and conclusions regarding the nature and origin of identity constitution, which the theorists assume to be indeterminant.

Hence, both positions because of their class origins and Cartesian ontological and epistemological (transcendental) activities and vantage points inadequately address the issue of how their intellectual assumptions and the practical consciousnesses in black communities within the global capitalist matrix of domination of the West historically and ontologically became constituted within and by the dialectical unfolding of racial-class divisions and social relations of production organized via mode of production, language, ideology, ideological apparatuses, and communicative discourse. They fail to synthesize their transcendental academic rhetoric with structural Marxist dialectics, which captures the racial-class divisions, ideological apparatuses, and the dialectical economic structure within which the practical consciousnesses of the black masses, the academic theories of ambivalence, hybridity, créolité, négritude, double consciousness, intersectionality, and the identities of the theorists emerged.

In other words, building on both the post-structural notion of the indeterminacy of meaning in ego-centered communicative discourse, i.e., linguistic communication and interaction is between endless signifiers and not signifiers and signified which allows for meaning to be deferred during interaction, as highlighted by Jacques Derrida; and the postmodern notion of the decentered subject, the rejection of the notion of individual subjectivity as autonomous, self-critical, unified, and stable, i.e., the transcendental subject of Kantian discourse, for the understanding of the subject as a locus of multiple, dispersed or decentered discourses, of Michel Foucault, bell hooks and Patricia Hill Collins, paradoxically from a transcendental academic perspective, offer an intersectional approach to the constitution of black consciousnesses and communities, which emphasizes the diverse and different levels of domination, class, race, gender, global location, age, and sexual identity, by which individual black consciousnesses and communities get constituted. Cornel West and Paul Gilroy in keeping with the logic of the transcendental subject of Kantian discourse offer Du Boisian double consciousness as an epistemological mode of critical inquiry into modernity as being the fundamental characteristic of black individual consciousness with a touch of religiosity and jazz improvisation. However, in doing so, like Derrida and Foucault, who neglect the fact that the indeterminacy of meaning and the decentered subject operate relationally within structures of domination, since the seventeenth century within the modern form of the state and racial-class divisions, which derives from the mode of production, language, communicative discourse, ideology, and ideological apparatuses of Protestant capitalist relations of production, West, Gilroy, hooks, and Collins overlook the fact that their theories and the different levels of domination they point to as constituting black communities and consciousnesses derive from the contemporary organization of the modern state and class division in postindustrial capitalist societies.

That is, the social phenomenon of Du Boisian double consciousness (adopted by West and Gilroy) and the indeterminacy of meaning and the decentered subject highlighted by Derrida and Foucault in the intersectionality language of hooks and Collins occur in relation to the state and its ideological apparatuses and racial-class divisions of *postindustrial* capitalist societies. They both have their basis in the relations of production, exploitation, and organization of the state following the failed diverse student revolutions of the 1960s, which gave rise to local formations and heterogeneity as the theoretical theme for the new philosophers and social scientists of the late twentieth century who sought equality of opportunity, recognition, and distribution for the diverse groups (standpoints) of the student movements within the class division and global social relations of capitalist production and organization, which became triumphant with the fall of communism or state capitalism in Eastern Europe (Fraser, 1994).

That is to say, the double consciousness and intersectionality discourses of Du Bois, West, Gilroy, hooks, and Collins have their basis in globalization, neoliberalism, and the postindustrial relations of production and exploitation as organized under the hegemony of the American nation-state following the civil rights and hippie movements of the 1960s, which diversified and fragmentized subjectivities and social movements for the philosophy of the person, individual human rights, and (positive) freedoms to (speak, assemble, etc.). Gilroy and West articulated their intellectual activities within the embourgeoisement and proletarianization of blacks during an industrial and an emerging postindustrial modernism and organization of the state that juxtaposed, like Du Bois, the bodies, language, and material conditions of an emerging black underclass, which moved to Northern urban ghettoes from the agricultural South during the process of deindustrialization and suburbanization that saw industrial work transferred overseas, vis-à-vis the material conditions of a black bourgeois professional class working in professional high-end service occupations and the entertainment industry clamoring for equality of opportunity, recognition, and distribution for the former via education and redistribution of wealth by the welfare state. Both hooks and Collins, on the contrary, articulate their standpoint theories within a narcissistic postindustrial capitalism that fosters the self, sexuality, and identity politics for capital accumulation via financialization and cultural consumption. Hence, Du Bois, West, Gilroy, hooks, and Collins fail to realize that their identities and theories derive from the state and class division within the processes of globalization and postindustrial capitalist relations of production and its ideological apparatuses.

Put differently, the logic here is that the theories of West, Gilroy, hooks, and Collins regarding the constitution of black consciousnesses derive from the structure of the conjuncture of neoliberal policies of globalizing capitalist processes under American hegemony and postindustrial capitalist relations of the nation-state and its ideological apparatuses. It is the class division and social relations of production coupled with the experience of white American capital with the liberal hybrid embourgeoised black American's struggle for equality of opportunity, recognition, and distribution beginning in slavery and ending in the civil rights movement of the 1960s, which led to the passage of civil rights legislation that integrated blacks into the fabric of the society under the purposive-rationality of their liberal black hybrid leadership in the likes of W.E.B. Du Bois, Martin Luther King Jr., Barack Obama, etc., which would come to constitute the contemporary processes of globalization and this adoption of postcolonial, postmodern, and post-structural theory highlighted in the works of Gilroy, West, hooks, and Collins, in other words.

Following the civil rights movement of the 1960s and adoption of civil rights legislation such as the Civil Rights Act of 1964, the experience of white American capital with embourgeoised liberal hybrid blacks would give rise to hybridization as the mechanism of social integration for all ethnic, racial, cultural, sexual, etc., minorities into American postindustrial capitalist relations of production locally and globally. Locally, discrimination was outlawed throughout American society and its ideological apparatuses, which in theory became a color-blind multicultural, multiracial, multisexual, etc., postindustrial social setting with emphasis on personal responsibility, individual human rights, and freedoms to, speak, assemble, etc., amidst class differentiation and diversified consumerism. Subsequently, the global outsourcing of industrial work by American capital beginning in the 1970s would be coupled with hybridization, individuality, human rights and *freedoms to* as the mechanisms of social integration for ethnic, racial, cultural, sexual, etc., others into global capitalist relations of production under American hegemony. That is, under the passage of civil rights legislation such as the Civil Rights Act of 1964 to integrate liberal hybrid blacks into the fabric of American society and its ideological apparatuses, the American nation-state reinforced its liberal/conservative bourgeois Protestantism without regards to race, creed, nationality, sex, religion, etc. With the advent of outsourcing or globalization under American hegemony beginning in the 1970s, other ethnic, racial, gender, and other minorities the world-over were integrated or socialized, like the liberal hybrid black Americans, via ideology and ideological apparatuses such as human rights, freedom, education, the streets, prisons, media, Protestant churches, World Bank, International Monetary Fund (IMF), etc., to work for American capital within the global framework of this color-blind new world economic order with its ideological emphasis on human rights and *freedoms to.* In the processes of globalization, American capital sought and seeks to hybridize other ethnic, cultural, sexual, and racial others the world over via the retrenchment of the nation state and color-blind neoliberal economic legislation in order to make social actors of other cultures known for two reasons, however: first, to socialize them to the work ethic of the globalizing capitalist relations of production; and second, to accumulate surplus-value as American capital sought and seeks to service the elite others of ethnic, racial, gender, and other communities as agents of and for capital, i.e., cultural producers, consumers, and administrative bourgeoisie controlling production for global capital, for their postindustrial economy. Conversely, the interpellated and embourgeoised hybridized ethnic, cultural, sexual, and racial others the world-over dialectically respond by seeking equality of opportunity, recognition, and distribution within the class division and social relations of production of the capitalist world-system for themselves and their masses.

Postcolonial, postmodern, and post-structural theories are the academic and political discourses of globalization and postindustrial capitalist relations of production of the contemporary age. The concepts, i.e., ambivalence, double consciousness, créolité, négritude, intersectionality, etc., developing from these theories represent the psychological pathologies and practical consciousness of the bourgeoisies of once discriminated against "others" within the capitalist world-system. As a result of the emergence of a post-industrial capitalism intent on allowing divergent meanings and individual experiences, which were once discriminated against, to emerge around their class positions for capital accumulation in a service/financial economy focused on entertainment and financial service (diversified consumerism). Non-class meanings and subjective/individual experiences, homosexuality, transgenderism, black feminism, etc., which were, and to some extent continue to be, discriminated against by both the black underclass and bourgeoisie of earlier capitalist relations of production are fostered and allowed to emerge within the dialectic of the global (postindustrial) capitalist social class structure or relations of production. These non-class meanings and subjective experiences, homosexuality, black feminism, Pan-Africanism, etc., practical consciousnesses, i.e., standpoint theories, which are the product of the deferment of meaning in ego-centered communicative discourse, contemporarily, are seeking equality of opportunity, recognition, and distribution within the dialectic of a postindustrial capitalist social structure that stratifies and commodifies these non-class (standpoints) identities, meanings, and subjective/individual experiences around their class positions or social relations to production for capital accumulation in the service economies of core, postindustrial nations, such as the US, UK, etc. What has emerged, as a result, are these theories of ambivalence, hybridity, créolité, négritude, double consciousness, and intersectionality among bourgeois academics of once discriminated against others highlighting the discourse by which these variant subjective positions have been alienated, marginalized, and prevented from achieving equality of opportunity, recognition, and distribution with whites within the global (postindustrial) capitalist social structure of racial-class inequality and differentiation. Their theories are universalized and extrapolated globally under the ideological umbrella of identity politics, the fight for social justice, truth, and love. However, by no means can these theories, as applied in the black diaspora, be viewed, against the discourse of the pathological-pathogenic and adaptive-vitality positions, as the universal mechanism by which black consciousnesses and communities were constituted. Their rhetoric, like black consciousnesses and black communities in the US, UK, Africa, and the diaspora, are the by-product of the global (industrial and postindustrial) capitalist social structure of class inequality and differentiation and its ideological apparatuses, which attempt to interpellate and structure the practices of subjective experiences within class differentiation and thereby control the practices of diversity and meaning constitution, which contemporarily juxtaposes the bodies, language, ideology, and material conditions of a transnational, multiracial, multicultural, multisexual, etc., upper-class of owners and high-level executives against the bodies, language, ideology, and material conditions of a transnational, multiracial, multicultural, mulitsexual underclass in poverty the world-over seeking equality of opportunity, recognition, and distribution with the former. The postmodern, post-structural, post-colonial theories of ambivalence, hybridity, créolité, négritude, double consciousness, and intersectionality are the concepts, psychological processes, pathologies, and practical consciousness of the bourgeoisies of the once-discriminated against, and do not represent the nature of identity constitution. They are standpoint theories, the ambivalent psychology of the oppressed black others, which do not offer an alternative form of system and social integration to the global Protestant capitalist social structure of class inequality. They simply seek to convict the power elites of the system of not identifying with their values in order to achieve equality of opportunity, recognition, and distribution. As such, their theories do not speak to the nature of identity constitution in general. They speak to one aspect of identity constitution, i.e., structural reproduction and differentiation.

Given the neglect of this (historical) relational problem and the Cartesian (transcendental) ontological and epistemological problematic in the writings of post-sixties and post-segregationist era blacks to understanding black practical consciousnesses, contemporarily, the purpose of the present work is to historically understand the origins of double consciousness, intersectionality, and the constitution of black communities and consciousnesses by focusing on black practical consciousnesses, i.e., the ideas (which are the product of structural differentiation and reproduction) the majority of blacks recursively reorganize and reproduce in their material practices to constitute their being-in-the-world or the capitalist social structure of inequality of the United States (US), Africa, and the diaspora. Within this structurationist logic, I demonstrate how the emergence of the two dominant structurally differentiated social class language games of the black American community, a black underclass under the leadership of rappers, athletes, and "gangstas" and a black bourgeoisie under the leadership of educated professionals and preachers, influenced and gave rise to the "my nigga" Haitian identity emerging in Haiti and the US Haitian diaspora.

CHAPTER II

PHENOMENOLOGICAL STRUCTURALISM: A THEORY OF HUMAN ACTION

Against the Hegelian dialectical, postmodern, post-structural, and postcolonial logics of many white Western and black bourgeois scholars exploring black identity and consciousness, my structurationist position, phenomenological structuralism, suggests an anti-dialectical perspective grounded in Haitian epistemology, i.e., Haitian/Vilokan Idealism, and the Weberian (1958 [1904-1905]) sociology of *The Protestant Ethic and the spirit of capitalism* coupled with the structural Marxism of structuration theory. From the former my phenomenological structural sociology borrows the logic of the internalization of the ideas and ideals of the ideological superstructure of a society (stemming from its language, mode of production, communicative discourse, ideology, ideological apparatuses), in relation to two other structural processes and the ability to defer meaning in ego-centered communicative discourse, as the basis by which social actors go about recursively reorganizing and reproducing their being-in-the-world as their purposive-rationality or practical consciousness, which is the language of the latter, structurationism. Phenomenological structuralism seeks to fix structurationism to account for the origins, nature, and relations of alternative agential moments outside of structural reproduction and differentiation to the latter as represented by the lakou system and the Vodou Ethic and the spirit of communism of the Africans of Haiti, for example. In this work, I utilize phenomenological structuralism to understand the constitution of black identity and consciousness in general and the emergence of the "my nigga" Haitian identity in the Haitian-American diaspora in particular.

Paul C. Mocombe's (2018, 2019) structurationist theory of phenomenological structuralism, in keeping with the logic of structurationist sociology, assumes practical activity and consciousness, i.e., practical consciousness, to be the basis for understanding human behavior and consciousness in the world. Consciousness here refers to subjective awareness of phenomenal experiences (ideology, language, self, feelings, choice, control of voluntary behavior, thoughts, etc.) of internal and external worlds. The academic literature "describes three possibilities regarding the origin and place of consciousness in the universe: (A) as an emergent property of complex brain neuronal computation, (B) as spiritual quality of the universe, distinct from purely physical actions, and (C) as composed of discrete 'proto-conscious' events acting in accordance with physical laws not yet fully understood" (Hameroff and Penrose, 2014, pg. 70). The latter position, (C), represents the ORCH-OR ("orchestrated objective reduction") theory of Stuart Hameroff and Roger Penrose (2014), which includes aspects of (A) and (B), and posits that "consciousness consists of discrete moments, each an 'orchestrated' quantum-computational process terminated by... an action [,objective reduction or OR,] rooted in quantum aspects of the fine structure of space—time geometry, this being coupled to brain neuronal processes via microtubules" (pg. 70). In this view, the understanding is that a proto-conscious experience existed in the universe, panpsychism, and as a result of emergent structures of the brain it (proto-conscious experience, psychion) became embodied and evolved as a result of quantum neuronal computations of "brains".

Paul C. Mocombe's (2016, 2017, 2018, 2019) structurationist sociology, phenomenological structuralism, which attempts to resolve the structure/agency problematic of the social sciences, builds on the ORCH-OR theory and panpsychism of Hameroff and Penrose, while holding on to the multiverse hypothesis of quantum mechanics and Haitian ontology/epistemology, which the authors reject, the former, because it is not "a more down-to-earth viewpoint" (Hameroff and Penrose, 2014, pg. 51). For Mocombe (2016, 2017, 2018), quantum superposition, wave-function realism, entanglement, and evidence in Haitian Vodou of spirit possession, which represent ancestors from a parallel world, Vilokan, of the earth's on which we ought to pattern our behaviors and structures, are grounding proofs for the acceptance of the multiple worlds hypothesis of quantum mechanics. Within the latter hypothesis, the understanding is that "each possibility in a superposition evolves to form its own universe, resulting in an infinite multitude of coexisting 'parallel' worlds. The stream of consciousness of the observer is supposed somehow to 'split', so that there is one in each of the worlds—at least in those worlds for which the observer remains alive and conscious. Each instance of the observer's consciousness experiences a separate independent world, and is not directly aware of any of the other worlds" (Hameroff and Penrose, 2014, pg. 50). Albeit each instance of the observer's consciousness is entangled and superimposed by the phenomenal properties of subatomic particles constituting it. It is within this multiple worlds hypothesis that Mocombe constitutes the notion of consciousness in the universe according to his theory of phenomenological structuralism. For Mocombe, consciousness is a fifth force of nature, a quantum material substance/energy, psychion, the phenomenal property of which is recycled/entangled/superimposed throughout the multiverse and becomes embodied via the microtubules of brains. It is manifested in simultaneous, entangled, superimposed, and interconnecting material resource frameworks as embodied praxis or practical consciousness, which in-turn becomes the phenomenal properties of material (subatomic particle energy, psychion) consciousness that is recycled/entangled/superimposed throughout the multiverses as practical activity/consciousness.

Structurationist sociology synthesizes structure and agency via the concept of praxis or practical consciousness; accounting for agency or practical consciousness via the actions associated with structural reproduction and differentiation within a particular material resource framework (Crothers, 2003; Ortner, 1984). This latter paradigm overlooks alternative praxes not associated with structural reproduction and differentiation, however. Building on structurationist sociology and the multiple worlds theory of quantum mechanics to account for the agency problematics overlooked by the structurationist position, Mocombe argues that the "moments, or movements, which escape from the compound of socially constructed identifications" are the product of an individual actors' (mental) stance/analytics (Martin Heidegger's term) vis-à-vis three types of structures/systems of signification amidst the practical consciousness associated with societal structural reproduction and differentiation (the social system): 1) the (chemical, biological, and physiological) drives (forms of sensibility and understanding) of the body and brain (the biological system), 2) impulses or phenomenal properties of residual past consciousnesses or recycled/entangled/superimposed subatomic/chemical particles encapsulated in and as the neuronal energies of the brain via microtubules (the physical system), 3) and actions or practical consciousnesses resulting from the deferment of meaning in ego-centered linguistic and symbolic communicative discourse (the linguistic system) (2018, 2019).

Generally speaking, consciousnesses, actions (practical consciousness), learning, and development within Mocombe's phenomenological structural ontology are the product of the embodiment of the phenomenal properties of recycled/entangled/superimposed subatomic neuronal energies/chemicals, psychion, of a psychonic/panpsychic subatomic field of the multiverse objectified in the space-time of multiverses via the aggregated body and the microtubules of the brain. Once objectified and embodied the phenomenal properties of the neuronal energies/chemicals encounter the space-time of physical worlds via a transcendental subject of consciousnesses (the aggregation of a universal-self superimposed and entangled across the multiple worlds of the multiverse) and the drives and sensibilities of the aggregated body and brain in reified structures of signification, language, ideology, ideological apparatuses, and communicative discourse defined and determined by other beings that control the resources (economics), and modes of distributing them, of a material world required for physical survival in space-time. The Heideggerian (mental) stances/analytics, "ready-to-hand," "unready-to-hand," and "present-at-hand," which emerge as a result of conflict between the embodied transcendental ego vis-à-vis its different systems, 1) the sensibilities and (chemical, biological, and physiological) drives of the body and brain, 2) drives/impulses of embodied residual memories or phenomenal properties of past recycled/entangled/superimposed subatomic/chemical particles, 3) the actions produced via the body in relation to the indeterminacy/deferment of meaning of linguistic and symbolic signifiers as they appear to individuated consciousnesses in ego-centered communicative discourse, 4) and the dialectical and differentiating effects, i.e., structural reproduction and differentiation, of the structures of signification, social class language game, of those who control the economic materials (and their distribution, i.e., mode of production) of a world are the origins of practical consciousnesses. All four types of actions, the drives and sensibilities of the body and brain, drives or phenomenal properties of embodied recycled/entangled/superimposed past consciousnesses, structural reproduction/differentiation stemming from the mode of production, and deferential actions arising from the deferment of meaning in ego-centered communicative discourse via the present-at-hand stance/analytic, exist in the material world with the social class language game, i.e., the physical, mental, emotional, ideological, etc. 5) powers of those who control the material resource framework as the causative agent for individual behaviors. In other words, our (mental) stances in consciousness vis-à-vis the conflict between the (chemical, biological, and physiological) drives and sensibilities of the body and brain, (societal) structural reproduction and differentiation, drives of embodied past consciousnesses of recycled/entangled/superimposed subatomic/chemical particles, and deferential actions arising as a result of the deferment of meaning in ego-centered communicative discourse determines the practical consciousness we want to recursively reorganize and reproduce in the material world. The power and power positions of those who control (via the mode of production, language, ideology, ideological apparatuses, and communicative discourse) the resources (and their distribution, i.e., mode of production) of a material resource framework, and the threat it poses to the ontological security of an actor, in the end determines what actions and identities are allowed to organize and reproduce in the material world without the individual actor/agent facing marginalization or death.

It is Being's (mental/cognitive) stance/analytic, "ready-to-hand," "unready-to-hand," and "present-at-hand," in consciousness vis-à-vis the conflict, or lack thereof, between the (chemical, biological, and physiological) drives and sensibilities of the aggregated body and brain, drives/impulses (phenomenal properties) of residual past/present/future consciousnesses of recycled/entangled/superimposed subatomic particles, alternative practices which arise as a result of phenomenological meditation and deferment of meaning, along with the differentiating logic or class divisions of the social relations of production, which produces the variability of actions and practices in cultures, social structures, or social systems. All four types of actions are always present and manifested in a social structure to some degree contingent upon the will and desires of the economic social class that controls the material resource framework through its body (practical consciousness), language/symbols, ideology, ideological apparatuses, and social relations of production. They choose, amidst the class division of the social relations of production, what other meaning constitutions and practices are allowed to manifest themselves in the material world without facing alienation, marginalization, domination, or death.

Hence, we never experience the things-in-themselves of the world culturally and historically in consciousness. We experience them structurally or relationally, the structure of the conjuncture of the mode of production, its language, ideology, ideological apparatuses, etc., and our (mental/cognitive) stances/analytics, ready-to-hand, unready-to-hand, present-at-hand, vis-à-vis these things as they appear to and in consciousness determine our practical consciousness or behaviors.

We initially know, experience, and utilize the things of and in consciousness in the preontological ready-to-hand mode, which is structural and relational. That is, our bodies encounter, know, experience, and utilize the things of the world in consciousness, intersubjectively, via their representation as objects of knowledge, truth, usage, and experience enframed and defined in the relational logic and practices or language game (Wittgenstein's term) of the institutions or ideological apparatuses of the other beings-of-the-material resource framework whose historicity comes before our own and gets reified in and as the actions of their bodies, language, ideology, ideological apparatuses, mode of production, and communicative discourse. This is the predefined phenomenal structural, i.e., ontological, world we and our bodies are thrown-in in coming to be-in-the-world. How an embodied-hermeneutically-structured Being as such solipsistically view, experience, understand, act, and utilize the predefined objects of knowledge, truth, and experienced defined by others and their conditions of possibilities in consciousness in order to formulate their practical consciousness is albeit indeterminate. Martin Heidegger in *Being in Time* is accurate, however, in suggesting that three stances or modes of encounter (Analytic of Dasein), "presence-at-hand," "readiness-to-hand," and "un-readiness-to-hand," characterizes our views of the things of consciousness represented intersubjectively via bodies, language, ideology, and communicative discourse, and subsequently determine our practical consciousness or social agency. In "ready-to-hand," which is the preontological mode of human existence thrown in the world, we accept and use the things in consciousness with no conscious experience of them, i.e., without thinking about them or giving them any meaning or signification outside of their intended usage. Heidegger's example is that of using a hammer in hammering. We use a hammer without thinking about it or giving it any other condition of possibility outside of its intended usage as defined by those whose historicity presupposes our own. In "present-at-hand," which, according to Heidegger, is the stance of science, we objectify the things of consciousness and attempt to determine and reify their meanings, usage, and conditions of possibilities as the nature of reality as such. Hence the hammer is intended for hammering by those who created it as a thing solely meant as such. The "unready-to-hand" outlook is assumed when something goes wrong in our usage of a thing of consciousness as defined and determined by those who adopt a "present-at-hand" view. As in the case of the hammer, the unready-to-hand view is assumed when the hammer breaks and we must objectify it, by then assuming a present-at-hand position, and think about it in order to either reconstitute it as a hammer, or give it another condition of possibility. Any other condition of possibility that we give the hammer outside of its initial condition of possibility which presupposed our historicity becomes relational, defined in relation to any of its other conditions of possibilities it may have been given by others we exist in the world with who either ready-to-hand, unready-to-hand, or present-at-hand attempts to maintain the social class language game of power. In the ready-to-hand stance the latter unconsciously practices and attempts to reproduce the social class language game of power by discriminating against and marginalizing any other conditions of possibilities of their social class language as determined by those in ideological power positions. They may move to the unready-to-hand stance in response to those who they encounter that attempts, present-at-hand, to alter the nature of the dominant social class language game they recursively reorganize and reproduce as outlined by those in power positions who are present-at-hand of the dominant social class language game. In either case, not all beings achieve the present-at-hand stance. The latter is the stance of science and ideologies, which are tautologies when they profess that their stances represent the nature of reality as such, and those in power positions, who choose, among a plethora of alternative present-at-hand social class language games, what alternative practical consciousnesses outside of their social class language game that are allowed to manifest in the material world.

Hence, as outlined above, phenomenological structuralism posits consciousness to be the by-product or evolution of subatomic particles, psychion, unfolding with increasing levels of abstraction within a material resource framework enframed by the mode of production, language, ideology, ideological apparatuses, and communicative discourse of bodies (who control the material resource framework) recursively reorganizing and reproducing the ideals of the latter factors as their practical consciousness. Thus, in phenomenological structuralism the understanding is that the structure of reality determines language (via its generative grammar) and how we ought to live in the world. However, the language, and its usage, i.e., social class language game, of those who control the material resource frameworks of the world conceals that relationship via their mode of production, ideologies, ideological apparatuses, and communicative discourse, which is evolutionary. In other words, like the Wittgensteinian position of the *Tractatus*, Mocombe's theory of phenomenological structuralism assumes that there is a uniform (grammatical) structure to language determined by the logical-empirical structure of (quantum and physical) reality. The grammatical structure of linguistic utterances attempts to capture the subjects and objects of that reality and how we ought to live in it and with them. In being-in-the-world with others, this logical-grammatical structure, however, is concealed by the developmental knowledge, and its usage (practical activity), of those who control the material resource framework of the world via the stage of development of their language, ideology, ideological apparatuses, social relations of production, and communicative discourse. Be that as it may, the latter comes to constitute an evolutionary social class language whose linguistic systemicity and usage comes to determine our conception of reality, and the classes, categories, and forms of life we belong to and interact in and with, which depending on its stage of development and relation to the True nature of reality as such, is either accepted or constantly deferred by those in its speech community who are marginalized or not represented in its evolutionarily developed linguistic systemicity. The latter process under the guise "language game," language as a tool, is what Wittgenstein captures in his second treatise on language as developed in the *Philosophical Investigations*. That is, the classes and categories created by the dominant social class language game of a material resource framework constitute reified classes, categories, and forms of life, "language games," whose meanings and praxes as defined by the dominant social class language game are either accepted or deferred by those classified in them.

So in Mocombe's theory of phenomenological structuralism, Wittgenstein's two theories of language and meaning must be read as one philosophy as opposed to two, one supported by analytical philosophy and the other by postmodernism/post-structuralism. We have a plethora of language games (classes, forms of life, and categories) in the world, which structures our language, because of the ability to defer meaning in ego-centered communicative discourse and the developmental stage of the human mind and body vis-à-vis the actual structure of reality. The language of science, like its predecessor religion, attempts to capture the logical-empirical structure of (quantum and physical) reality, and how we ought to live within it, amidst the utterances and practical consciousnesses of the masses given their abilities to defer meaning in ego-centered communicative discourse and the classes, categories, and forms of life they are classed in/with by the dominant social class language game.

Hence in the end, consciousness (praxis) and subject constitution is a product of conflict, or lack thereof, and an individual's (mental/cognitive) stance, i.e., analytics, vis-à-vis three structures of signification and the ability to defer meaning in ego-centered communicative discourse stemming from the social class language game (i.e., language, symbols, ideology, ideological apparatuses, and communicative discourse) of those who control the mode of production of a material resource framework. It is the ready-to-hand drives of the body and brain, ready-to-hand and present-at-hand manifestation of past/present/future recycled/entangled/superimposed residual consciousnesses/subatomic particles, the present-at-hand phenomenological meditation and deferment of meaning that occurs in embodied consciousness via language, ideology, and communicative discourse as reflected in diverse individual practices, within the ready-to-hand, unready-to-hand, and present-at-hand differentiating logic or class divisions of the social relations of production, which produces the variability of actions and practices in cultures, social structures, or social systems. All four types of actions, the (chemical, biological, and physiological) drives/impulses of the body and residual past consciousnesses of subatomic particles, structural reproduction/differentiation, and actions resulting from the deferment of meaning in ego-centered communicative discourse, are always present and manifested in a social structure (which is the reified ideology via ideological apparatuses, their social class language game, of those who control a material resource framework) to some degree contingent upon the will and desires of the economic social class that controls the material resource framework through the actions of their bodies (practical consciousness), language, symbols, ideology, ideological apparatuses, and social relations of production. They choose, amidst the evolutionary class division of the social relations of production, "the structure of the conjuncture," (Marshall Sahlins's term) what other meaning constitutions and practices are allowed to manifest without the Beings of that practice facing alienation, marginalization, domination, or death.

The individual being is initially constituted as superimposed, entangled, recycled, and embodied subatomic particles, psychion, of multiple worlds of the multiverse, which have their own predetermined form of understanding and cognition, phenomenal properties (qualia), based on previous or simultaneous/entangled/superimposed experiences as aggregated matter (this is akin to what the Greek philosopher Plato refers to when he posits knowledge as recollection of the Soul). Again, the individual's actions are not necessarily determined by the embodiment and interconnecting drives of these recycled/entangled/superimposed subatomic particles. It is conflict and an individual's stance, ready-to-hand, unready-to-hand, and present-at-hand, when the subatomic particles become aggregated matter or embodied, which determines whether are not they become aware, present-at-hand, of the subatomic particle drives and choose to recursively reorganize and reproduce the content of the drives as their practical consciousness.

This desire to reproduce the cognition and understanding of the (chemical, biological, and physiological) drives of the recycled/entangled/superimposed subatomic particles, however, may be limited by the structuring structure of the aggregated body and brain of the individual subject. That is to say, the second origins and basis of an individual's actions are the structuring drives and desires, for food, clothing, shelter, social interaction, and sex, of the aggregated body and brain, which the subatomic particles constitute and embody. In other words, the aggregated body and brain is preprogrammed with its own (biological/physiological) forms of sensibility, understanding, and cognition, structuring structure, by which it experiences being-in-the-world as aggregated embodied subatomic particles. These bodily forms of sensibility, understanding, and cognition, such as the drive and desire for food, clothing, shelter, social interaction, linguistic communication, and sex, are tied to the material embodiment and survival of the embodied individual actor, and may or may not supersede or conflict with the desire and drive of an individual to recursively (re) organize and reproduce the structuring structure of the superimposed, entangled, and recycled (phenomenal properties of) subatomic particles. If these two initial structuring structures are in conflict, the individual moves from the ready-to-hand to the unready-to-hand stance or analytics where they may begin to reflect upon and question their being-in-the-world prior to acting. Hence just as in the case of the structuring structure of the subatomic particles it is an individual being's analytics vis-à-vis the drives of its body and brain in relation to the impulses/frequencies of the subatomic particles, which determines whether or not they become driven by the desire (actions/praxis) to solely fulfill the material needs of their body and brain at the expense of the drives/desires of the subatomic particles or the social class language game of the material resource framework they find their existence unfolding in.

The social class language game, and its differentiating effects, an individual find their existence unfolding in is the third structuring structure, which attempts to determine the actions of individual beings as they experience being-in-the-world as embodied subatomic particles. The aggregated individual finds themselves objectified and unfolding within a material resource framework controlled by the actions of other bodies, which presuppose their existence, via the evolutionary actions of their bodies (practical consciousness), language, communicative discourse, ideology, and ideological apparatuses stemming from how they satisfy the desires of their bodies and subatomic particle drives (means and mode of production). What is aggregated as a social class language game by those in power positions via and within its mode of production, language, ideology, ideological apparatuses, and communicative discourse attempts to interpellate and subjectify other beings to its interpretive frame of satisfying their bodily needs, fulfilling the impulses of their subatomic particles, and organizing a material resource framework at the expense of all others, and becomes a third form of structuring individual action based on the mode of production and how it differentiates individual actors.

That is to say, an individual's interpellation, subjectification, and differentiation within the social class language game that presupposes their being-in-a-world attempts to determine their actions or practical consciousness via the reified language, ideology, etc., of the social class language game, the meaning of which can be deferred via the communicative discourse of the individual actors. Hence, the deferment of meaning in ego-centered communicative discourse of the language and ideology of a social class language game is the final means of determining an individual's action or practical consciousness outside of, and in relation to, its stance, i.e., analytics, vis-à-vis the drives of subatomic particles, drives and desires of the body and brain, and structural reproduction and differentiation.

Whereas the practical consciousness of the transcendental ego stemming from the impulses of embodied subatomic particles are indeterminant as with its neuronal processes involved with the constitution of meaning in ego-centered communicative discourse (Albeit physicists are in the process of exploring the nature, origins, and final states of subatomic particles, and neuroscientists are attempting to understand the role of neuronal activities in developing the transcendental ego and whether or not it continues to exist after death). The form of the understandings and sensibilities of the body and brain are determinant as with structural reproduction and differentiation of the mode of production and physiological mapping of the brain and body, and therefore can be mapped out by neuroscientists, biologists, and sociologists to determine the nature, origins, and directions of societal constitution and an individual actor's practical consciousness unfolding.

The interaction of all four elements or processes in relation to the stance of the transcendental ego of the individual actor is the basis for human action, praxis/practical consciousness in a world. However, in the end, consequently, the majority of practical consciousness will be a product of an individual actor's embodiment and the structural reproduction and differentiation of a social class language game given 1) the determinant nature of embodiment, form of understanding and sensibility of the body and brain amidst, paradoxically, the indeterminacy of impulses of embodied subatomic particles and the neuronal processes involved in ego-centered communicative discourse; and 2) the consolidation of power of those who control the material resource framework wherein a society, the social class language game, is ensconced and the threat that power (consolidated and constituted via the actions of bodies, mode of production, language, ideology, ideological apparatuses, and communicative discourse) poses to the ontological security of an aggregated individual actor who chooses (or not) either ready-to-hand or present-at-hand to recursively reorganize and reproduce the ideals of the society as their practical consciousness. It should be mentioned that in response to this latter process, those in power positions who internalize the ideals of the social structure and recursively (re) organize and reproduce them as their practical consciousness are in the unready-to-hand stance when they encounter alternative forms of being-in-the-world within their social class language game. They dialectically attempt to reconcile the practical consciousness of their social class language game with the reified practical consciousness of those who have deferred their meanings for alternative forms of being-in-the-world within their social class language. They can either accept, marginalize, or seek to eradicate the deferred or decentered subject or their practices.

Hence within the theory and methodology of phenomenological structuralism, there is, contrary to David Hume's "bundle of perception" hypothesis, a human essence, which is tied to the embodiment and structuring structure of the phenomenal properties of superimposed, entangled, embodied, and recycled subatomic particles, the processes of which are unbeknownst to us as of the writing of this work, as they are recursively reorganized and reproduced via the superverse and its multiverses. Just the same, Universalism and Truth are also tied to the science and physics of the remaining processes of phenomenological structuralism. Subatomic/chemical particles with phenomenal properties constitute objects and subjects that are external and internal to the perceiving human actor who know them (the objects and subjects) as both external and internal phenomenon endowed with, and mediated by, linguistic and ideological meanings, stemming from the evolutionary modes of production, of other human actors who presupposed their aggregated existence. The essence, universalism, and Truth of an object and subject lies in the phenomenal properties of their subatomic and chemical particles once demystified and demythologized, from linguistic and ideological meanings and understandings associated with the evolutionary mode of human production, by the techniques of phenomenology and the scientific process. Be that as it may, for phenomenological structuralism, in keeping with the empiricist logic of Bertrand Russell, "outside of human desires there are no moral standards." Morality or moral standards are associated with the linguistic and ideological desires (power and power positions) of those who control the resources and mode of production of a material resource framework via their language, ideology, ideological apparatuses, and communicative discourse (i.e., social class language game). It (moral practices and statements) constitutes a part of the superverse/multiverse as phenomenal properties of subatomic particles once disaggregated as lived-experience in the multiple worlds of the multiverse. This does not mean that morality is universal; instead, it is contingent upon the material resource frameworks of the multiverse and the evolutionary stage of practical consciousness as constituted in the aforementioned frameworks. In that sense, assuming the phenomenal properties of subatomic particles get recycled between the superverse and its multiverses as I am positing here, morality is an epiphenomenon of lived-experience and becomes an emergent property of the superverse and its multiverses, which constitute the *lwas* (platonic forms or concepts such as beauty, justice, egalitarianism, etc.) of Haitian metaphysics that human reason, which are the recycled subatomic neuronal/chemical particles of the superverse and multiverse operating through DNA and its aggregation as the brain and mind (perception), can reflect upon to constitute their being-in-the-world (practical consciousness) in relation to the language, ideology, etc., i.e., social class language game, of those who precede individual existence. Ostensibly, social change, following subatomic particle aggregation, is tied to both the 1) differentiating effects and techniques of the social class language game of those who control the material resource framework of (an) earth, 2) and the ability to defer meaning in ego-centered communicative discourse, via symbols, language, ideology, etc., which encapsulates or is the medium by which the *lwas* (concepts) of the superverse and its multiverses are expressed as human practical consciousness in material worlds.

Background to Phenomenological Structuralism

The linguistic turn in meaning and identity constitution, whether in linguistics or the social sciences, presupposes that meaning and the nature of human identity or consciousness are nothing more than the relationships which pertain within a given linguistic system, structure, culture, or social structure. Thus, such questions as those pertaining to matters of human agency, individual or shared interests, community, etc., have generally been ignored by so-called "structuralists" (Edgar and Sedgwick, 1999, pg. 383). This in turn makes most structural approaches synchronic; that is, most structuralists approach a phenomenon at a single moment in history, or as something existing outside history, which is unchanging.

It is well known that Ferdinand de Saussure in linguistics, to Claude Lévi-Strauss in anthropology, and Talcott Parsons and Louis Althusser in sociology postulate this synchronic world ordered into an interconnected semiotic system. In Saussurean structuralism, which serves as the model for the social sciences, language "is viewed as a purely arbitrary system of signs in which *parole* or speech is subsidiary to *langue*, the formal dimension of language. *Parole* is the world's messiness that the semiotic order [or formal dimension] shuns" (Obeyesekere, 1997, pg. 18), subjecting social actors to its binary rules that gives them their conceptual framework, rather than the other way around (Levi-Strauss, 1963; Marshall, 1998; Saussure, 1972 [1916]).

In anthropology, Lévi-Strauss extends this idea to culture, and culture too becomes a system of external signs, which reflect the structure or categories of the mind, exercised in social relations to order experience (Lévi-Strauss, 1963, pg. 279). Just the same, in sociology Talcott Parsons employs the notion of structure or system to refer to modern capitalist society as an "organic" whole or totality consisting of interrelated parts (i.e., structurally differentiated) that perform specific functions in relation to each other and contribute to the maintenance of the whole, i.e., structural functionalism (Parsons, 1951, pg. 5-6). The structural Marxism of Louis Althusser, and many others, replaces both Parsons's conservative holism and Levi-Strauss's mental categories by positions in modes of production and relations to the means of production for the structure or system that governs meaning and gives social actors their conceptual framework (Althusser, 2001[1971]).

The logical consequence of the adoption of the Saussurean position by Lévi-Strauss, Parsons, and Althusser in philosophy and the social sciences, however, is the implication that human action, or consciousness, lies in the reproduction of the relational (binary rules for inclusion and exclusion) objective models of society as either structured by our minds, or the external interrelated structures of signification as internalized by social actors. Therefore, to understand human social agency, one only needs to understand either how the mind structures reality (transcendental idealism), or the differentiating rules of a culture, social structure, or social system. Both positions, however, are problematic. In the psychologism of the former case, social structure reflecting the structure of the mind, social practice or action and its variability are inconceivable in that there is no analytical means to explain how the internal "binary" processes of the mind give rise to the external empirical phenomena of social structures, practices, and their variabilities. In the latter case, structure or social structure as a reflection of the internalization of external functional structures of signification, i.e., part/whole relationship, the possibility for, and the origins of, the variability of practices, which have ontological status in the world, amongst irreducibly situated subjects are inconceivable, as human subjects or social actors are only reproducing in their actions the relational meaning and representation of the external objective social world (society), without any alternative practices, deviations, or improvisations outside of the structural differentiation of the social structure.

Moreover, since the 1960's with the advent of postmodern and post-structural theories into the theoretical discourses of social science academics a new struggle regarding the origins and nature of identity and consciousness vis-à-vis the aforementioned problematics has dominated social science and philosophical theories. The issue centers on several factors raised by postmodern and post-structural thinkers in the likes of Michel Foucault, Jacques Derrida, and Jacques Lacan against the structuralism of the sciences, 1) they question the validity regarding the Cartesian rational individual, which Foucault and Derrida deny in favor of their attempt to dissolve the subject altogether; 2) they question the interdependency of the constitution of a stable structure and a distinct subject with agency, in denying the latter they undermine the former; 3) they question the status of science; 4) finally, they question the possibility of the objectivity of any language of description or analysis. Although these factors raised in the writings of Jacques Lacan, Jacques Derrida, and Michel Foucault are theoretically legitimate and have posed tremendous problems for the social sciences and their constitution as a science based on the notion of a stable structure constituted by stable subjects with agency. These problems have not adequately been addressed by Marxist social theorists in the likes of Louis Althusser, Pierre Bourdieu, Jürgen Habermas, Anthony Giddens, and Marshall Sahlins working to resolve these issues by attempting to synthesize the rationality of the individual with the phenomenological discourses of the former theorists, and Marxist and structural Marxist philosophy.

Hence the structure/agency debate in the social sciences emphasize the rational origins of the reproduced and transformed social actions of social actors that constitute a social structure: are social actors determined and driven by internal invariable structures of the mind (Lévi-Strauss, 1963; Bell, 1985 [1982]), or are social actors automatons determined and driven by external relational structures of signification (Parsons, 1951; Althusser, 2001 [1971]))? Thus, in the social scientific form of the debate, biological determinism, i.e., innate senses of anything, as well as the Lévi-Straussian sense, i.e., innate structure of the mind, were out rightly rejected. Also, the idea that social actors are irreducibly situated subjects who act and react based on rational calculations as they respond to particular external social processes (social structure) or stimuli was for the most part dismissed. Total rationality was viewed as an impossibility given the inability of social actors to either know all the choices available to them in the present or know the complete future outcomes of those choices. This made rationality necessarily relative to a frame of reference or structure of signification, which rejects the indeterminacy of meaning and decentered subject of postmodern/post-structural theorizing.

Hence, the focus in the study of action and interaction in the social sciences was thus not a matter of denying or minimizing the rational potential of social actors, but expressed rather an urgent need to understand where 'the system' or structure that limits their knowledge and stabilizes society "comes from—how it is produced and reproduced, and how it may have changed in the past or be changed in the future" (Ortner, 1984, pg. 146). In other words, thinkers plagued by this debate, sought "to explain the relationship(s) that obtain between human action, on the one hand, and some global entity which we may call the system, [or social structure, structure, or culture] on the other" (Ortner, 1984, pg. 148), when the latter (i.e., the system) is not a necessary reflection of neither biology, nor the structure of the mind, but an external force of rules of conduct, i.e., categorical boundaries, that stabilizes society and thereby constitute the identity of social actors as argued by Talcott Parsons and Louis Althusser.

From roughly 1975 to the present, an enormous strand of critical writings, expounding a great many strands of theoretical schools of thought, combined to challenge this post-World War II structuralist matrix which denied alternative agencies, outside the relational logic of a structure, system, or culture to social actors. Some were advanced by rationalist thinkers seeking to preserve the idea of individuals as solitary thinkers who act in a purposive rational way, while others were offered by theorists dedicated to preserving the tenets of structural-functionalism and structural-Marxism while explicating the functional role of difference or the variability of practices amongst social actors within social structure not as an invariable by-product of the mind but as an external unified structure of signification or system. Considering this action-oriented response to account for the different provinces of meaning within systems or structures of signification, the term praxis or structurationist theorists will serve as the dominant label for the arguments expounded in opposition to Parsonian structural-functionalism and variants of structural Marxism by prominent theorists such as Pierre Bourdieu, Marshall Sahlins, Anthony Giddens, and Jürgen Habermas (Crothers, 2003; Ortner, 1984). These arguments are complex, and to examine them together is necessarily to do violence to the purity of notions advanced separately by various authors. The exercise is nevertheless useful at least for revealing their main and common objective, i.e., to resolve the structure/agency debate of the social sciences.

The Structurationist Response and its Problems

Structural-functionalists and Structural-Marxists in attempting to understand social action (i.e., praxis) within social structures of signification privilege social relations and reproduction via linguistic and symbolic representation over biological determining elements (i.e., race, sex, etc.), for meaning, human action, and consciousness constructions. In doing so, however, they fail to account for the origins and nature of the different provinces of meaning, human action, and consciousness existing within, but at the same time, outside the relational or dialectical prescribed logic of the social structure (structural reproduction and differentiation). Neo-structuralists or structurationists in the likes of Pierre Bourdieu (1990 [1980], 1984) with his theory of practice (habitus or constructivist structuralism), Marshall Sahlins (1976, 1995 [1981]) through mythopraxis, Anthony Giddens (1984) through his theory of structuration, and Jürgen Habermas (1987 [1981], 1984 [1981]) with his theory of "communicative action," however, attempt to do just that, "explain the relationship(s) that obtain between human action, on the one hand, and some global entity which we may call the system, [or social structure, structure, or culture] on the other" in order to capture the nature of social action, reproduction, transformation, and differentiation within structures of signification. They attempt to do so, for the most part, through "the central notion of the 'duality of structure' which refers to 'the essential recursiveness of social life, as constituted in social practices: structure is both medium and outcome of the reproduction of practices'" (Archer, 1985, pg. 60). That is, structures are not only external to social actors, but are internal rules and resources ("form of consciousness") produced and reproduced by actors "unconsciously" (intuitively) in their practices.[1] From this perspective, accordingly, structure, i.e., culture or, sociological speaking, social structure, "may set conditions to the historical process, but it is dissolved and reformulated in material practice, so that history becomes the realization, in the form of society, of the actual [(embodied rules)] resources people put into play" (Sahlins, 1995 [1981], pg. 7). In this understanding, the structure is not an epiphenomenon of the structure of the mind, but is a result of the internalization by social actors of external (social structural) rules of conduct which are sanctioned, recursively (re) organized, reproduced, and differentiated in material practice. Thus, social structure, human action, meaning, and consciousness are mutually constituted and united together as "practical consciousness," i.e., a duality.

Ostensibly, like structuralism, structural functionalism, and structural Marxism, the structurationist response to account for the nature of human action within structures of signification, however, is also problematic.

That is, the central notion of the duality of structure prevents praxis theorists from accounting for the origins and relational nature of the variability of praxis or "practical consciousnesses" within a particular structure of signification. That is to say, the part/whole dialectic of the "duality" concept cannot account for the origins of alternative "practical consciousnesses" that arises as a result of 1) the drives and sensibilities of the body and brain, 2) the drives and impulses, phenomenal properties, of embodied recycled subatomic particles, and 3) the deferment of meaning in ego-centered communicative discourse during the internalization process as suggested by postmodern and post-structural theory (Mocombe, 2016). In essence, structurationists are only able to account for the dialectic of 4) structural reproduction and differentiation stemming from the means and mode of production of a society and their ideological apparatuses (Mocombe, 2016).

Pierre Bourdieu

The central notion of the duality of structure in Pierre Bourdieu (1990 [1980]) is described as a "dialectic of objective structures and incorporated structures (*habitus*) which operates in every practical action" (Bourdieu, 1990, pg. 41; insert added). Action, therefore, is a result of the *habitus* of individuals, an "embodied history, internalized as a second nature and so forgotten as history . . ." (56); a "system of structured, structuring dispositions" (52) that are "deposited in each organism in the form of schemes of perception, thought and action [,]" (54) derived from "the conditionings [(fields)] associated with a particular class of [material] conditions of existence . . ." (53). In short, in his application of this theory to capitalist society in his work *Distinctions* (1984) cultural, economic, political, and social capital become the system of structured, structuring dispositions that are deposited in social actors in their form of schemes of perception, thought, and action that differentiates them and their conditioning fields from each other in the society. More concretely speaking, the bourgeois class of capitalist society possesses the capital forms, i.e., linguistic, social, economic, cultural, and political capitals, which constitute the social structure of modern societies and gets distributed throughout the society and differentiates the middle and working classes from the upper-class of owners and high-level executives based upon the amount of capital they possess in their material conditions. Albeit, all classes in the society seek to possess the capital of the bourgeois upper-classes whose institutions or ideological apparatuses transmit these structuring dispositions to them.

Although Bourdieu's materialization of social structure by synthesizing the objectivity of the latter with the subjectivity of action is able to capture the actual nature of human social action and societal reproduction, the movement of the body as a result of the embodiment of a "system of structured, structuring dispositions" within "fields" associated with a particular class of material conditions, his theory is only able to capture the origins and nature of structural reproduction and differentiation produced by the relational logic and praxis of the "[(capitalist)] system of structured, structuring dispositions" and not the origins and role of difference arrived at through the deferment of meaning in the incorporation process and the other two processes I have highlighted above. In other words, Bourdieu's praxis response is unable to capture the relation and role of the different means (practical consciousnesses) of organizing a "field," which arises because of the deferment of meaning in the internalization "of schemes of perception, thought and action derived from the conditionings" within a dominant structure of signification. That is, the central notion of the duality of structure prevents Bourdieu from accounting for the origins and relational nature of the variability of praxis or "practical consciousnesses" within a particular structure of signification. The part/whole dialectic of the "duality" concept cannot account for alternative "practical consciousnesses" that arises as a result of not structural differentiation, but the drives of the body, phenomenal properties of embodied subatomic particles, and the deferment of meaning in ego-centered communicative discourse during the internalization process of signifiers (Habermas, 1987 [1981], 1984 [1981]; Mocombe, 2014, 2016). In a word, he is unable to account for Jacques Derrida's notion of *différance*, alternative structures of signification and actions that are outside the structuring structure of capitalist structural differentiation, on the one hand; and Mocombe's (2016, 2017) *drives/impulses*, phenomenal properties, vis-à-vis the body and embodied subatomic particles, on the other.

Marshall Sahlins

In Marshall Sahlins's (1976, 1995 [1981]) cultural structuralist history, the interrelationship is also between structures of significance and social action. That is, action, "structure of the conjuncture," emerges from the dialectic between culture (structure) and the cultural schemes in the individual, prefigured myths (mythopraxis) in his application of his theory to the ancient Hawaiians or prefigured "interests" in the case of contemporary "man," which are actually symbols and categories constituting a received system that gives persons, events, and objects their historical effect (1995 [1981]). So that, situations are ordered by culture (structure), and history, or agency, is the product of structures of significance: the recursively organized and reproduced cultural schemes (*habitus* in Bourdieu's approach) of the individual or social actor "dissolved or reformulated" in the material world (7).

Like Bourdieu, Sahlins is able to demonstrate the material nature of social action derived from the internalization of external structures of signification. However, also like Bourdieu, he is unable to account for the relation of the analytics (mental states) of an individual actor vis-à-vis the different provinces of meaning within the structure of signification, which arises as a result of the drives of the body, phenomenal properties of embodied subatomic particles, and the deferment of meaning in ego-centered communicative discourse. In other words, as in the case of the ancient Hawaiians, who Sahlins argue assumed Captain Cook to be a god because their internalization of the mythical structures of signification which structured their social action or gave them their historical effect posited such a being, he is unable to account for the nature and relation of those Polynesians who upon internalizing this "mythical reality" rejected it for another interpretation, i.e., he was a "thug" seeking to steal their land, women, children, and resources. Sahlins' conflating of action and structures mutual constitution prevents such a materialized happening or conclusion. The part/whole dialectic by which Hawaiian consciousness is constituted via the structure of the conjuncture of their mythopraxis in Sahlins' theorizing cannot account for how the Polynesians could reach any other conclusion outside that which is determined by their dialectic totality, mythopraxis, "which are actually symbols and categories constituting a received system that gives persons, events, and objects their historical effect."

Anthony Giddens

Just the same, Anthony Giddens (1984), like Bourdieu and Sahlins, also highlights this "*duality*" of structure." His theory of structuration, which has no obvious single statement of explanation, is a social ontology describing what it means to be an individual invested with "practical consciousness"—a structure's or culture's rules and resources. Thus, "one of the main propositions of structuration theory is that the rules and resources drawn upon in the production and reproduction of social action are at the same time the means of system reproduction (duality of structure)" (19). Action in this understanding is a result of the structural properties of social systems consciously and unconsciously manifesting themselves in the practices that individuals, in order to maintain their ontological security, recursively organize and reproduce (25).

Whereas Giddens, unlike Bourdieu and Sahlins, posits difference through the notion of structural differentiation as a result of the threat to a social actor's ontological security, he is still unable to account for the origins, nature, and relation, within the dominant structure of signification, of those who upon internalizing a structure's rule of conduct which are sanctioned reject them for ontological insecure ways of reproducing their material resource framework. In other words, Giddens, through his notion of "ontological security," is able to demonstrate how and why social actors choose to reproduce the external structural properties of social systems, which after a while simply become a second nature forgotten as history. What he is unable to demonstrate, however, given his notion of the "duality" of structure, is how alternative practices may emerge, and the relation and functioning of these practices to the dominant social system.

Jürgen Habermas

Jürgen Habermas's (1987 [1981]) ought to be "organic" conclusion regarding the constitution of present modern conditions, unlike Giddens, account for the constitution of alternative practices through the distinction he draws between system and lifeworld. Habermas's evolutionary social ontology, "communicative action," is based on the Weberian understanding of the rationalization process in modernity. That is to say, for Habermas the rationalization process in modern communicative discourse has historically developed into a differentiated lifeworld of varying cultural traditions, networks of solidarity groups, and institutions of socialization, "enframed" by, but differentiated from, the rational formation of the secular systems of economy and politics derived from linguistically arrived at "mutual understanding" amongst these varying groups and institutions. This Durkheimian "organic solidarity" which emphasizes mutual cooperation, takes *différance*, or the variability of alternative practices derived through the deferment of meaning in ego-centered communicative discourse, to be the basis for the constitution of modern society. For the rational system of economy and politics in the Habermasian sense is distinguished from the lifeworld of a myriad of meaningful subjective pragmatic positions or categorical boundaries, which it "organically" stabilizes and governs. This, according to Habermas, like Emile Durkheim, differentiates modern societies from primitive ones, which "mechanically" marginalized all differences and *différance* for the underlying "sacred rules" governing meaning that is the social structure.

Like the traditional structural structurationism of Bourdieu, Sahlins, and Giddens, which views the (post) modern social structure or system as a reified symbolic order in which its representations, practices, and meanings are fixed and must be internalized or embodied by social actors as their practical consciousness, part/whole relation, my attempt to understand the constitution of modern society as difference and *différance* assumes that the distinction between the lifeworld and its manifestation as a system (organized around the mode of production), is more enduring just as in primitive societies. Habermas, who refers to this notion as "the colonization of the lifeworld," sees it as a "crisis" in the constitution of modern society; I see it as the more valid means or framework to understanding the nature of systems and social integration up till this point in the human archaeological record.

To put it simply, whereas Habermas, building on the works of George Herbert Mead, Emile Durkheim, and Max Weber, sees the "linguistification of the sacred, as an unfettering of the rationality potential of action oriented to mutual understanding" (Habermas, 1987 [1981], pg. 288), i.e., "communicative action" between subjective positions of the lifeworld within the rational agreed upon boundaries of the economic and political system, which distinguishes modernity from "primitive societies." I, building on the structural duality outlined by the more traditional structurationists, view Habermas's liberal position and the constitution of modern society in terms of a *re-sacrilization* of society based on the substantive and purposive rationality of the Protestant ethic and the spirit of capitalism. That is, (post) modern society is no different from primitive ones. It is an enchantment of the world via the Protestant Ethic and the spirit of capitalism. As such, so-called modern society is a Durkheimian "mechanical solidarity" *re-sacrilized* through the universal claims embedded in a substantive and purposive-rationality, which is an avatar of a sacred linguistic worldview, i.e., the cultural or social structural conditions of Protestantism and its discursive practice the spirit of capitalism and its modes of production.

This mechanical constitution of modern society via bodies (practical consciousnesses), language, ideology, ideological apparatuses, and communicative discourse structuralizing the class division and social relations of production of the Protestant ethic and the spirit of capitalism worldview on the earth, captures the constitution of modern society in our universe, galaxy, and the earth, through the Habermasian rejected notion of "the colonization of the lifeworld." Habermas fails to realize that the lifeworld he speaks of is structuralized and differentiated within the systemic dialectic, class division and social relations of production, of the Protestant Ethic and the spirit of (postindustrial) capitalism, which juxtaposes his embourgeoised position within the system against the differentiated lifeworld of the underclass masses, he is theorizing about. That is to say, the lifeworld is not magically protected from the systemicity of the Protestant Ethic and the spirit of capitalism by which modern society is constituted. It is also structured and differentiated within the systemicity, class division and social relations of production, of the Protestant Ethic and the spirit of capitalism via bodies, language, ideology, ideological apparatuses (media, education, etc.), communicative discourse, and the mode of production of the upper-class of owners and high-level executives. It is within this (their enchantment) mechanical constitutive framework that the origins and relations of alternative practices arrived at as a result of an individual actor's stance/analytics vis-à-vis the drives of the body, drives/impulses (phenomenal properties) of residual past consciousnesses of recycled subatomic particles, and through the deferment of meaning in ego-centered communicative discourse must be understood. It is not that these alternative practices arrived-at, ready-to-hand, unready-to-hand and present-at-hand, vis-à-vis the drives and sensibilities of the body and brain, residual past/present/future consciousnesses of recycled/entangled/superimposed subatomic particles, and through the deferment of meaning in ego-centered communicative discourse are given free rein to reproduce their practices within the social system, which is grounded in the reproduction and differentiation of the social relations of production. On the contrary, their practices are relationally constrained within the structure and differentiation of the system or social structure as determined by class division and the social relations of production through, contemporarily, bourgeois/underclass bodies, mode of production, language, ideologies, ideological apparatuses, and communicative discourse, dialectically, seeking equality of opportunity, recognition, and distribution for these once discriminated against alternative practices within the social class language game of the postindustrial bourgeois state. In essence, by accounting for both structural reproduction and differentiation and social practices arriving through the deferment of meaning in ego-centered communicative discourse, Habermas is highlighting the power dynamics or mechanical solidarity of postindustrial capitalist society, which marginalizes against previous discriminatory practices, i.e., sexism, patriarchy, racism, and homophobia, for its post-racial, post-sexual, etc. constitution where the bourgeoisies of once-discriminated against subjective positions marginalize and discriminate against the underclasses of their communities. In a word, Habermas overlooks, by labeling the phenomenon "a crisis," the power relations by which postindustrial (Protestant/Capitalist) society, even Durkheim's mechanical solidarity, is constituted in favor of the bourgeoisies, which have internalized the practical consciousness of the social structure, of once discriminated against subjective positions.

In sum, the structurationist or praxis school in the social sciences is commonly associated with Jürgen Habermas (1987 [1981], 1984 [1981]), Pierre Bourdieu (1990 [1980], 1984), and Anthony Giddens (1984) in sociology, and Marshall Sahlins (1976, 1995 [1981]) in anthropology (Crothers, 2003; Ortner, 1984). Elaborated in a series of theoretical works and empirical studies, structurationists or praxis theorists account for agency and consciousness in social structure or system, "by clamping action and structure together in a notion of 'practice' or 'practises'" (Crothers, 2003, pg. 3). That is, structures are not only external to social actors, as in the classic structural functional view, but are also internal rules and resources produced and reproduced by actors "unconsciously" (intuitively) in their practices. In structurationist or praxis theory, as Marx one-hundred years before suggested, the structure is "not a substantially separable order of reality", but "simply the 'ideal' form in which the totality of 'material' relations…are manifested to consciousness…" (Sayer, 1987, pg. 84). From this perspective, accordingly, structure or, sociological speaking, social structure, "may set [(ideological)] conditions to the historical process, but it is dissolved and reformulated in material practice [(through mode of production and ideological apparatuses)], so that history becomes the realization, in the form of society, of the actual [(embodied rules)] resources people put into play" (Sahlins, 1995 [1981], pg. 7): consciousness, as a result, refers to "practical consciousness" or the dissolution and reformulation of a social structure's terms (norms, values, prescriptions, and proscriptions) in material practice.

Although this Neo-Marxist "clamping together" of structure, praxis, and consciousness descriptively accounts for "the individual moment of phenomenology" by explaining the unanimity, closure, and "intentionality" of a form of human action or sociation, the capitalist social (material) relations of production and its class divisions and differentiations, which constitute the integrative actions of modern society. It fails, however, as pointed out in the epistemological postmodern/post-structural positions of Michel Foucault, Jacques Derrida, Jacques Lacan, bell hooks, and Patricia Hill-Collins, to account for the origins and nature of fully visible alternative forms of practices (i.e., "the variability of the individual *moments* of phenomenology") within the dominant order that are not class based, but are the product of the deferment of meaning in ego-centered communicative discourse, a la the Vodou Ethic and the spirit of communism social class language game of the Vodou leadership of Haiti, for example. Structurationists fail to see that society and its dominant institutionalized identity and behavior are not solely "one-dimensional," i.e., a duality, and differentiated by the dialectic of capitalist social relations of production, but is constituted, through power relations, as transition, relation, and difference. This difference, akin to Jacques Derrida's *différance*, is not biologically (racially) hardwired in the social actor. It is a result of self-reflective and non-impulsive social actors, upon internalizing the arbitrary structural terms or signifiers of their society via their consciousness, bodies, language, and linguistic communication, conceiving of and exercising other forms of being-in-the-world from that of the dominant symbolic order and its structural differentiation or relational logic through the deferment of meaning in ego-centered communicative discourse (Habermas, 1987 [1981], 1984 [1981]; Giddens, 1984).

By "clamping" action, structure, and consciousness together, i.e., part/whole totality, however, structurationists do not account for, nor demonstrate, the nature and relation of this non-biologically and non-impulsive determined difference (*différance*) to that of the dominant practices of the social structure as highlighted in the theorizing of postmodern and post-structural scholars. Instead, they re-introduce the problem in a new form: How do we know or *exercise* anything at odds with an embodied received view grounded in, and differentiated by, capitalist social relations of production? Paul C. Mocombe's (2013, 2014, 2015, 2016, 2018) phenomenological structural ontology/sociology, phenomenological structuralism, seeks to fix structurationism to account for this problematic by synthesizing Haitian epistemology, i.e., Haitian/Vilokan idealism, the materialism of physics, with the agential initiatives highlighted in the phenomenological method and discourses of Haitian/Vilokan idealism, Husserl, Heidegger, Merleau-Ponty, and Sartre, the Neo-Marxist structuralism of Althusser and structurationism, and Wittgenstein's notion of language game.

For Mocombe, in building on the duality concept of structuration theory, human social action, consciousness, and identity is not only a duality determined by their relation to the mode of production and its differentiation. But, in building on the work of Margaret Archer (1985) in her critique of structurationism, it is also a dualism. Not a conceptual dualism as Archer points out, but a reified external one, the externalized structure of a society reified, in the words of Louis Althusser (1970, 2001), through language, ideology, ideological apparatuses, communicative discourse, and the mode of production. As such, social action and identity/consciousness constitution are not necessarily a duality, i.e., the internalization of the external language, ideology, etc., of a social structure recursively (re) organized and reproduced as the practical consciousness of a social actor. Duality is a contingent phenomenon based on a human subject's stance/analytics (mental state) vis-à-vis the reified structure, which presupposes their existence and the will of those in power positions. In other words, alternative actions or practical consciousnesses are distinct reified languages, ideologies, ideological apparatuses, communicative discourses, and modes of production from that of the dominant social structure within which they operate. These alternative actions or practical consciousnesses are the product of four sources, and Being's stance, ready-to-hand, unready-to-hand, and present-at-hand, vis-à-vis them: 1) the (physiological) drives of the body and brain, 2) impulses/frequencies of residual actions/memories (phenomenal properties) of embodied recycled past consciousnesses of subatomic particles, 3) ideologies of a social system along with its differentiating logic (structural reproduction and differentiation), which produces the variability of actions and practices in cultures, social structures, or social systems as highlighted by structurationist theorists, and 4) the "present-at-hand" phenomenological meditation/deferment that occurs on the latter actions via linguistic/symbolic communication. The exercise of power by social actors in power positions in the ideological apparatuses social actors are interpellated and subjectified in, in the end, determines what practical consciousnesses are allowed to manifest in a material resource framework without a social actor facing alienation, marginalization, or death. Hence structural reproduction and differentiation for Mocombe is always a product of power and power positions in relation to a social actor's stance or analytic.

To this end of fixing structurationism to account for the nature and origins of alternative practical consciousnesses outside the structural reproduction and differentiation of capitalist relations of production, Paul C. Mocombe's (2014, 2015, 2016) phenomenological structuralism builds on Haitian/Vilokan idealism and the material relationship highlighted in physics between the identity and indeterminate behavior of subatomic particles highlighted in quantum mechanics and the determinate behavior of atomic particles in their aggregation as highlighted in general relativity to understand the material constitution of consciousness at the subatomic/neuronal level in, and as, the brain and its manifestation as human practical consciousness at the atomic level as revealed by modes of production, language, ideologies, ideological apparatuses, communicative discourse, and the actions of the body. I go on, in the subsequent chapters, to utilize Mocombe's structurationism, phenomenological structural ontology, to account for the emergence of the "my nigga" Haitian identity in Haiti and the Haitian diaspora in the US.

Theory

Normally referred to as "animism," "fetishism," "paganism," "heathenism," and "black magic" in the Western academic literature, Vodou (spelled Vodun, Voodoo, Vodu, Vaudou, or Vodoun) is the oldest monotheistic religion in the world. Commonly interpreted as "Spirits" or "introspection into the unknown," Vodou is the structuring structure (metaphysics) of the Fon people of Dahomey and other tribes of the continent who would arrive on the island of Haiti/Ayiti as named by the Taino natives (Métraux, 1958; Deren, 1972; Rigaud, 1985; Desmangles, 1992; Bellegarde-Smith and Michel, 2006). Unlike German Idealism whose intellectual development from Kant to Schopenhauer, Hegel, Marx, Nietzsche, Husserl, Heidegger, and the Frankfurt school produced the dialectic, Marxist materialism, Nietzscheian antidialectics, phenomenology, and deontological ethics. The epistemology of Haitian Vodou, Haitian/Vilokan Idealism, produces a hermeneutical phenomenology, materialism, and an antidialectical process to history enframed by a reciprocal justice as its normative ethics, which is constantly being invoked by individual social actors to reconcile the noumenal (sacred—ideational) and phenomenal (profane—material) subjective world in order to maintain balance and harmony between the two so that the human actor can live freely and happy with all of being without distinctions or masters. As such, Haitian epistemology as a form of transcendental realism and idealism is phenomenological, in the Heideggerian sense (i.e., hermeneutical), material in the Marxian sense, and antidialectical. It refutes Hegel's claims for the importance of historical formations and other people to the development of self-consciousness. Instead, Haitian/Vilokan idealism, phenomenologically, emphasizes the things in the consciousness (lwa or concepts, ideas, ideals) of the individual as they stem from the noumenal/Vilokan world, and get interpreted according to their level of learning, development, capacity for knowledge, and modality, i.e., the way they know more profoundly—kinesthetically, visually, etc., as they antidialectically seek to reproduce them in the phenomenal world as their practical consciousness against other interpretive formations of these same concepts in the material world as recursively organized and reproduced by others.

Haitian Ontology and Metaphysics, i.e., Vodou/Vilokan

Ontologically speaking, within the Haitian metaphysical worldview, Vilokan/Vodou, the world is a unitary (energy) material world created out of Bondye. The world is a creation of a good God, *Bondye Bon*, which created the world and humanity out of itself composed of two intersecting spheres, the profane (the phenomenal world) and sacred (noumenal/Vilokanic, mirrored world of the profane). Embedded in that pantheistic material world are concepts, *lwa yo* in Haitian metaphysics, from the parallel mirrored (Vilokanic) world, that humanity can ascertain via experience and the structure of its being, form of understanding and sensibility (dreams, reason and rationality, extrasensory perceptions), to help make sense of their experience and live in the world, which is Bondye, and therefore sacred, as they (via their nanm) seek perfection and reunification (reintegration) with God, the energy force/source.

That is to say, it, Bondye, provided humanity with objects, concepts, ideas, ideals, and practices, i.e., *lwa yo* of Vodou, proverbs, rituals, dance, geometry, knowledge of herbal medicine, trades, and skills, by which they ought to know, interpret, and make sense of the external (phenomenal profane) world and live in it comfortably. These transcendentally real objects, concepts, ideas, ideals, and practices can either be known through dreams, divinations, experience or rationality, and becomes the structure (once reified and institutionalized as proverbs, husbandry, dance, rituals, institutions, etc.), form of sensibility and understanding, through which humanity come to know, hold beliefs and truth-claims. So Bondye, a powerful energy force that always existed created the world and humanity out of itself using four hundred and one transcendentally real concepts (God and four-hundred lwa), ideas, and ideals (geometric principles, mathematics, etc.). Humanity and the world around it is an aggregation of bondye's material energy, the energy of God, which constitutes its existence. In humanity this existence is composed of three distinct aggregation of energy (*ti bon anj*; *gwo bon anj*; *ko*, the body), all of which are material stuff, which constitute our *nanm* (souls) where personality, truth-claims, knowledge, and beliefs are deposited, via dreams, revelations, extrasensory perceptions, divinations, experience, reason, the energy source of a God as manifested via a lwa, and can be examined and explored as the synthetic a priori form of the understanding of the human agent.

For humanity to constitute its existence and be in the world according to the will of God or Bondye, in other words, transcendentally real concepts stemming from God's will (the mirrored world of the profane, Vilokan) are embedded in the material world, which is God, and can be ascertain and embodied by humanity via their constituted being as a material being with extrasensory perceptions, reason and rationality, and or through experience. As these transcendentally real concepts are ascertain, they are constituted and institutionalized, and passed on through humanity via priests/priestesses and early ancestors who institutionalized (reify)/ institutionalize them (as ideology, ideological apparatuses, and communicative discourse) in the natural world via religious ceremonies, dance, rituals, herbal medicine, trades, concepts, and proverbs. These trades, ideals, proverbs, and or concepts are truisms, mechanisms to ascertain and constitute knowledge, which although they are deduced from the constituted make-up (i.e., consciousness) of the human being, in Haitian metaphysics they are attributed to God and the ancestors who institutionalized (reified) them in order to be applied in the material world so that their descendants can live freely in the world, satisfy their needs, be happy, and achieve perfection in the profane material world in order to reunite with God after their sixteen life cycles.

Haitian Epistemology, i.e., Haitian/Vilokan Idealism

Hence, the Haitian epistemological position that would emerge out of the metaphysical worldview, Vodou, of the African people of Haiti and their form of system and social integration is a strong form of Kantian transcendental idealism and realism, which would be institutionalized throughout the provinces and mountains of the island (Desmangles, 1992; Author, 2016). This position suggests that Haitian epistemology is not a synthesis between modernity and Vodou magic and spiritualism as proposed by many scholars such as Susan Buck-Morss (2009), for example. On the contrary, my argument is that the process of demystification and rationalization of Vodou metaphysics, and only Vodou metaphysics, reveals an epistemological position, Haitian/Vilokan Idealism, which parallels Kantian transcendental idealism coupled with a transcendental realism found in Haitian Vodou with its emphasis on the knowability of the noumenal world via trances, revelations, and extrasensory perceptions.

Kantian transcendental idealism "attempts to combine empirical realism, preserving the ordinary independence and reality of objects of the world, with transcendental idealism, which allows that in some sense the objects have their ordinary properties (their causal powers, and their spatial and temporal position) only because our minds are so structured that these are the categories we impose upon the manifold of experience" (Blackburn, 2008, pg. 356). Haitian epistemological transcendental idealism, Haitian Idealism or Vilokan Idealism, is a form of transcendental idealism in the Kantian sense in that it attempts to synthesize empiricism, idealism (rationalism), and realism via synthetic a priori concepts/ideals the Haitians believe can be applied not only to the phenomenal but also the noumenal (Vilokanic) world in order to ascertain the latter's transcendentally real absolute knowledges they call, *lwa*, gods/goddesses (401 concepts, ideas, and ideals represented as gods/goddesses), of Vilokan/Vodou. So like Kant, Haitian epistemological transcendental idealism, holds on to analytic truths, truths of reasons or definitions, as outlined in their proverbs (*pwoveb*); a posteriori truth, truths of experience or experiments, also embedded in their proverbs, geometry (*veves*), rituals, magic, sorcery, and herbal medicine; and synthetic a priori concepts (categories in Kantian epistemology supplemented with trances, dream-states, extrasensory perceptions), truths stemming from the form of the understanding and sensibility of the mind and apparatuses of experience embedded not only in their proverbs and Vodou rituals, beliefs, and magic, but also their understanding of trances, dream-states, and extrasensory perceptions as categories of the mind applicable to the noumenal or Vilokanic realm where transcendental real concepts, lwa yo, exist (as Platonic forms) which they must ascertain in order to live life happily in the phenomenal world without masters or owners of production. The latter (trances, dream-states, and extrasensory perceptions) they believe, in other words, can be applied to the noumenal or Vilokanic world in order to know gods/goddesses, *lwa yo*, which are immutable/absolute concepts, ideas, and ideals God has created and imposed upon and in the material world, from the mirrored world of the earth (Vilokan), which the people, who embody these concepts, ideas, and ideals, should utilize to recursively reorganize and reproduce their being-in-and-as-the-world in order to achieve perfection over sixteen life cycles (Desmangles, 1992; Beauvoir, 2006; Mocombe, 2016). Hence, unlike Kantian transcendental idealism, which removes God out of the equation via the categories, which imposes the order we see in the phenomenal world, Haitian epistemological transcendental idealism and realism, Haitian/Vilokan Idealism, holds on to the concept of God, supernatural, and the paranormal to continue to make sense of the plural tensions between the natural (material) world, i.e., the world of phenomenon, and the world as such, ideational, noumena, i.e., the supernatural and paranormal world, transcendental real world, which is knowable as truth-claims, knowledge, and beliefs, through dreams, divinations, revelations, experience, reason and rationality, and the synthetic a priori, for pure (development of science, i.e., herbal medicine, etc.) and practical reason (i.e., morals and values). Thus Haitian/Vilokan Idealism, unlike Kantian Transcendental Idealism, implies that the objects, concepts, ideals, ideas, etc., of the (ideational) noumenal world are transcendentally real and the form of sensibilities and understandings, which include dream states, trances, and extrasensory perceptions are other categories of the understanding, which can be applied beyond the phenomenal world, where the objects are really subjective (interpretive) ideas, in order to ascertain the nature of the absolute concepts of the Vilokanic/noumenal world in order to achieve balance and harmony with it in the phenomenal.

Within this pantheistic (Spinozaian) conception of the multiverse and material world, knowledge, truth-claims, and beliefs arise from transcendentally real ideational concepts (lwa yo) of bondye/God as embedded in the earth's mirrored world (Vilokan) and gets deposited in our *nanm* (souls) intuitively, in dreams, revelations, divinations, extrasensory perceptions, reason, rituals, and or experiences which in turn constitutes and structures the form of the understanding of our minds and bodies (senses) so that we can experience the material world according to our interpretations of these concepts in consciousness and developmental track over sixteen reincarnated life cycles (Beauvoir, 2006; Mocombe, 2016). The human being recursively (re) organize and reproduce these (Platonic) transcendentally real ideational concepts as their practical consciousness in the phenomenal material world not always in its absolute form as defined noumenally (the sacred mirrored world of Vilokan), but according to their level of learning, development, capacity for knowledge, and modality, i.e., the way they know more profoundly—kinesthetically, visually, etc.

As defined, Haitian epistemology is an epistemological transcendental idealism and realism, Haitian Idealism or Vilokan Idealism, which posits that both phenomena (the profane world) and noumena (its mirror image where wisdom, ideals, and ancestors reside) are knowable through experience and the form of human sensibility and understanding (the categories of Kantian epistemology supplemented with, dreams, divinations, extrasensory perceptions, and trance states), which stems from the energy force of a God, which constitutes our nanm (a material thing), and used to recursively organize and reproduce their being-in-and-as-the-world.

So on top of the twelve Kantian schematized categories of the understanding, divided into four groups of three (1. The axioms of intuition, i.e., unity, plurality, and totality; 2. The anticipations of perception, i.e., reality, limitation, and negation; 3. The postulates of empirical thought, i.e., necessary, actual, and possible; 4. The analogies, i.e., substance, cause, and reciprocity), necessary for experience by making objective space and time possible, Vilokanic/Haitian idealism adds dream states, trances, and extrasensory perceptions as a fifth group of three to make known the concepts, lwa, of the Vilokanic world knowable so that human actors can achieve balance between the phenomenal world and the former (Vilokanic/noumenal) by recursively organizing and reproducing them as their material practice.

For Kant experience requires both the senses, the a priori forms of sensibility, i.e., space and time, and the understanding, i.e. the twelve categories. A unified consciousness (not a self or the Cartesian "I"), which is a structural feature of experience necessary to provide the unity to our experience, what Kant calls, "the transcendental unity of apperception," rule-governed and connected by the categories, experiences real objects that we perceive and exist independently of our perception of them. Thus, the spatio-temporal objects are necessarily relative to and subject to the a priori forms of experience, i.e., forms of sensibility and the understanding. In this sense, Kant does away with the noumenal world of absolutes, which is unknowable as the independent objects are phenomenal, relative to the a priori forms of experience. Unlike Kant, however, Haitian/Vilokan Idealism posits that the nanm, which provides unity to our experiences is a material thing, a Cartesian material "I" composed of three distinct entities (sometimes more as Haitian metaphysics suggests that a fourth entity, *lwa met tet*, may constitute the nanm of serviteurs in order to guide them in their decision-making) that are also tied to the natural world and can be manipulated in life as well as death. On top of it's a priori forms of sensibility and Kantian categories are dream-states, trances, and extrasensory perceptions, which allows the nanm to have access to the world of Vilokan/noumenal world where we can perceive the things that are phenomenal, relative to our a priori forms of experience, as they are in-themselves in order to achieve balance between the world as it appears to us and how it ought to be so that we can live abundantly as individual masters of our own destiny.

Hence Haitian epistemological transcendental idealism (Haitian Idealism, Vilokanism, Vodouism, or Vilokan Idealism) and realism is not only natural, but supernatural and paranormal to the extent that it supplements the synthetic a priori concepts Kant attributes to the categories of the mind with divinations, revelations, dream states, and extrasensory perceptions in order to ascertain the absolute (transcendentally real) concepts, ideals, ideas, etc., (lwa) of God as embedded in the noumenal (Vilokanic) world. Moreover, it posits that these absolute *lwa yo*, transcendentally real concepts, ideas, ideals, etc., are part of the noumenal world (sacred world of Vilokan), which is not a plural world as plurality, in keeping with the logic of Arthur Schopenhauer, belongs to the world of phenomenon, and can eventually be known by extrasensory perceptions, human reason, understanding, and experience. However, in the human sphere the world of phenomenon and its plurality is a result of interpretations and the different levels of development (reason, experience, capacity, and modality) of the consciousness of the human subjects (not all humans develop their form of sensibilities and understanding at the same rate or in the same life cycle) where the concepts of lwa yo are embedded and embodied and recursively organized and reproduced as the practical consciousness of the human actor. Albeit humanity is reincarnated until they have ascertained all of the true concepts of the unitary world, which can be done so through experience and a priori, and will seize to exist (will seize to experience reincarnation) once they do so.

Haitian/Vilokan Idealism and Realism as such indicates a condition of transcendentally real absolutes on the one hand as it pertains to the Vilokanic or noumenal world; and relativity in our notions of objects and reality on the other as it pertains to the transcendentally ideal phenomenal world. In terms of the latter, the phenomenal world, in other words, is simply the world of plurality constituted by imperfect beings, anti-dialectically (constantly fighting against the praxis of others for their own understanding and praxis), living through their aggregated material bodies and imperfections according to their interpretations of the concepts and level of learning, development, capacity for knowledge, and modality, i.e., the way they know more profoundly—kinesthetically, visually, etc.

This is why, epistemologically speaking, the phenomenal world in Haiti, looks like an epistemological anarchic world where everyone exists for their own liberty and existence according to their own developmental track, capacities, modalities, belief systems, and methods governed by an eye for an eye normative worldview, which prevents others from encroaching on an individual's (regardless of their level of development) method and right to exist.

The Phenomenology of Haitian/Vilokan Idealism

Hence Haitian/Vilokan Idealism is phenomenological, material, and antidialectical in the sense that the emphasis is on the things (concepts, ideas, ideals) of consciousness as revealed to, and interpreted by, human individuals (via the form of sensibility and understanding) from the noumenal world of Vilokan. These things (concepts, ideas, and ideals) of consciousness they in-turn recursively reorganize and reproduce as their practical consciousness in the material world antidialectically against the interpretive practical consciousnesses of others within a normative ethic of reciprocal justice of the socioeconomic/political structure of the Lakou as organized in a material resource framework. The human actor, in other words, encounter contents in their consciousness, which, with the aid of an elder, priest, or priestess, of a lakou, they must interpret in the material world as their practical consciousness, when things in their lives go awry, in order to have balance within themselves, nature, and their social interactions within the lakou system. The lakou is a community of people and houses organized and gathered around a common yard under the directions of a oungan (Vodou priest), manbo (Vodou priestess), or family elder that promoted and promotes an egalitarian existence rooted in the Vodou religion and ancestor worship, land ownership arrangements, and working the soil. Within the lakou system, each individual or nuclear family owned/own their own land, through which they provided/provide for basic necessities by growing food and raising livestock for their own consumption and for sale in local markets. They also grew and grow export crops, such as coffee, in order to buy imported consumer goods such as clothes and tools. The lakou thus divided power in a way that allowed rural residents to live and work as they wished (through land and garden ownership to provide for their own subsistence), while preventing the consolidation of wealth, and therefore control and inhibitor of equality, in the hands of any one person within the community through a set of customs and secret societies of the Vodou religion that regulate(d) land ownership, land transfers, family relationships, and community affairs. Communal assistance and exchange, via food sharing, harvesting, house building, religious life, and ancestral worship, under the leadership of women also characterized and characterizes lakou life. In essence, the purpose of lakou life is to promote total liberty and equality, via land ownership and self-sufficiency, for all without distinctions and economic differentiation. Hence the lakou system helps to institutionalize the antihumanism that would come to constitute Haitian rural life in that the emphasis is not on promoting the universality of the autonomous rational individual as the purpose of socialization. Instead, the emphasis is on allowing total liberty and equality so that the individual actor can experience Being or existence as they interpret the concepts of the noumenal/Vilokanic world as their practical consciousness. The autonomous rational self is simply one aspect (analytics) of being amongst a plethora of other forms and agential moments by which the individual social actor can choose (based on their analytics in consciousness) to recursively reorganize and reproduce their existence without facing marginalization from their community unless their choice harms other individuals. Hence, like Martin Heidegger's phenomenology, the phenomenology of Haitian/Vilokan Idealism highlights the things of consciousness as they are interpreted by a human actor as their practical consciousness vis-à-vis their analytics, i.e., their conscious awareness or not of these concepts, lwa yo, as they experience being-in-the-world with others who may inhibit their existence.

Introduction to Phenomenological Structuralism

So what does Haitian Idealism, its metaphysics, phenomenology, materialism, antidialectics, and reciprocal justice, has to say to modern science, both physical and social, in terms of the development of a theory and methodology. As far as I am concerned it is the materialist holism of Haitian idealism, which attempts to connect cosmology, cosmogony, social relations, the phenomenology of subjective experience, and the process of antidialectics, which is important. For they offer a new conception of human agency, which is tied to physics, phenomenology, and human social relations, that is relevant for the social sciences and its ongoing debate to resolve its structure/agency problematic. That is, Haitian idealism is tied to a materialist holism that directs human social action, via its antidialectical historical process, towards the transcendentally real ideational concepts, lwa yo, of the natural and supernatural world above social constructive identifications, which, as subjective positions, attempt to limit human phenomenological agency as it experiences being-in-the-world. In this vision, it offers, through the concept and process of antidialectics and phenomenology, an agential theory of social action that is relevant for the construction of a social theory and methodology for the social sciences. In modern social science discourse, Paul C. Mocombe's phenomenological structuralism, which seeks to fix structurationist sociology, anthropology, and social psychology for human agency, is the closest thing to a theory and methodology that can be associated to/with the interconnections between cosmology, cosmogony, social relations, phenomenology, and antidialectics as found in Haitian/Vilokan idealism.

Paul C. Mocombe's (2014, 2016, 2017, 2019) phenomenological structural ontology seeks to fix structurationism to account for the structure/agency problematic by synthesizing the materialism of physics, quantum mechanics in particular, with the agential initiatives highlighted in the phenomenological discourses of Husserl, Heidegger, Merleau-Ponty, and Sartre (which parallels the phenomenology found in Haitian/Vilokan Idealism for Mocombe), the Neo-Marxist structuralism of structurationism and Althusser, and Wittgenstein's notion of language game (the latter two to capture the reification of the subjectivity of the phenomenal world via society by those who consolidate and control its resources and prevent human actors from achieving balance and harmony with the noumenal world). It is the metaphysics of Haitian idealism, its phenomenology, and antidialectic viewpoint of Haitian social practice, which Mocombe attempts to tie to the phenomenology of German idealism that it parallels in his structurationist theory and methodology. As defined, phenomenological structuralism is a mix-method paradigm, theory and methodology, which incorporates three worldviews associated with the research process: The postpositivist worldview, with its emphasis on scientific research into the psychology of the forms of sensibility and understanding of the brain, and the physics of subatomic particle embodiment and its relevance for human social action; Constructivism and critical theory, with its emphasis on the sociology of the mode of production and understanding and meaning as it pertains to individuals and networks of solidarity groups, which defer the meaning of the ideologies of the mode of production and are marginalized by those in power positions for doing so; and Pragmatism/Advocacy/ Participatory, with its emphasis on finding solutions to the increasing problems associated with the enchantment of the world around the contemporary ideology, the Protestant Ethic and the spirit of capitalism, which threatens all life on earth and prevents humanity from achieving balance and harmony with the material/noumenal world.

To this end of fixing structurationism to account for the nature and origins of alternative practical consciousnesses outside the structural reproduction and differentiation of capitalist relations of production in modernity, Paul C. Mocombe's (2014, 2016, 2017, 2019) phenomenological structuralism builds on the material relationship highlighted in physics between the identity and indeterminate behavior of subatomic particles highlighted in quantum mechanics and the determinate behavior of atomic particles in their aggregation as highlighted in general relativity to understand the material constitution of consciousness at the subatomic/neuronal level in, and as, the brain. And it's (consciousnesses') unfolding and manifestation as human practical consciousness at the atomic level as revealed by language, ideologies, ideological apparatuses, communicative discourse, and the actions of the bodies (i.e., practical consciousness) of those who control a material resource framework, and the mode of distributing its resources, where a society is constituted and ensconced. So borrowing from Haitian Idealism, this interconnectedness between the world of phenomenon and noumenon and the human being as a material subject whose nanm is a material thing capable of constructing their own phenomenological experiences, Mocombe begins his analysis by demonstrating the connection between the noumenal world of contemporary quantum mechanics and the phenomenal world of subject constitution where the Haitian concept of antidialectics and phenomenology as it parallels the hermeneutical phenomenology of Heidegger serves as a mechanism for agential initiative against social reproduction and differentiation, which is simply the reification of an adverse subjective experience, which attempts to curtail the human actors full connection to the noumenal world.

For Mocombe, all aggregated matter in our dispensation of spacetime is composed of subatomic particle energies. Thus, to understand the constitution and origins of human practical consciousness one must begin with not only the actions associated with these particles, but their essence or intrinsic nature, which is their inner conscious life (i.e., panpsychism). In other words, subatomic particles have or is consciousness (a material fifth force of nature), which becomes embodied during their aggregation via the Higgs-Boson field. According to the tenets of quantum physics as reflected in supersymmetry theory, wave-function realism, dark matter, parallel universes (multiverses), and the EPR (Einstein, Podolsky, and Rosen) paradox, the universe is composed of ordinary matter (atoms and molecules) and dark matter (axions, wimps, neutrinos, bosons, and fermions).[2] Dark matter, as opposed to ordinary matter, constitutes over eighty percent of the material substance that constitute the cosmos. This dark matter is not constituted by atoms and molecules like ordinary matter but consists of subatomic particles and energy. The particles in the nature of quarks are identified as wimps or axions, very tiny particles that contribute to the formation of nuclear components. These tiny particles are conceived of as coiled energies, strings of space-time, packets of energy-like photons. They are physical in nature but immaterial, and coexist, in a parallel/alternate universe, with ordinary matter in the same location without impediment or interference. They belong to the fermion family of invisible particles whose counterparts are named a boson, which is pure energy. So, as highlighted in supersymmetry theory, for every boson particle of matter, a symmetry counterpart, fermion, exists which manifests itself as force or energy. Thus, for every reality we discover in the solid world around us, we must assume that there exists a symmetric counterpart, or boson, which is invisible but is nevertheless as physical as its visible counterpart. These supersymmetric doubles constitute the backbone of alternate realities, parallel universes that are displayed in ten dimensions, including our ordinary three-dimensional Cartesian reality. Moreover, according to quantum theory, these particles have psychic properties (Frankish, 2016). That is, the particles are conscious, i.e., panpsychism. They have phenomenal properties and are aware of their position, of themselves, and of their surroundings. In other words, the multiverses created by these particles are endowed with consciousness and phenomenal properties whose information can never be destroyed, is immortal in principle, get recycled throughout the multiverse, and becomes embodied.

These phenomenal properties coupled with the consciousness of subatomic particles, according to Mocombe, help to explain the magic of action-at-a-distance highlighted in the physics of quantum mechanics, which contradicts action in real space and time and simultaneity as suggested by Albert Einstein's theory of general relativity, thus making the two physics incompatible. So in phenomenological structural sociology Mocombe interprets the quantum fact that the two phenomenon happening in the quantum world, i.e., one mathematical rule for the external objective world before a measurement is made, and another that jumps in after the measurement occurs by an observer, by siding with the *psi-ontologists* as Christopher Fuchs calls them, who want the wave function to describe the objective world, over the *psi-epistemologists* who see the wave function as a description of our knowledge and its limits (Frank, 2017). In the former, also known as wave-function realism, the understanding is that we live in a multiverse of many-worlds or parallel universes (similar to the connection between Vilokan and the world of earthly actions as seen in Haitian Idealism). Measurements do not suspend the equation or collapse the wave function, "they merely made the Universe split off into many (perhaps infinite) parallel versions of itself. Thus, for every experimentalist who measures an electron *over here*, a parallel universe is created in which her parallel copy finds the electron *over there*" (Frank, 2017). The latter, psi-epistemologists, suggests physics is no longer a description of the world in-and-of itself. Instead, it's a description of the rules for our interaction with the world, i.e., the perceiving subject determines the objective rules of physics (Frank, 2017).

In other words, according to quantum mechanics in contradistinction to Einstein's EPR paradox and theory of general relativity associated with the psi-epistemologists, which argued against quantum theory's action-at-a-distance, subatomic particles are recycled/entangled/superimposed throughout the multiverses maintaining, based on the assumption of panpsychism, the contents of their aggregated existence, i.e., experiences throughout the multiverses. This, for Mocombe, helps to explain Schrodinger's wave function mathematical entity, "which seemed to allow the position of an unmeasured particle to be spread out across an arbitrarily large region of space. When the particle's position was measured, the wave function was said to 'collapse', suddenly becoming localized where the particle was detected. Einstein objected that if this collapse was a real physical process, it would reintroduce action-at-a-distance, and so be incompatible with special relativity" (Price and Wharton, 2016). For Einstein, all that has occurred is not action-at-a-distance, but our information about the particle, and not the particle itself has changed. For Mocombe, in building on the logic of quantum mechanics and panpsychism associated with the psi-ontologists, which suggests that the particles have phenomenal properties and are conscious, the particle itself, impacted by the physical processes of the observer, either chooses to change under observation or collapses under the observable laws within which it is being observed. Physics and the physical sciences highlight the actions of the observable matter, but not what it is intrinsically, which is a fifth force in and of nature, mainly, consciousness and its aggregated experiences.

Hence the logical consequence regarding the evolution and constitution of the multiverses, and their contents, based on the assumptions of action-at-a-distance, phenomenal properties, wave-function realism, and panpsychism, for Mocombe, is similar to the intersecting worlds theory highlighted in Haitian Vodou, which parallels the physics, "membrane theory," of Lisa Randall and Raman Sundrum (1999). The proposal in keeping with the logic of Haitian Vodou and the "brane theory" of Randall and Sundrum is that there might be an additional dimension on the cosmological scale, the scale described by general relativity, which gives rise to four dimensional multiverses within it. That is to say, our universe is embedded in a vastly bigger five-dimensional space (the four-dimensional space of relativity, plus a fifth dimension for the subatomic forces including consciousness), a kind of super-universe. Within this super-space, our universe is just one of a whole array of co-existing universes (Haitian Vodou only accounts for our universe), each a separate four-dimensional bubble within a wider arena of five-dimensional space where consciousness (a subatomic force) is recycled between the five-dimensional super-space, i.e., superverse, and its multiverses.

For Mocombe the multiverses originated, from the super-universe, either by fiat or quantum fluctuation. They are bosonic forces that were brought forth together with fermion counterparts. They are also the primeval pan-psychic field, stemming from the super-verse, whose fermion can be called a psychion, a particle of consciousness of a psychonic/panpsychic subatomic field. These have evolved together to produce the four forces of nature, electromagnetic force; gravity; the strong nuclear force; and weak nuclear force, in our universe, which in turn produced atoms, molecules, and aggregated life endowed with the recycled/superimposed/entangled consciousness and phenomenal properties of the primeval pan-psychic fields of the superverse and its multiverses (the fifth force of nature). In other words, according to quantum mechanics subatomic particles of energy constitute all the matter of our universe via the Higgs Boson Field, i.e., the god particle, which objectifies and materialize the matter that we are, see, hear, taste, feel, and touch. Subatomic particles constitute our material bodies and consciousness as neuronal energies, which constitute and operate the brain and the body (Hameroff and Penrose, 2014). However, subatomic matter, which are strings/waves at the subatomic particle level, operate differently from observable objectified energy, matter, in that their behavior are indeterminate and can exist in multiple places, dimensions or parallel universes, simultaneously prior to being observed or even during observation as aggregated matter. In fact, the subatomic particles that constitute our material bodies and consciousness as neuronal energies are the same subatomic particles that constitute everything that we consider to be the world, universe, other species, etc. At the subatomic particle level, we are not subjects contemplating an object, i.e., the world, multiverse, etc., we are the world, an undifferentiating energy, endowed with consciousness and phenomenal properties, which are immortal in principle. Hence, the implication suggested by the Standard Model of physics is that the observable and non-observable matter that constitutes our universe exists elsewhere in other unseen dimensions and parallel universes simultaneously with our own dispensation of space-time. We do not occupy a universe. We are part of a superverse and multiverse with a plethora of I (s) and other sentient beings, or not, existing in them indistinguishable from one another at the subatomic level as recycled energy. They become distinguishable at the atomic level through subatomic particle aggregation, i.e., matter. Subatomic particles aggregate to form objectified matter, universes, worlds, species and sentient beings, etc. The plethora of I (s) and other sentient beings are constituted and connected via subatomic particles that are recycled/superimposed/ entangled throughout and as the superverse and multiverse to constitute and operate consciousness as subatomic neuronal energies of the body and the brain, which encounters objectified matter as objectified matter via the actions and senses of the brain, body, language, ideologies, ideological apparatuses, and communicative discourse. In essence, consciousness is recycled/superimposed/entangled subatomic energies of the multiverses objectified and embodied, similar to the nanm in Haitian idealism and Hegel's conceptualization of *Geist*. Whereas for Hegel *Geist* is distinct from the world and unfolds dialectically in it, via embodiment of certain individuals, towards an ever-increasing rationalization of the world. For Mocombe the historical manifestation, Being-in-Spacetime, of the objectification of subatomic particles of the universe as consciousnesses and bodies has no definitive end-goal and is indeterminate, but constrained in materialized space-time by our material bodies (forms of sensibility and understanding) and power relations or the social class language games of those whose objectification or historicity precedes individual consciousnesses and control the economic (material) conditions (and mode of production) of a material resource framework (Ratner, 2011).

Like the laws of physics, which attempts to regulate and determine subatomic particle activity as general law (Theory of general relativity) once they are aggregated in our universe and galaxy, the social class language game of those who control the economic conditions, and their distribution, of a material resource framework attempts to regulate and determine the indeterminacy of meaning unfolding in and as the consciousnesses of social actors via the actions of bodies, mode of production, language, ideology, ideological apparatuses, and communicative discourse. Unlike, postmodern and post-structural theorizing, which utilize the indeterminacy of meaning as highlighted by the unconscious in the psychoanalytic works of Sigmund Freud and Jacques Lacan, phenomenological structuralism analogously builds on the material relationship in physics between the identity and indeterminate behavior of subatomic particles highlighted in quantum mechanics and the determinate behavior of atomic particles in their aggregation as highlighted in general relativity to understand the material constitution of consciousnesses at the subatomic/neuronal level in, and as, the brain and their manifestation as human practical consciousnesses, via the body, at the atomic level.

Unlike psychoanalysts like Lacan and Freud or phenomenologists like Edmund Husserl, Mocombe does not claim to know how the embodiment of recycled/superimposed/entangled subatomic neuronal energies endowed with consciousness come to constitute consciousnesses in and as the brain and their subsequent revelation as an "I," nanm, the practical consciousnesses of bodies and brains with phenomenal properties, i.e., the way colors look, pain feels, etc. That is, the transcendental ego, nanm, or "I" of a differentiated individual subject with phenomenal properties, which we do not have access to, could just as much be the past I (impulses/drives of recycled subatomic particles of previous beings) of a sentient being from an alternative universe, as suggested in Haitian Vodou metaphysics via their concept of a *lwa met tet*, and not necessarily the product of repression and the rule of the father. Psychoanalysis and the indeterminacy of the processes of the unconscious and the universal mapping of consciousnesses by Edmund Husserl's transcendental phenomenology and contemporary neuroscientists, for Mocombe, in other words, neither adequately captures the indeterminate behavior of embodied recycled subatomic particles as neuronal energies of the brain and the myriad of practical consciousnesses they may produce as revealed by diverse practices of bodies in the phenomenal world, nor can they account for the origins of the transcendental ego, nanm, or I. Husserl, Freud, Chomsky, and contemporary neuroscientists attempt to highlight and capture the Kantian form of the understanding and sensibilities of the aggregated body and brain, which is unable to explain how aggregated subatomic particles give rise to the transcendental ego of consciousness with phenomenal properties, which in turn produces praxis via the body. Mocombe is not claiming that his phenomenological structural ontology captures this process. The only thing of consciousness, which is a ghost in a machine via the microtubules of neurons, subatomic particles, of the brain, he is claiming to be phylogenetically universal is the stance of the transcendental ego, what Martin Heidegger (1927) in *Being and Time* calls the *analytic of Dasein*, vis-à-vis the drives of the aggregated body, impulses or phenomenal properties of embodied recycled/superimposed/ entangled drives of subatomic particle energies, and the language, ideology, ideological apparatuses, structural reproduction and differentiation of those who control a material resource framework. Hence Mocombe holds on to Haitian phenomenology with its emphasis on the phenomenal world as the world of subjective plurality (based on the developmental track, modality, capacity, etc., i.e., analytics/stances, of the human actor) and the phenomenological logic of Husserl, Heidegger, Merleau-Ponty, and Sartre here to capture, in a behavioral sense, the how, via Heidegger's three stances/analytics ready-to-hand, unready-to-hand, present-at-hand, of identity constitution amidst indeterminacy of consciousnesses and actions produced by recycled subatomic neuronal energies with consciousness and phenomenal properties, which produce the structure of actions, practical consciousnesses, revealed by actions of bodies as and in the material resource framework of the earth, which is already structured (via language, ideology, and ideological apparatuses) by those whose historicity precedes individual consciousnesses.

In other words, what Mocombe is suggesting in phenomenological structuralism, which seeks to highlight the phenomenology of being-in-the-structure-of-those-who-control-a-material-resource-framework and the origins of our practical consciousness vis-à-vis our aggregation as subatomic particles, is that embodiment is the objectification of the transcendental ego. This transcendental ego is a part of a universal *élan vital*, the superverse and multiverses, which has ontological status in dimensions existing at the subatomic particle level and gets embodied via, and as, the body and connectum of Being's brains. Hence, as highlighted in Haitian metaphysics, the transcendental ego, nanm, is the universal *élan vital*, which is the neuronal energies of past, present, and future Beings-of-the-multiverse, embodied, and encounters a material world via and as the body and brain in mode of production, language, ideology, ideological apparatuses, and communicative discourse. Once embodied in and as human individual consciousnesses in a particular universe, world, and historical social formation, the transcendental ego, nanm, becomes an embodied hermeneutic structure that never encounters the world and the things of the world in themselves via the aggregated built in ontogenetics' of the body, brain, and the neuronal energies. Instead embodied hermeneutic individual consciousness is constituted via the recycled/superimposed/entangled subatomic neuronal particle energies which are aggregated as a transcendental ego and the body in their encounter and interpretation of past recycled neuronal memories and things enframed in and by the language, bodies, ideology, ideological apparatuses, and practices of those who control the economic conditions of an aggregated material resource framework and its social relations of production. In consciousness, as phenomenology posits, it (individual subjective consciousness of embodied beings) can either choose to accept the structural knowledge, differentiation, and practices of, the drives of the body, the impulses (phenomenal properties) of recycled/entangled/ superimposed past/present/future consciousnesses of subatomic neuronal particles, the actions of those who control, via their bodies, mode of production, language, ideology, ideological apparatuses, and communicative discourse, the economic conditions of the material resource framework and recursively reorganize and reproduce them in their practices, or reject them, through the deferment of meaning in ego-centered communicative discourse, for an indeterminate amount of action-theoretic ways-of-being-in-the-world-with-others, which they may assume at the threat to their ontological security. It is Being's stance or analytic, ready-to-hand, unready-to-hand, and present-at-hand vis-à-vis 1) the ontogenetic drives of the aggregated body and brain, 2) impulses, phenomenal properties, of residual actions/memories of embodied recycled/superimposed/entangled past consciousnesses/subatomic particles, 3) the phenomenological meditation/deferment that occurs on the latter actions, and ideologies of a social system along 4) with its dialectically determined differentiating logic, which produces the variability of actions and practices in, and as, cultures, social structures, or social systems that enframe the material world. In the end, however, 5) power and power relations of those who internalize the structural reproduction and differentiation, stemming from the mode of production, of the social structure as their practical consciousness, as well as the antidialectical disposition of those who do not, determine what alternative actions are allowed to manifest in the world.

As such, as in Haitian and Heidegger's phenomenology, phenomenology here is not just transcendental, it is also hermeneutical, which means like in Haitian Idealism, the social actor is always in an antidialectical position seeking to defend their hermeneutical interpretive positions at all cost against the interpretive positions of others. The act of interpretation or an embodied hermeneutic structure via the body, language, ideology, and communicative discourse is a universal precondition of being-in-the-world-with-other-human-beings. However, whereas Heidegger is interested in the question of the meaning of Being-as-such, i.e., the phenomenology of Being, phenomenological structuralism is concerned with the Vygotskyian sociocultural question of the meaning or constitutive nature of embodied Being-as-such's-being-in-the-world-with-others who attempt to constrain practical consciousnesses via the actions of their bodies (practical consciousness), language, ideologies, ideological apparatuses, and communicative discourse derived from social relations of production, and the different modes of existence that have emerged as a result of the aforementioned processes.

That is, as in Martin Heidegger's phenomenological ontology, Mocombe is interested in the necessary societal relationship and practical consciousnesses that emerge out of the phenomenology of Being-in-the-world-within-structures-of-signification-of-others, who control the economic conditions of the material resource framework we find ourselves existing in, that presuppose our historicity, and Being's perceptions, responses, and practices, i.e., relations, to these structures-of-signification in order to be in the world. Unlike Heidegger, however, the concern is not with the phenomenology of being-in-the-world because for Mocombe Being never encounters the world as the-thing-itself. Instead being encounters the world via its aggregated brain and body, recycled/superimposed/entangled past/present/future consciousnesses or subatomic particles and their phenomenal properties, and structures of signification, which derive from class division and social relations of production as reified in the bodies (as agential initiative), language, ideology, ideological apparatuses, and communicative discourse of those who control the resources of a material resource framework.

Be that as it may, whereas Mocombe accept the Husserlian phenomenological understanding that the facts of the world and their conditions of possibility are present in consciousness, i.e., the notion of intentionality, consciousness is always consciousness of something as we experience being-in-the-world-with-other-beings via our consciousness, i.e., transcendental ego, bodies, language, ideologies, and communicative discourse. His position, however, is that as an embodied hermeneutic structured being we never experience the facts of the world and their conditions of possibility as the "the things in themselves." This position of Mocombe's is contrary to Haitian/Vilokan Idealism, which suggests that we can know both noumena and phenomena via trances, dream-states, and extrasensory perceptions. Mocombe is not saying that we cannot know noumena. Instead, for Mocombe, we experience the facts of the world not noumenally, culturally, and historically, which is a present-at-hand viewpoint, but structurally and relationally, via the bodies, language, ideology, and communicative discourse in institutions or ideological apparatuses, i.e., the social class language game, of those who control the economic conditions of the material resource framework we find ourselves thrown-in, via our bodies, language, and communicative discourse. Thus, the reified ideology of a subjective position of the phenomenal world attempts to prevent us from seeing/knowing the truth-claims and knowledge of the noumenal world.

Theoretically speaking, in other words, Mocombe's phenomenology of embodied Being-in-the-world-as-such's-Being-with-others, phenomenological structuralism, synthesizes Merleau-Ponty's and Heidegger's phenomenology, with Haitian idealism and phenomenology, Karl Marx's materialism, Althusser's structural Marxism, and Ludwig Wittgenstein's language game to suggest that being-in-the-world with others, our practical consciousness, is a product of our acceptance or antidialectical rejection of the symbols of signification, social class language game, of those bodies in institutional/ideological power positions who control via their bodies (practical consciousness), language, ideologies, ideological apparatuses, and communicative discourse the economic conditions (mode of production) of a material resource framework as we encounter them and their symbols/signifiers in institutions or ideological apparatuses via our own transcendental ego, bodies, language, and communicative discourse. Hence, we never experience the things-in-themselves of the world culturally and historically in consciousness. We experience them structurally or relationally, "the structure of the conjuncture" (Marshall Sahlins's term) of the mode of production, and our stances/analytics, ready-to-hand, unready-to-hand, present-at-hand, vis-à-vis these ideological structures as they stand in relation to the drives (forms of sensibilities and understanding) of our bodies/brains, impulses of subatomic particles, and the ability to defer meaning in ego-centered communicative discourse determine our practical consciousness or behaviors we recursively organize and reproduce in the material resource framework. So Mocombe rejects the ability to know noumena, as posited by Haitian Idealism, via divinations, revelations, intuitions, etc., because of ideology, which requires the human agent and their viewpoint, gaze, or disposition to change in order to access it.

"Presence-at-hand," "Readiness-to-hand," and "Un-readiness-to-hand,"

We initially know, experience, and utilize the things of the world in the preontological ready-to-hand mode, which is structural and relational. That is, our bodies (nanm in Haitian Idealism) encounter, know, experience, and utilize the things of the world in consciousness, intersubjectively, via their representation as objects of knowledge, truth, usage, and experience enframed and defined in the relational logic and practices or language game (Wittgenstein's term) of the institutions or ideological apparatuses of the other beings-of-the-material resource framework whose historicity comes before our own and gets reified in and as language, ideology, ideological apparatuses, communicative discourse, and social action stemming from the mode of production (i.e., how they organize and distribute the resources of the material resource framework). This is the predefined phenomenal structural, i.e., ontological, world we and our bodies are thrown-in in coming to be-in-the-world. How an embodied-hermeneutically-structured Being as such solipsistically view, experience, understand, and utilize the predefined objects of knowledge, truth, and experienced defined by others and their conditions of possibilities in consciousness in order to formulate their practical consciousness is albeit indeterminate. Heidegger's description of Being is accurate, however, in suggesting that three stances or modes of encounter (Analytic of Dasein), "presence-at-hand," "readiness-to-hand," and "un-readiness-to-hand," characterizes our views of the things of consciousness represented intersubjectively via bodies, language, ideology, and communicative discourse, and subsequently determine our practical consciousness or social agency. In "ready-to-hand," which is the preontological mode of human existence/consciousness thrown in the world, we accept and use the things in consciousness with no conscious experience of them, i.e., without thinking about them or giving them any meaning or signification outside of their intended usage. Heidegger's example is that of using a hammer in hammering. We use a hammer without thinking about it or giving it any other condition of possibility outside of its intended usage as defined by those whose historicity presupposes our own. In "present-at-hand," which, according to Heidegger, is the stance of science (and ideology for me), we objectify the things of consciousness and attempt to determine and reify their meanings, usage, and conditions of possibilities. Hence the hammer is intended for hammering by those who created it as a thing solely meant as such. The "unready-to-hand" outlook is assumed when something goes wrong in our usage of a thing of consciousness as defined and determined by those who adopt a "present-at-hand" view. As in the case of the hammer, the unready-to-hand view is assumed when the hammer breaks and we have to objectify it, by then assuming a present-at-hand position, and think about it in order to either reconstitute it as a hammer, or give it another condition of possibility. Any other condition of possibility that we give the hammer outside of its initial condition of possibility which presupposed our historicity becomes relational, defined in relation to any of its other conditions of possibilities it may have been given by others we exist in the world with. Hence for Heidegger, the ontological status of being-in-the-world-with-others, via these three stances or modes of encountering the objects of consciousness hermeneutically reveal, through our view, experience, understanding, and usage of the predefined objects of knowledge, truth, and experience. Whereas Heidegger in his phenomenological work goes on to deal with the existential themes of anxiety, alienation, death, despair, etc. in Mocombe's phenomenological stance regarding societal constitution or Beings-as-such's-being-in-the-world-with-others via our stances to the body, language, ideology, ideological apparatuses, communicative discourse, and social relations of production he is not concerned with the phenomenological preoccupation of individual solipsistic existence as defined in Jean-Paul Sartre's work who claims to take off from Heidegger. Instead, he is interested in the universal ontological structure, i.e., social structure or societal constitution and practical consciousness, which arise out of Heidegger's three stances vis-à-vis embodiment, language, ideology, ideological apparatuses, communicative discourse, and social relations of production, which prevents Being from relating their existence to the noumenal world, which is possible as suggested in Haitian/Vilokan Idealism. That is, Mocombe is not concerned with Sartre's phenomenologization of the Cartesian *res cogitans*/ transcendental ego, i.e., the present-at-hand transcendental ego, which he gives ontological status in the world as a solipsistic individual seeking to define themselves for themselves lest they be declared living in bad faith. In his view, the overemphasis of that particular aspect of *Dasein* is a product of a specific historical and relational mode of production, and only accounts for one of its analytics as highlighted by Heidegger.

For Mocombe, the transcendental ego, which is a part of a universal *élan vital*, the superverse and multiverses, existing in another dimension at the subatomic particle level, does not, initially, originate out of the historical material world, but several variations of it becomes objectified via embodiment and the aforementioned stances in a universe, galaxy, and historical material world structured, via mode of production, language, ideology, ideological apparatuses, by other embodied Beings and their stances. Upon death its historicity via subatomic neuronal particles (and their properties) either collapses unto other versions of its aggregated matter where it still exists in the multiverse, or gets reabsorbed into the *élan vital*, the pan-psychic field of physics, to be recycled to produce future beings. As such consciousness, i.e., practical consciousness, is a product of the stances of *Dasein* or the human subject vis-à-vis the structures of 1) its embodied recycled/entangled/superimposed past/present/future consciousnesses via the microtubules of neurons, 2) the physiological drives and sensibilities of the aggregated body and brain, 3) language and ideology, which can be deferred in ego-centered communicative discourse, and 4) structural reproduction and differentiation resulting from the social relations of production. Be that as it may, as with Heidegger, who refutes Sartre's existential rendering of his phenomenological ontology, Mocombe is interested in the objectified societal constitution and practical consciousnesses of the transcendental egos and their relations that emerge within a dominant constitution of Being that controls a material resource framework of the world via bodies, mode of production, language, ideology, ideological apparatuses, and communicative discourse vis-à-vis the stances of the transcendental ego, which if they are truly to be free, ought to assume the antidialectical unfolding highlighted in Haitian/Vilokan Idealism over the dialectical one of its German counterpart.

The individual being is initially constituted as recycled/superimposed/ entangled and embodied subatomic particles of the multiverse, which have their own predetermined form of understanding and cognition, phenomenal properties, based on previous experiences as aggregated matter (this is akin to what the Greek philosopher Plato refers to when he posits knowledge as recollection of the Soul and reincarnation to achieve perfection as highlighted in Haitian/Vilokan Idealism). Again, the individual's actions are not necessarily determined by the embodiment and drives of these recycled/entangled/superimposed subatomic particles. It is an individual's stance, ready-to-hand, unready-to-hand, and present-at-hand, when the subatomic particles become aggregated matter or embodied and the conflict with the other forms of human actions, which determines whether are not they become aware, present-at-hand (the stance of science and ideology), of the subatomic particle drives and choose to recursively reorganize and reproduce the content of the drives as their practical consciousness.

This desire to reproduce the cognition and understanding, phenomenal properties, of the drives of the recycled subatomic particles, however, may be limited by the structuring structure of the aggregated body and brain of the individual subject. That is to say, the second origins and basis of an individual's actions are the structuring physiological drives and desires, for food, clothing, shelter, social interaction, and sex, of the aggregated body and brain, which the subatomic particles constitute and embody. In other words, the aggregated body and brain is preprogrammed with its own (biological) forms of sensibility, understanding, and cognition, structuring structure, by which it experiences being-in-the-world as aggregated embodied subatomic particles. These bodily forms of sensibility, understanding, and cognition, such as the drive and desire for food, clothing, shelter, social interaction, linguistic communication, and sex, are tied to the material embodiment and survival of the embodied individual actor, and may or may not supersede or conflict with the desire and drive of an individual to recursively (re) organize and reproduce the structuring structure, phenomenal properties, of the recycled subatomic particles. If these two initial structuring structures are in conflict, the individual moves from the ready-to-hand to the unready-to-hand stance or analytics where they may begin to reflect upon and question their being-in-the-world prior to acting. Hence just as in the case of the structuring structure of the subatomic particles it is an individual being's analytics vis-à-vis the (chemical and physiological) drives of its body and brain in relation to the impulses of the subatomic particles and their conflict or lack thereof, which determines whether or not they become driven by the desire to solely fulfill the material needs of their body and brain at the expense of the drives/desires of the subatomic particles or the social class language game of the material resource framework they find their existence unfolding in.

The social class language game, and its differentiating effects, an individual find their existence unfolding in is the third structuring structure, which attempts to determine the actions of individual beings as they experience being-in-the-world as embodied subatomic particles. The aggregated individual finds themselves objectified and unfolding within a material resource framework controlled by the actions of other bodies, which presuppose their existence, via the actions of their bodies (practical consciousness), language, communicative discourse, ideology, and ideological apparatuses stemming from how they satisfy the desires of their bodies and subatomic particle drives (means and mode of production, i.e., relations of production). What is aggregated as a social class language game by those in power positions via and within its praxis, language, ideology, ideological apparatuses, and communicative discourse attempts to interpellate and subjectify other beings to its interpretive frame of satisfying their bodily needs, fulfilling the impulses of their subatomic particles, and organizing a material resource framework at the expense of all others, and becomes a third form of structuring individual action based on the mode of production and how it differentiates individual actors.

That is to say, an individual's interpellation, subjectification, and differentiation within the social class language game that presupposes their being-in-the-world attempts to determine their actions or practical consciousness via the reified language, ideology, etc., of the social class language game, the meaning of which can be deferred via the communicative discourse of the individual actors. Hence, the deferment of meaning in ego-centered communicative discourse of the language and ideology of a social class language game is the final means of determining an individual's action or practical consciousness outside of, and in relation to, its stance, i.e., analytics, vis-à-vis the drives of subatomic particles, desires of the body and brain, and structural reproduction and differentiation.

Whereas the practical consciousness of the transcendental ego stemming from the impulses of embodied subatomic particles are indeterminant as with its neuronal processes involved with the constitution of meaning in ego-centered communicative discourse (Albeit physicists are in the process of exploring the nature, origins, and final states of subatomic particles, and neuroscientists are attempting to understand the role of neuronal activities in developing the transcendental ego and whether or not it continues to exist after death). The form of the understandings and sensibilities of the body and brain are determinant as with structural reproduction and differentiation of the mode of production, and therefore can be mapped out by neuroscientists, biologists, and sociologists to determine the nature, origins, and directions of societal constitution and an individual actor's practical consciousness.

The interaction of all four elements in relation to the stance of the transcendental ego of the individual actor are the basis for human actions in the world. In the end, consequently, the majority of practical consciousness will be a product of an individual actor's embodiment and the structural reproduction and differentiation of a social class language game given 1) the determinant nature of embodiment, form of understanding and sensibility of the body and brain amidst, paradoxically, the indeterminacy of impulses, phenomenal properties, of embodied subatomic particles and the neuronal processes involved in ego-centered communicative discourse; and 2) the consolidation of power of those who control the material resource framework wherein a society, the social class language game, is ensconced and the threat that power (consolidated and constituted via the actions of bodies, mode of production, language, ideology, ideological apparatuses, and communicative discourse) poses to the ontological security of an aggregated individual actor who chooses, dialectically, (or not by assuming an antidialectical position) either ready-to-hand or present-at-hand to recursively reorganize and reproduce the ideals of the society as their practical consciousness. Those who seek to antidialectically maintain their subjective positions do so at the constant threat to their ontological security.

Hence the understanding here is that the transcendental ego of Being becomes embodied and objectified in a material resource framework enframed by bodies, the mode of production, language, ideology, ideological apparatuses, and communicative discourse of those who precede them and control a material resource framework. As embodied consciousness, the transcendental ego initially encounters itself and the world in the ready-to-hand preontological mode interpellated by the subjects of the reified social class language game. This means as aggregated recycled/entangled/superimposed subatomic particle endowed with consciousness and phenomenal properties, Being is, initially, unconsciously driven by the drives of its aggregated body and the agential initiatives or impulses (phenomenal properties) of recycled/entangled/superimposed past/present/future subatomic neuronal particles as limited by their embodiment via the microtubules of the brain. If its bodily and neuronal drives/impulses are uninhibited by the bodies (practical consciousness), mode of production, language, ideology, ideological apparatuses, and communicative discourse, i.e., social class language game, of those who control the material resource framework, Being may spend all of their existence in this stance. However, should they encounter resistance vis-à-vis their drives/impulses and the social class language game of those who control the material resource framework, Being moves to the unready-to-hand stance where they think about and question their own drives and or those of the material resource framework. At which point, they may become present-at-hand and may opt for either the practices associated with their internal drives/impulses, which they reify as culture, or that of the social class language game in power. If they choose the latter, being simply seeks the structural practices and differentiation of power at the expense of their internal drives/impulses and cognitive developments. In the former case, choosing to reproduce their internal drives, Being, attempts to recursively reproduce either the drives of its body or what was/is the unconscious drives/impulses of recycled/ entangled/superimposed past/present/future consciousnesses in the conscious present-at-hand stance at the threat to their ontological security in the material resource framework. At which point they may seek other Beings who share their drives/impulses/cognitive developments or seek to change the ideology of power to accept what has become a decentered subject who has deferred the meaning of power. The latter position is the basis for postmodern and post-structural thought, and alternative practices outside of structural reproduction and differentiation.

Phenomenological structuralism, therefore, seeks to highlight the ontological universal modes of embodied human existence with others, which relationally has emerged out of the phenomenological processes (Heidegger's three stances) of the transcendental ego experiencing, interpreting, and using the representational facts of its embodiment vis-à-vis the world as defined by and in the reified language game of others who control objects of a material resource framework, and how these modes of human existence come to (re) shape practical consciousness and constitute social structure or societal constitution.

That is to say, phenomenological structuralism synthesizes, the notions of the materialism and indeterminacy of behavior of recycled/entangled/ superimposed subatomic particles in quantum mechanics as they get objectified as neuronal energies of the brain and body to produce the transcendental subject of consciousness; with the potentiality for the multiplicity of choice or meaning in Haitian and Heideggerian phenomenology to capture the process of indeterminacy and deferment of meaning highlighted by postmodern and post-structural theory; with Marxist dialectic, Althusserian structural Marxism, and Wittgensteinian notions of language games to highlight the reified atomic structures, bodies, mode of production, language, communicative discourse, ideology, and ideological apparatuses, collectively understood here under the concept social class language game, which attempts to structure the indeterminacy of consciousness at the atomic human level as revealed in the practices, i.e., practical consciousnesses, of social actors, and prevent them from connecting with the noumenal world.

The notion of *language game* utilized here is an adoption of the "language-games" later philosophy of Ludwig Wittgenstein (1953) conceptualized within a neo-Marxian and Althusserian structural Marxian understanding of the constitution of identities based on the practical consciousness and ideology of those who control the economic conditions, social relations of production, of a material resource framework. For the Wittgenstein of the *Philosophical Investigations* language is a tool and must be thought of as a rule-governed, self-contained practice, like a game, of activities associated with some particular family of linguistic expressions, which have no point outside themselves, but is simply associated with the satisfactions they give to the participants and their form of life. What Mocombe is suggesting, against the genetic ontology of Christopher Macann (1993) who views the transcendental ego as "a subjectification of embodied human being," is that embodiment is the objectification of the transcendental ego, which is a part of an universal *élan vital* (which is a material thing, the subatomic particles of past consciousnesses, the eternal recurrence of past consciousnesses, that gets encapsulated in the brain of breathing subjects we see in any given historical formation) that has ontological status in dimensions existing at the subatomic particle level and gets embodied as and via the connectome of Beings' brains and their bodies. Embodiment is the multiverse manifesting itself as embodied consciousness or a transcendental ego. Once objectified, materialized, and embodied as human individual consciousnesses in a present historical formation the transcendental ego becomes an embodied hermeneutic structure that never encounters the world and the things of the world in themselves as highlighted by Jacques Lacan through his conception of the symbolic; instead embodied hermeneutic individual consciousnesses are constituted via, and as, recycled/entangled/superimposed neuronal energies of past/present/future consciousnesses, i.e., subatomic particles, the body, language, and ego-centered communicative discourse in their encounter and interpretation of things either ready-to-hand, unready-to-hand, and present-at-hand enframed in and by the historical consciousness, language, bodies, ideology, ideological apparatuses, and practices of those who control the economic conditions, social relations of the mode of production (as suggested by Althusser), of the material resource framework it finds itself thrown in. As embodied consciousness, whose ideas and practices are revealed and manifested through the body and language, it (individual consciousnesses of beings) can either accept (ready-to-hand) the signified historical structural knowledge, differentiation, and practices (social class language game) of those who control the economic conditions, social relations of production, of the material resource framework and recursively reorganize and reproduce them in their practices and institutions, or reject them (in the unready-to-hand and present-at-hand stance), by assuming an antidialectical stance, as demonstrated by the African participants of Bois Caiman of the Haitian Revolution, for an indeterminate amount of action-theoretic ways-of-being-in-the-world-with-others-in-space-time, which they may assume at the threat to their ontological security. It is the ready-to-hand drives of the body and brain, ready-to-hand and present-at-hand manifestation of past/present/future recycled/entangled/superimposed residual consciousnesses/subatomic particles, the present-at-hand phenomenological meditation and deferment of meaning that occurs in embodied consciousness via language, ideology, and communicative discourse as reflected in diverse individual practices, within the ready-to-hand, unready-to-hand, and present-at-hand differentiating logic or class divisions of the social relations of production, which produces the variability of actions and practices in cultures, social structures, or social systems. All four types of actions, the drives/impulses of the body and residual past consciousnesses of subatomic particles, structural reproduction/differentiation, and actions resulting from the deferment of meaning in ego-centered communicative discourse, are always present and manifested in a social structure (which is the reified ideology via ideological apparatuses, their social class language game, of those who control a material resource framework) to some degree contingent upon the will and desires of the economic social class that controls the material resource framework through its body, language, symbols, ideology, ideological apparatuses, and social relations of production, and the antidialectical stance of the human actor who rejects the latter position as a nonobjective/subjective position. The former choose, amidst the class division of the social relations of the mode of production, what other meaning constitutions and practices are allowed to manifest themselves without the Beings of that practice facing alienation, marginalization, domination, or death, and the latter chooses their own subjective positions at the threat to their ontological security.

Phenomenological Structuralism Diagrammatically

As outlined, phenomenological structuralism agrees with structurationist sociologists that in the constitution of society—which is the reification, by those who control the resources of a material resource framework, of the social relations of production via their bodies (practical consciousness), language, ideology, ideological apparatuses, and communicative discourse—the individual elements incorporate the structure of the whole and get differentiated by the dialectical and relational logic, structural reproduction and differentiation, of that whole.

Mocombe's phenomenological structural understanding, unlike that of the traditional structurationists, attempts to provide an analytical tool to explain and examine the relation of the "others" within the totality who do not, however: the relationship between "the individual elements [, who,] internalize [and recursively reproduce,] the structur[ing ideology] of the whole," and those who as a result of their ready-to-hand, unready-to-hand, and present-at-hand stances vis-à-vis the drives of their bodies, residual past consciousnesses (of phenomenal properties) of recycled subatomic particles or through self- reflection or phenomenological meditation in the unready-to-hand and present-at-hand mode of encountering the reified structural terms of a society conceive of, or choose among, fully visible "alternative" ways of being-in-the-world, which they attempt to, antidialectically, exercise in the "totality" at the threat to their ontological security.

This "mechanical" relationship can be expressed diagrammatically (see Figure 2.1). The model is an adaptation of Stephen Slemon's (1995) description of colonialism's multiple strategies for regulating Europe's others (Slemon, 1995, pg. 46), and whether in Mocombe's usage of it or Slemon's slightly different depiction, it is a macro, at the societal level, extrapolation of Hegel's and Marx's master/slave dialectical power model, which would proceed along line A1, since they both suppose that their respective concepts (colonialism for Slemon and society, culture, structure, what have you, stemming from the social relations of the mode of production, for me) are ideological or discursive formations constituted through power and power relations reified via mode of production, actions of bodies, language, ideologies, ideological apparatuses, and communicative discourse.[3] Whereas Slemon extrapolates the dialectic to colonialism in particular, Mocombe does so to society in general.

The general understanding, within a phenomenological structural understanding of the constitution of society and practical consciousness, is that individual actors or network of solidarity or cultural groups (irreducibly "mediating" situated subjects), represented by lines "A" and "B" on the diagram, are interpellated and relationally socialized within society—its semiotic field or predefined and predetermined lexicons and representations of signification (at the bottom of the diagram) i.e., the field of socialization "and its investment in reproducing and naturalising the structures of power" (Slemon, 1995, p. 47)—through "ideological apparatuses" (at the top of the diagram) controlled by socialized institutional regulators ("As"), power elites or those in power positions, who recursively reorganize and reproduce the rules of conduct (which appear to be natural and commonsensical) of the social structure, which in modern times represent an ideological flanking for the protestant economic (capitalist) subjugation running along line "A1." Where in the first instance (A) there is encountering of the reified rules of conduct of the society (which is its structure, i.e., social structure stemming from the social relations of the mode of production) at the preontological ready-to-hand mode of encountering, there is adoption or internalization (the Structurationist view) on behalf of the individual or network of groups of the prescribed understanding of the representations and practices of the semiotic field, i.e., the recursively organized and reproduced rules of conduct, associated with the social relations of the mode of production, which are sanctioned. In the second (B), the individual encounters the facts and values of the world in either unready-to-hand or the present-at-hand mode, and through a form of phenomenological meditation on the structural terms (i.e., norms, values, prescriptions and proscriptions of power) that presuppose their existence, conceives of, or chooses among other or fully visible alternatives (other "Bs" discriminated by the social structure), a different understanding (, i.e., practical means, arriving from the drives of the body, unconscious drives of recycled subatomic particles, or through the deferment of meaning in ego-centered communicative discourse) of being-in-the-world ; or as in the case of racism, sexism, and classism is prescribed a structurally differentiated unalterable subordinate role based on the relational binary logic (rules for inclusion and exclusion) of the semiotic field of those in power positions ("As"). In this structurally differentiated mode the encountering is always either at the ready-to-hand or unready-to-hand mode of encountering, in the latter because something, discriminatory effects of the totality, is wrong in allowing the social actor to partake in the rules of conduct of the society. So regardless if they accept or reject the rules of conduct, they are still classified by the power elites as (Bs).

The socialized individuals or groups ("As")—socialized in the "constitutive power of societal (ideological) apparatuses like education, media, church, family, etc., and the constitutive power of fields of knowledge [, which stems from the semiotic field,] within those apparatuses" (46)—possess the potential to become, if they so choose, power elites and as such institutional regulators (at the top of the diagram), who subordinate through the manufacture of consent. Now to maintain power, those who become regulators (some "As") must address "B's" signification, which relationally undermines (it gives social actors an "alternative" form of being-in-the-world), as well as define, delimits, and stabilizes the predefined and reified lexicons and representations of signification that is the society's semiotic field. In other words, their

("Bs'''") interpretations or structurally differentiated identity in relation to "A's" reject the singularity and realism or naturalism attached to the representations and meanings of the social field, while at the same time helping to constitute it by defining, delimiting, and stabilizing the field, i.e., "B's" interpretation in relation to "A's" helps to define, because it is not, "A's" interpretation. Hence, the "As" must negotiate, appropriate, and reinflect "Bs" interpretive-practices into the semiotic field in order to delimit, their own; this is done, or has been done, up to this point in the human archaeological records on the constitution of society, by having them ("Bs") remain outside the field, by dismissing their interpretive-claims, in which case the field justifies their permanent outsider status (oppressed or discriminated against minorities, i.e., marginalized "other").

The "Bs," for the most part, can either accept (if their gaze is upon the eye of power—"As"—for recognition as a structurally differentiated "other," i.e., a class-in-itself) their appropriation, the rationale the institutional regulators ("As") prescribe to their ("B$_1$s'''") interpretive-practical consciousness which legitimates it as a representation, or they ("B$_2$s''") may choose (by averting their gaze as a class-for-itself) to remain *quasi*-outsiders if the meaning disclosed by the dominant institutional regulators is not in accordance with their own, or a previously discriminated subculture's, interpretive-practical understanding of the signifiers of the social structure. Regardless of what choice they ("Bs") make, however, they, "Bs," because the validity claims the institutional regulators provide for their (Bs') understanding validates their existence to start with, constantly attempt incorporation and acceptance, either, as a "class-in-itself," pushing for integration as a structurally differentiated "other" (hybrid) who recursively reproduce the rules of conduct of the social structure ("B$_1$s'''"); or separation ("B$_2$s''"), as a "class-for-itself," for their own rules of conduct which are sanctioned by the power elites of the subculture. The former is the position of the bourgeoisie's of once discriminated against groups, such as blacks, women, etc., in contemporary postindustrial Protestant capitalist societies seeking to partake as a hybrid other in the social class language games of the society.

Thus there are two fundamental paths which are open to "Bs": first, if they (B) accept the understanding of (A), regarding their interpretation as an "other," and seek integration, as a structurally differentiated "class-in-itself," they have to give up their interpretive-practical consciousness, which on the one hand undermines the legitimation of the interpretive community they are classed with, while on the other hand, legitimating society's semiotic field, which has appropriated their ("Bs'''") understanding and representation to substantiate and delimit their (As') power position

and "practical consciousness." From this perspective, the "Bs," "B₁s'",
who accept appropriation, are socialized (institutionalized) and attempt to
live as ("As"), which entail recursively organizing and reproducing, as a
hybrid "other," the rules of conduct of the society which are sanctioned.
Those who do not (the second path), that is, those in the present-at-hand
mode of encountering who reject the rules of conduct of the society, for
their own, "B₂s'", may seek to reconstitute society in line with their
interpretive-practical consciousness, which gives rise to another (warring)
structure of signification or form of being-in-the-world, which, as a
segregated categorical boundary or alternative practical consciousness,
relationally and differentially delimits that of the society or social
structure, which they initially constituted.⁴

From the perspective of power, "As," "Bs'" interpretations, their
interpretive-practical consciousness, are always represented in the semiotic
field in order to define, delimit, and stabilize the power structure. Thus,
"Bs" are always oppressed minorities or majorities, i.e., "others," in the
Hegelian master/slave relationship (A1), who must construct their
identities or consciousness within two or more ideals: that of the social
structure (master's own understanding of themselves) and what it says of
the discriminated against "other" (the slave). Hence, the "Bs," as long as
their gaze is turned back upon the eyes of power (vector of motion of
"B₁s'") for recognition in the unready-to-hand mode of encountering,
which seeks to fix the status quo for their participation, pose no real
danger to the semiotic field, unless—following the aforementioned second
path,"B₂s',"—they should take-up arms against it as a distinct structuring
structure, i.e., "class-for-itself" or categorical boundary, which has averted
their gaze, and are attempting to preserve or universalize their
"alternative" ontology or "practical consciousness." This latter position is
represented by Islamic fundamentalists contemporarily, and the African
participants of Bois Caiman during the Haitian Revolution (1791-1804),
for examples.

In other words, in having to construct their (Bs) identities or
consciousness by warring against the ideals of the social structure, which
become the relational terms that defines, delimits, and stabilizes the social
structure and that by which all ("As" and "Bs") must construct their
consciousness, the gaze back upon the eye of power is a sign of
recognition of the validity claims of the social structure, which necessarily
implies that in order to be recognized the "Bs" must attempt to be what
they are not, like "As." This agential move to be like "As," however,
constrains the variability of practices, which, as the diagram highlights,
can only be maintained if the gaze of Bs' (vector of motion of "B₂s'") are

averted away from the eyes of power in order to establish another segregated structuring structure, which celebrates and reproduces the practices' of their "otherness." So long as the aim of "B" is for acceptance into the structure of social relations that constitute the society, their "otherness" can only be expressed as those ("As") who recursively reorganize and reproduce the rules of conduct of the social structure. For it is only upon the world of existing state of affairs, i.e., the valid norms and subjective experiences of power (the structure of the conjuncture of the social relations of production), which is taken to be the nature of reality and existence as such, will they ("Bs") be admitted into the structure of social relations that constitute the society, for any other form may undermine the whole of social relations that is the constituted society.[5]

Institutional regulators
(Society's educational/ideological apparatuses)

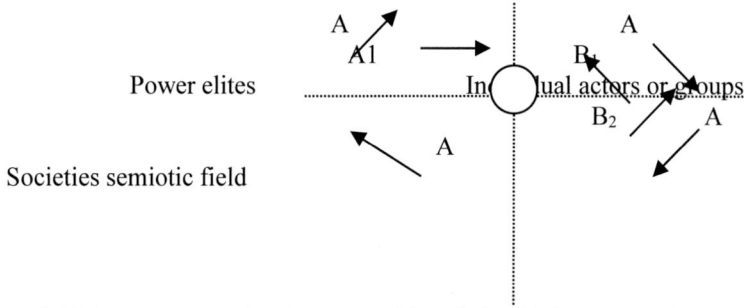

Figure 2.1 Diagram representing the nature of the relationship between society and the individual or group in phenomenological structuralism. "A" represent the power elites of the social structure; B_1 represent those "others" (hybrids) with their gaze upon the eye of power seeking to be like "A"; B_2 represent those with their gaze averted from the eye of power seeking to exercise an alternative practical consciousness from that of "As" and "B_1s."

The Role of Power in the Diagram

Whereas, figure 2.1 demonstrates the action of individual actors or groups within "a" reified consciousness, social class language game, that forms the structure of relations that is their society via the practical consciousness of bodies, language, ideology, ideological apparatuses, communicative discourse, and mode of production; figure 2.2 makes evident the actions of social actors (As), if and when, they become institutional regulators or power elites.

The understanding here is that it is the legal regulations of a society, its "lexicons and representations of signification," its rules of conduct that are sanctioned, as outlined by the power elites, or institutional regulators in power positions, which represent the objective conditions (social structure) of society that structure the social relations of the mode of production and constitute the materials by-which consciousness is to be cultivated for the ontological security of the individual. In other words, the general understanding, within a phenomenological structural understanding, is that individual actors or groups (irreducibly situated subjects), lines A and B, are socialized within society—its semiotic field or predefined and predetermined lexicons and representations of signification (at the bottom of the diagram) i.e., the field of socialization "and its investment in reproducing and naturalising the structures of power" (Slemon, 1995, pg. 47)—through "ideological apparatuses" (at the top of the diagram) controlled by socialized institutional regulators ("As"), which represent an ideological flanking for the economic subjugation running along line "A1." The relation between the two runs this way: societal power operates through a complex relationship between apparatuses (i.e., the law, education, rituals, family etc.) placed on line "C," where in the first instance institutional regulators ("As")—at the top of the line— appropriate and manufacture, based on what is already understood, lexicons and representations of signification of individuals in order to consolidate and legitimate itself as a natural "order" and to reproduce individuals as deployable units of that order. So, in the first instance, societal power runs not just through the middle ground of this diagram (A1) but through a complex set of relations happening along line "C;" and since the argument here is that a function (i.e., socialized social actor) at the top of this line is employing those representations created at the bottom of the line in order to make up "knowledges" that have an ideological function, one can say that the vector of motion along line C is an upward one, and that this upward motion is part of the whole complex discursive structure whereby society manufactures individuals and thus helps to regulate societal relations. This is the first position.

The second position, as the diagram demonstrates, is the downward movement of societal power, where the institutional regulators of society's apparatuses are understood to be at work in the production of a purely unique and entirely projected idea of the individual, relationally delimited by other fully visible marginalized "alternative" forms of the individual being-in-the-world. The point this movement, which is inextricably tied to the first, is trying to articulate is that society is a product of the working and reworking of reified psychic projections associated with the social relations of the mode of production operating through line A1. Hence, society has to be understood as a structure or system of power relations in which those in power positions attempt to structure, via bodies, language, ideology, ideological apparatuses, and communicative discourse individuals toward an unchangeable unified end associated with the social relations of the mode of production.[6] This does not mean that there is no agency, for who or what acts oppositionally, in this understanding of the constitution of society, is demonstrated through an understanding of the movements of lines A and B described above, which represents the Haitian concept of antidialectics.

Essentially, then, in this phenomenological structural understanding, society develops from the interpretive-practical consciousness of those (power elites or social actors in power positions) who maintain control of and integrate its material resource framework via the social relations of the mode of production.[7] Through this economic and political process, all individual actors ("As" and "Bs"), unless they choose (as a "class-for-itself" under the auspices of their own power elites) to, antidialectically, establish their own institutions, are socialized in apparatuses controlled by these social actors, institutional regulators (at the top of the diagram), who employ their representations, the reified symbolic objects that constitute the semiotic field (society)—at the bottom of the diagram, in institutions—so as to control, guide, and incorporate the ambivalence that lies in the act of interpretation (Bhabha, 1995, pg. 208)—in order to make up and reproduce ideological "knowledges" that maintain the functioning of the society as a whole.[8] Mocombe is arguing that this model, up to this point in the human archaeological research on societal relations, is a general structure for understanding the multivalent strategies at work in the reproduction and transformation of societies. Furthermore, it resolves the issue of agency, which is problematic when one posits ideology or discourse or psychic processes as constructing human subjects, for who or what acts is clearly demonstrated in the model through the praxis of the structure ("As") and anti-structural elements ("Bs" if they form interpretative communities, "B₂s'", which, antidialectically, do not seek incorporation or cooptation).

Institutional regulators
(Society's educational/ideological apparatuses)

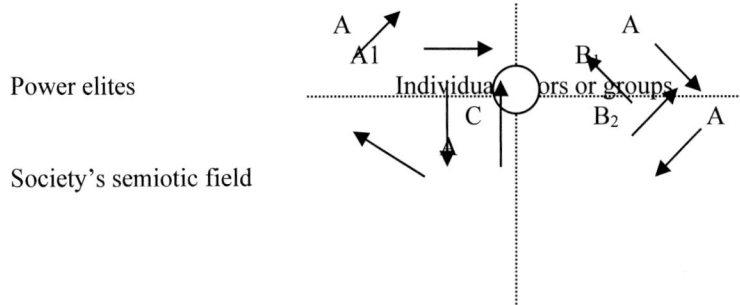

Power elites

Society's semiotic field

Figure 2.2 Diagram representing the nature of the relationship—C—between society's semiotic field (bottom of diagram) and the institutional regulators (top of diagram) in phenomenological structuralism.

Methods

In sum, phenomenological structuralism as a theory and method for the social sciences suggests that Being-in-the-world-with-others is the product of an embodied hermeneutic beings' encounter with and interpretation of the *social class "language game"* (Ludwig Wittgenstein's term) of those who control the economic conditions of a material resource framework (a la Karl Marx) via the actions of their bodies (practical consciousness), language, ideology, institutions or ideological apparatuses, and communicative discourse, which individual being's consciousness (which is a material thing in the brain constituted by recycled subatomic particles of other consciousnesses) encounter via the stances of their consciousness vis-à-vis their embodiment, the bodies of others, mode of production, language, ideology, ideological apparatuses, and communicative discourse.

The notion of *social class language game* utilized here is an adoption of the "language-games" later philosophy of Ludwig Wittgenstein (1953) conceptualized within an Althusserian structural-Marxist understanding of the constitution of identities based on the practical consciousness and ideology, social class language game, of those who control the economic conditions of a material resource framework. For the Wittgenstein of the *Philosophical Investigations* language is a tool and must be thought of as a rule-governed, self-contained practice, like a game, of activities associated with some particular family of linguistic expressions, which have no point outside themselves, but is simply associated with the satisfactions they give to the participants and their form of life. What Mocombe is suggesting is that embodiment is the objectification of the transcendental ego, which is a part of a universal *élan vital* (which is a material thing, the subatomic particles of past consciousnesses, the eternal recurrence of past consciousnesses, that gets encapsulated in the brain of breathing subjects we see in any given historical formation) that has ontological status in dimensions existing at the subatomic particle level and gets embodied via the connectum of Beings' brains and their bodies. Once objectified, materialized, and embodied as human individual consciousness in a present historical formation the transcendental ego becomes an embodied hermeneutic structure, consciousness, which never encounters the world and the things of the world in themselves as highlighted by Jacques Lacan. Instead, embodied hermeneutic individual consciousness is constituted via the stance/analytics of its transcendental ego vis-à-vis the drives (forms of sensibilities and understanding) of the body and brain, impulses (phenomenal properties) of recycled past consciousnesses of subatomic particles, mode of production, language, ideology, and ego-centered communicative discourse in their encounter and interpretation of things enframed in and by the historical consciousness, bodies, ideology, ideological apparatuses, and practices (i.e., social class language game) of those who control the economic conditions of the material resource framework it finds itself thrown in. As an embodied hermeneutic consciousness, whose ideas and practices are revealed and manifested through the body and language as practical consciousness, it (individual consciousness of beings) can either choose to accept the signified historical structural knowledge, differentiation, and practices of those who control the economic conditions of the material resource framework and recursively reorganize and reproduce them in their practices and institutions, or antidialectically reject them, given the ability to, present-at-hand, defer meaning in ego-centered communicative discourse, for an indeterminate amount of action-theoretic ways-of-being-in-the-world-with-others, which they may assume at the threat to their ontological security. It is the impulses or phenomenal properties of recycled/ entangled/superimposed subatomic particles, the drives and sensibilities of the body and brain, manifestation of the phenomenological meditation and deferment of meaning that occurs in embodied consciousness via language and communicative discourse as reflected in social practice or practical consciousness, along with the differentiating logic or class divisions of the social relations of production, which produces the variability of actions and practices in cultures, social structures, or social systems. All four types of praxis are always present and manifested in a social structure to some degree contingent upon the will and desires of the economic social class that controls the material resource framework through the actions of its body (practical consciousness), language, communicative discourse, ideology, ideological apparatuses, and social relations of the mode of production and the antidialectical stance of certain human actors. The former dialectically choose, amidst the class division and differentiating effects of the social relations of the mode of production, what other meaning constitutions and practices are allowed to manifest themselves in the ideological apparatuses of the material resource framework without facing marginalization, domination, or death by other embodied hermeneutic consciousnesses who accept their dominant discourse and discursive practice. While the latter, antidialectically, recursively reorganize and reproduce their existence in the world by viewing the structure of social relations as a subjective position that does not have the natural right to determine individual existence, which ought to be in harmony with nature as opposed to prescribe rules of conduct that are sanctioned by power and power relations.

Be that as it may, the emphasis of the social scientist in the academy is to present-at-hand (the stance of science and ideology) determine (via qualitative research methods, i.e., ethnographies, historiographies, sociometry, etc.) the origins and nature of an individual's and social group's practical consciousness—i.e., structural reproduction and differentiation as in the case of the black American underclass and bourgeoisie; the drives of the body and brain wherein the individual, and the groups they constitute, are solely driven by innate biological drives of the body and brain for their material survival; impulses of subatomic particles wherein the individual, and the groups they constitute, are driven by unconscious drives encoded in the recycled subatomic particles that constitute the individual (i.e., in Haitian Vodou that is the origins of homosexuality. The individual is biologically born a male or vice a versa constituted by the subatomic particles of past lives where they experienced being in another dispensation of space-time as the opposite sex); and the deferment of meaning in ego-centered communicative discourse as in the case of certain subgroups in the black American community wherein certain words (i.e., "bad" for "good"; "dope" for "nice," etc.) are deferred or given alternative meanings from that of the dominant group of the society—in relation to, and amidst, the structural reproduction and differentiation of the larger society or social class language game (social roles, ideological apparatuses, rituals, rules, norms, and goals), while simultaneously fighting against the objectification and reification of the latter for simply subsistence living.

As defined, phenomenological structuralism proposes a mix-method research paradigm, which incorporates three worldviews associated with the research process: The postpositivist worldview, with its emphasis on scientific research into the psychology of the forms of sensibility and understanding of the brain, and the physics of subatomic particle embodiment; Constructivism and critical theory, with its emphasis on the sociology of the mode of production and understanding and meaning as it pertains to individuals and networks of solidarity groups, which defer the meaning of the ideologies of the mode of production and are marginalized by those in power positions for doing so; and Pragmatism/Advocacy/ Participatory, with its emphasis on finding solutions to the increasing problems associated with the enchantment of the world around the contemporary ideology, the Protestant Ethic and the spirit of capitalism, which threatens all life on earth and prevents the human subject from relating to the noumenal world.

Be that as it may, methodologically speaking, the sociology of the structure of the conjuncture of the mode of production must be outlined in any research project, while accounting for the nature of an individual's or network of solidarity groups's agential initiatives—1) product of the drives of the physical body and brain; 2) impulses (phenomenal properties) of embodied recycled subatomic particles; 3) structural reproduction and differentiation according to the rules of conduct which are sanctioned for the material relations (mode) of production; and 4) the deferment of meaning in ego-centered linguistic and symbolic communicative discourse—amidst a change-oriented discourse of the researcher, which emphasizes the de-reification of the mode of production towards exploitation and marginalization in favor of subsistence living vis-à-vis the material resource framework. For phenomenological structuralism seeks to highlight the ontological universal modes of embodied human existence with others, which relationally has emerged out of the phenomenological processes (Heidegger's three stances) of the transcendental ego experiencing, interpreting, and using the representational facts of its embodiment vis-à-vis the world as defined by and in the language game of others who control objects of a material resource framework, and how these modes of human existence come to (re) shape practical consciousness and constitute social structure or societal constitution. It is within this Wittgensteinian/Marxian/Heideggerian derivative ontology I explore the emergence of the "my nigga" Haitian practical consciousness, which is a product of structural reproduction and differentiation.

Phenomenological structuralism posits consciousness to be the by-product or evolution of subatomic particles unfolding with increasing levels of abstraction within a material resource framework enframed by the mode of production, language, ideology, ideological apparatuses, and communicative discourse of bodies recursively reorganizing and reproducing the ideals of the latter factors as their practical consciousness. Subatomic particles, via the Higgs boson particle, gave rise to carbon atoms, molecules and chemistry, which gave rise to DNA, biological organisms, neurons and nervous systems, which aggregated into bodies and brains that gave rise to the preexisting consciousness of the subatomic particles, bodies, and languages. In human beings, the indeterminate behavior of subatomic neuronal energies that produced the plethora of consciousnesses and languages in the neocortex of the brain gave rise to ideologies, which in turn gave rise to ideological apparatuses and societies (sociology) under the social class language game or language, ideology, and ideological apparatuses of those who organize and control the material resources (and their distribution) required for physical (embodied) survival in a particular resource framework. So contrary to Karl Marx's materialism which posits human consciousness to be the product of material conditions, the logic here is a structural Marxist one in the Althusserian sense. That is, the aggregated, atomic, mature human being is a body and neuronal drives that never encounters the (ontological) material world directly. Instead, they encounter the (ideological) world via structures of signification, which structures the world or a particular part of it through the body, language, ideology, and ideological apparatuses, i.e., social class language game, of those whose power and power positions dictate how the resources of that framework are to be gathered, used, and distributed (means and mode of production).

Hence in the end, subject constitution is a product of an individual's stance, i.e., analytics, vis-à-vis three structures of signification and the ability to defer meaning in ego-centered communicative discourse stemming from the social class language game (i.e., language, symbols, ideology, ideological apparatuses, and communicative discourse) of those who control the mode of production of a material resource framework. It is the ready-to-hand drives of the body and brain, ready-to-hand and present-at-hand manifestation of past recycled residual consciousnesses/subatomic particles, the present-at-hand phenomenological meditation and deferment of meaning that occurs in embodied consciousness via language, ideology, and communicative discourse as reflected in diverse individual practices, within the ready-to-hand, unready-to-hand, and present-at-hand differentiating logic or class divisions of the social relations of production, which produces the variability of actions and practices in cultures, social structures, or social systems. All four types of actions, the drives/impulses of the body and residual past/present/future consciousnesses of subatomic particles, structural reproduction/differentiation, and actions resulting from the deferment of meaning in ego-centered communicative discourse, are always present and manifested in a social structure (which is the reified ideology via ideological apparatuses, their social class language game, of those who control a material resource framework) to some degree contingent upon the will and desires of the economic social class that controls the material resource framework through the actions of their bodies (practical consciousness), language, symbols, ideology, ideological apparatuses, and social relations of production. They choose, amidst the class division of the social relations of production, what other meaning constitutions and practices are allowed to manifest themselves without the Beings of that practice facing alienation, marginalization, domination, or death.

Discussion and Conclusions: Hypothesis/Thesis

Hence within the theory and methodology of phenomenological structuralism, the logic here is that Karl Marx's materialism is the product of the first group of embodied human beings initial encounter with the material world. Upon that initial ready-to-hand encounter, driven by the drives of the body and impulses of subatomic particles, two present-at-hand worldviews emerged and became reified via mode of production, language, ideologies, ideological apparatuses, and communicative discourse. In a fruitful and bountiful environment, as early humankind encountered ready-to-hand in Africa prior to their migration elsewhere, a harmonious disposition towards the world took hold, which was juxtaposed against an antagonistic disposition arising from a lack of resources, etc., as was found among Europeans who migrated out of Africa to Europe. According to Cheik Anta Diop (1981, 1988, 1989), as a result of these experiences African and most people of color on the earth, the Taino people of the Caribbean, for example, who inherited hospitable environments, shared certain linguistic and cultural commonalities that formed a tapestry that laid the basis, present-at-hand, for African cultural unity, which was reified and diametrically opposed to the European cultural unity that would develop, unready-to-hand and present-at-hand, in the barren and harsh environments of Europe as early humans migrated out of Africa.

What Diop called the Southern Cradle-Egyptian Model (African): 1) Abundance of vital resources, 2) Sedentary-agricultural, 3) Gentle, idealistic, peaceful nature with a spirit of justice, 4) Matriarchal family, 5)

Emancipation of women in domestic life, 6) territorial state, 7) Xenophilia, 8) Cosmopolitanism, 9) Social Collectivism, 10) Material solidarity—alleviating moral or material misery, 11) Idea of peace, justice, goodness, and optimism, and 12) Literature emphasizes novel tales, fables, and comedy, emerged, present-at-hand, among the people of color in tropical climates with bountiful resources. This Southern Cradle-Egyptian Model was diametrically opposed to an unready-to-hand and present-at-hand Northern Cradle-Greek Model: (European), 1) Bareness of resources, 2) Nomadic-hunting (piracy), 3) Ferocious, warlike nature with spirit of survival, 4) Patriarchal family, 5) Debasement/enslavement of women, 6) City state (fort), 7) Xenophobia, 8) Parochialism, 9) Individualism, 10) Moral solitude, 11) Disgust for existence, pessimism, 12) Literature favors tragedy. The European/Greek model, over time became reified and recursively reorganized and reproduced, present-at-hand, as the Protestant Ethic and the spirit of capitalism under the leadership of Pastors, merchants, and owners in their encounter with Christianity; and the former, African model, as the Vodou Ethic and the spirit of communism under the leadership of priests, priestesses, healers, and elders (*oungan*, *manbo*, *gangan*, and *granmoun* in the Kreyol language of African/Taino/ Haitian Vodou).

Hence unlike Karl Marx, which views the origins of modern capitalist relations of production via the notion of primitive accumulation, phenomenological structuralism is in agreement with Max Weber and views it as the product of the (ideological) structures of signification of European Protestant Christianity, i.e., the Protestant Ethic and the spirit of capitalism reified via ideological apparatuses based on the mode of production, which I juxtapose against the African Vodou Ethic and spirit of communism of the original inhabitants of the earth who, because of their material abundance, did not develop an antagonistic present-at-hand (ideological) view of the world as their European counterparts who experienced hardship in satisfying their basic needs. In other words, African peoples, and other people of color originally inhabited the earth, ready-to-hand, in environments with abundance of vital resources. Over time, their tribal and village leaders developed present-at-hand structural ideologies, Vodou; ideological apparatuses, villages, Lakous, peristyles, *lwa yo*, and herbal medicine; and modes of productions, subsistence agriculture, husbandry, and komes that reified their experiences and formed a tapestry, i.e., social class language game under the leadership of *oungan yo*, *manbo yo*, and *granmoun yo* (elders) that laid the basis for African cultural/structural unity, which was diametrically opposed to an European cultural/structural unity that encountered, ready-to-hand, a barren material resource framework.[9]

The latter because they were unable to satisfy their bodily needs in the barren material resource framework of Europe, in other words, became unready-to-hand and developed an antagonistic stance vis-à-vis the world, which became reified, present-at-hand, as the Protestant Ethic and the spirit of capitalism when they encountered Christianity under the leadership, initially, of Pastors and merchants. Hence, what Cheikh Anta Diop called the Southern Cradle-Egyptian Model (African), which I call the Vodou Ethic and the spirit of communism social class language game, emerged, ready-to-hand and present-at-hand, among the Africans, and the Northern Cradle-Greek (European) Model, or the Protestant Ethic and the spirit of capitalism social class language game, emerged, unready-to-hand and present-at-hand, among the Europeans as the structures that attempt to limit the unfolding of human action in the material resource framework of the earth. An in ideal state, the latter sought embourgeoisement and domination, and the former, ounganification/manboification, egalitarianism, harmony, balance, perfection, and subsistence living. Both models, or structuring structures, interpellated and subjectified individual Beings of their material resource frameworks via different modes of production, languages, ideologies, ideological apparatuses, and communicative discourses. Both models converged on the island of Hispaniola, at the height of the slave trade and African enslavement during the eighteenth century, where the enslaved Africans of Haiti juxtaposed the latter against the former in the attempt to overthrow it on the island. However, the dialectical adoption of practices associated with the Catholic/Protestant Ethic and the spirit of capitalism by the mulatto elites and the petit-bourgeois blacks, Affranchis, has given rise to the "my nigga" Haitian identity dominating the ghettoes of Haiti and the US, contemporarily.

Notes

[1] See Paul C. Mocombe's (2019) *Theory of Phenomenological Structuralism*.

[2] Mocombe's phenomenological structuralism, as in Western epistemology and ontology which developed as a result of the ever-increasing rationalization and testing of Christian notions, reflects his rationalization of Vodou metaphysics as an ontology and sociology for understanding cosmic and societal constitution. As such, Mocombe's work builds from Reginald O. Crosley's (2006) essay, "Shadow-Matter Universes in Haitian and Dagara Ontologies: A Comparative Study," whose physics we summarize here.

[3] For an in-depth look at Slemon's diagram and description see: Slemon, Stephen (994). "The Scramble for Post-colonialism." In *De-Scribing Empire: Post-colonialism and Textuality*, Eds. Chris Tiffin and Alan Lawson. London: Routledge. Slemon

borrows this model (see figure 2.1 in the text) from De Saussure (1983 [1916], pg. 80), who prescribes the model as means for all sciences to map out the things they are concerned with. He calls the horizontal axis, "the axis of simultaneity." "This axis concerns relations between things which coexist, relations from which the passage of time is entirely excluded." The vertical axis, "the axis of succession:" "Along this axis one may consider only one thing at a time. But here we find all the things situated along the first axis, together with the changes they undergo."

Slemon, in using this model to understand Edward Said's depiction of colonialism and the role of the "other" argues, as many critics of structuralism have done, that there is no agency regardless of the practices taking place along the diachronic axis (i.e., the vertical axis; the horizontal axis for Saussure is the synchronic). Using this model to depict what Mocombe means by phenomenological structuralism, he is arguing that his description is not historically specific, and resolves the issue of agency in structure (in this case ideological structure or hegemony).

[4] Some may point to a third alternative, i.e., subversion from within, but this is a misconception because in order to be a subverter, the social actor must still recursively organize and reproduce the practical consciousness of the whole.

[5] In other words, although "Bs" in the diagram represent the variability of praxis within structure, "counter-movements" in the Polanyian (2001 [1944]) sense only refer to embodied variable practices—which diametrically oppose the structuring end of the society or social structure they constitute and delimit—which seek to reconstitute society. So long as the aim of the discriminated against minority ("Bs") is for recognition as an "other," the variability of praxis is negated by the non-subversive hybridity of the discriminated against social actor.

[6] According to the Structuralism of De Saussure, "[c]hange originates in linguistic performance, in *parole* [(i.e., speech, practice, or event)], not in *la langue* [(formal structure or institutions)], and what is modified are individual elements of the system of realization. Historical changes affect the system in the end, in that the system will adjust to them, make use of the results of historical change, but it is not the linguistic system which produces them" (Culler, 1976, p. 41). From a phenomenological structural perspective what this means is that the ends to which the structure of society is directed appears to be unchangeable, even though the interpretive-practices amongst individuals and groups are, and may even contradict that appearance. What happens in the end is that institutional regulators attempt to incorporate these differential interpretive-practices in a way to maintain the order of things so that the ends to which society is structured continues to be realizable in spite of the differential practices. In fact, these practices, defined by their relation with the practices of the structure come to delimit the actual structure.

[7] This, as André C. Drainville (1995) observes, "is the essence of what Nicos Poulantzas called the political task of transformation" (57).

[8]Whereas at issue for Bourdieu, Sahlins, and Giddens "is the being of *structure* in history and as history" (Sahlins, 1985, pg. 145), Mocombe's approach does not see structure and history as antinomies, and therefore, focuses on the issue of "being" in *a structure of history*, or the predefined and predetermined "lexicons and representations of signification" that attempt to reproduce an aspect of "Being."

Transformation in this understanding is in the development of the historical structure as played-out in the interpretive-practices of the "Beings" or subjects of the system. In other words, reproduction is only attempted in the actual use of the structural ideas in "ideological apparatuses." But this is only an attempt, for the ideas, as objectified by those in power, are distorted as a result of the interpretive-practices of irreducibly situated individuals. So what we have is a dynamic structure driven by interpretive-practices within what is already understood of the objectified concepts of those in power positions, who must attempt to appropriate and redirect interpretative-practices that oppose or threaten their symbolic order. In doing so the structure may or may not be transformed, for transformation rests *only* in the ability of those with contradictory understandings of the symbolic order (Bs in the diagrams) to reconstitute society based on their understanding. As long as, power (As) is able to appropriate and reinflect their (Bs) understanding, reproduction, and as such structural domination along the same structural line (horizontal axis), is the only necessary outcome.

[9] I am using the Haitian/African Kreyol language for priests (oungan), priestesses (manbo), gangan (healers) and elders (granmoun), here out of convenience.

CHAPTER III

THE CONSTITUTION OF THE GLOBAL CAPITALIST WORLD-SYSTEM: THE PROTESTANT ETHIC AND THE SPIRIT OF CAPITALISM

Hence contrary to Karl Marx's early materialism which posits human consciousness to be the product of material conditions, the logic here is a later structural Marxist one synthesized with a Weberian sociology, which posits that the aggregated mature human being is an aggregation of "conscious" subatomic particles that never encounters the material world directly. Instead, they encounter the world via structures of signification, which structures the world or a particular part of it through the actions of the body, consciousness, language, ideology, ideological apparatuses, communicative discourses, and mode of production, i.e., social class language game, of those whose power and power positions dictate how the resources of that framework are to be gathered, used, and distributed (means and mode of production). Therefore, unlike Marx, which views the origins of modern capitalist relations of production, the current form of system integration dominating the world in which the Affranchis of Haiti were socialized, via the notion of primitive accumulation, my phenomenological structural ontology and sociology is in agreement with Max Weber and views it as the product of the structures of signification of Protestant Christianity, i.e., the Protestant Ethic and the spirit of capitalism social class language game under the leadership of white, Protestant, pastors, merchants, and owners, which I juxtapose against the African Vodou Ethic and spirit of communism social class language game of the original inhabitants of the earth under the leadership of priests, priestesses, healers, and elders, who, because of their early material abundance, did not develop an antagonistic unready-to-hand and present-at-hand view of the world as their European counterparts. Instead, they developed a present-at-hand worldview based on their initial ready-to-hand encountering of a material world, which readily provided them everything they needed for their existence.

In other words, African peoples, and other people of color originally inhabited the earth, ready-to-hand, in environments with abundance of vital resources. Over time, they developed present-at-hand structural ideologies and ideological apparatuses, agricultural production/*komes*, Vodou, villages, Lakous, peristyles, under the leadership of priests, priestesses, healers, and elders that formed a tapestry that laid the basis for African cultural/structural unity, which sought to keep the egalitarianism, balance, harmony, perfection, and subsistence living they encountered within their material resource framework.

This African cultural/structural unity was diametrically opposed to a European cultural/structural unity that encountered ready-to-hand and unready-to-hand a barren material resource framework. Upon their initial ready-to-hand stance, the European was unable to satisfy their bodily needs in a barren and hostile environment. As a result, they became or took an unready-to-hand stance, because their environment did not fulfill their basic needs, and sought to fulfill their basic needs through the objectification and externalization of the world, which they sought to exploit and dominate in order to meet their (bodily) needs. They reified their experiences, present-at-hand, as the nature of reality as such, which they sought to extrapolate throughout the world via the Protestant Ethic and the spirit of capitalism upon their encounter with Christian dogma following the fall of the Holy Roman Empire.

What Cheikh Anta Diop calls the Southern Cradle-Egyptian Model (African), which I call the Vodou Ethic and the spirit of communism social class language game, emerged among the Africans and many other people of color, and the Northern Cradle-Greek (European) Model, or the Protestant Ethic and the spirit of capitalism social class language game, emerged among the Europeans when they encountered Christianity. The former is characterized as and based on, 1) Abundance of vital resources, 2) Sedentary-agricultural, 3) Gentle, idealistic, peaceful nature with a spirit of justice, 4) Matriarchal family, 5) Emancipation of women in domestic life, 6) territorial state, 7) Xenophilia, 8). Cosmopolitanism, 9) Social Collectivism, 10) Material solidarity—alleviating moral or material misery, 11) Idea of peace, justice, goodness, and optimism, and 12) Literature emphasizes novel tales, fables, and comedy. The latter is characterized as and based on, 1) Bareness of resources, 2) Nomadic-hunting (piracy), 3) Ferocious, warlike nature with spirit of survival, 4) Patriarchal family, 5) Debasement/enslavement of women, 6) City state (fort), 7) Xenophobia, 8) Parochialism, 9) Individualism, 10) Moral solitude, 11) Disgust for existence, pessimism, 12) Literature favors tragedy. Historically, the latter, European model, became constituted and reified present-at-hand as the Protestant Ethic and the spirit of capitalism under the leadership of pastors, owners, and merchants; and the former, African model, as the Vodou Ethic and the spirit of communism under the leadership of priests, priestesses, healers, and elders, i.e., oungan yo, manbo yo, gangan yo, granmoun yo, respectively.[1] Both models converged on the island of Hispaniola, at the height of the slave trade and African enslavement during the eighteenth century, where the enslaved Africans and Taino people of Haiti juxtaposed the latter against the former in an attempt to overthrow it on the island. However, the Affranchis, mulattoes and petit-bourgeois blacks, with the aid of their former colonial slavemasters were able to maintain it as a form of social and system integration in the cities of the island against the Vodou Ethic and the spirit of communism of the majority of the Africans, which emerged in the provinces, mountains, and urban slums. Through a plethora of economic structural practices, i.e., corvée system, structural adjustment policies, neoliberalism, etc., which they, Affranchis, implemented to achieve equality of opportunity, recognition, and distribution with their former colonial masters, the "my nigga" Haitian identity would emerge as a structural identity in Haiti and the US diaspora heavily influenced by the black American underclass.

Hence, the argument here is that the constitution of modernity is the by-product of the structuralizing and differentiating effects (enchantment of the world) of the Protestant ethic and the spirit of capitalism, via agricultural, industrial, and postindustrial modes of production, European languages, Protestant ideology, and ideological apparatuses, churches, schools, etc., initially, by the practical consciousness or social class language game of religious, rich, white, Protestant, heterosexual, bourgeois, men in their rejection of the class division and social relations of production of the Catholic feudal order beginning in the sixteenth century. Building on the rationalization of the primeval pan-psychic field (emerging from the superverse and multiverses) within the God and soul concepts of early Christian dogma, these white men from Europe would interpret the God of Judaism as "active in history and in current political events rather than in the primordial sacred time of myth" (Armstrong, 1993, pg. 211). Be that as it may, the traditions of Christianity and Islam inherited this sociohistorical metaphysical understanding of God, which made their central motif a confrontation or a personal meeting between God and humanity devoted to ensuring that God's will is done on earth as it is in heaven:

This God is experienced as an imperative to action; he calls us to himself; gives us the choice of rejecting or accepting his love and concern. This God relates to human beings by means of a dialogue rather than silent contemplation. He utters a Word, which becomes the chief focus of devotion and which has to be painfully incarnated in the flawed and tragic conditions of earthly life. In Christianity, the most personalized of the three, the relationship with God is characterized by love. But the point of love is that the ego has, in some sense, to be annihilated (Armstrong, 1993, pg. 210-211).

The barbarian tribes from Europe that eventually brought down the Holy Roman Empire in the fifth century of the common era transmogrified the orientalism and aforementioned historical understanding of Christianity highlighted by Karen Armstrong to fit with their initial calculating, crude, and barbarous existence, which would subsequently become embodied, once they converted to Christianity, in the discourse and discursive practices of the Protestant Ethic and the spirit of capitalism social class language game.

The fall of the Holy Roman Empire would coincide with the rise of imperial Christianity, which began with the evangelism and feudalism of the Roman Catholic Church. The Catholic Church, following Constantine's usurpation of Christianity from the margins of the Roman Empire the fourth century of the Common Era, sought to imperially convert the world's social actors, and constitute the city of God on earth via, the family, church, feudalism and the aristocratic demeanor. Following the Protestant Reformation of the fifteenth and sixteenth centuries, they would subsequently be displaced by the imperial Christianity of the American nation-state embodied in its discourse and discursive practice, the Protestant Ethic and the spirit of capitalism, by the heteronormativity or social class language game of rich, white, Protestant, heterosexual male merchants.

Beginning in the sixteenth century of the common era, God's will on earth was no longer constituted around the ideological apparatuses of the family, church, aristocracy, and feudalism of the Catholic Church, but became interpreted as a Hobbesian imperative material struggle of" all against all" in the "flawed and tragic conditions of earthly life" wherein the most pious and egoless souls, which God calls to himself, who accept him, obtained material wealth as a sign of their personal salvation and God's grace and mercy. Protestant reformers such as the Puritans and Pilgrims zealously sought to convert all of Europe and the known world to their Protestant interpretation of the gospel of Jesus via the social class language game of the patriarchal family, Protestant churches, the modern state, class division, and social relations of mercantile and agricultural capitalist production. Their inability to constitute the city of God or their social class language game in Europe, based on their Protestantism, led to their persecution and the eventual founding of the American nation-state as the city of God grounded in the imperial Christianity of the Protestant Ethic and spirit of capitalism social class language game and its individualism. This Protestant Ethic and the spirit of capitalism, which would zealously and imperially seek to displace the evangelism and feudal discourse and discursive practice of the Catholic Church, the Amerindian world worldviews, Islam, African tribalism, etc., via the patriarchal family, Protestant churches, education, the state, and capitalist relations of production, has nothing to do with the egalitarianism, compassion, and social altruistic message of Jesus as highlighted in the synoptic gospels and the gospel of John as interpreted by the Catholic church, however. Quite the reverse, it fosters class division, inequality, selfishness, self-interested individualism, and materialism reified initially in the discourse and discursive practices, social class language game, of a patriarchal, heterosexual, white male Protestantism and the spirit of capitalism, which discriminated against and marginalized all other practical consciousnesses or ways of organizing society and the world via the patriarchal family, protestant discourse of churches, schools, prisons, class division, the modern state, and the social relations of mercantile, agricultural, industrial, and post-industrial capitalist productions.

Hence with the rise to power of Western European tribes and their Protestant interpretations of Christianity over feudal aristocratic Catholic dogma, the class division and social relations of production of the Protestant ethic and the spirit of capitalism and not the egalitarian, compassionate, and social altruistic message of Jesus, as Max Weber (1958) points out, represents what was understood, the set of values—rationality, hard work, economic gain as a sign of one's predestination, systematic use of time, and a strict asceticism with respect to worldly pleasures and goods—which he claims gave rise to the contemporary capitalist practices that constitute modern societies, and thus American capitalist society, and the existing configuration of bureaucratic power relations, social class language game, within which modern social identity and practical consciousness developed.

The purposive-rationality of these Protestant ideas and practices, mediated and overdetermined by the concepts of class, race, and nation, in other words, historicized social positions, based on racial, national identity, and economic gain for its own sake (class) through the accumulation of capital or profit in a "calling," initially mercantile, agricultural, and industrial relations of production, by which social actors or subjects were differentiated and subjugated (predestined or capitalists/damned or laborers) in the society and the world. Rich, white, heterosexual men universalized, present-at-hand, their ideology, through ideological apparatuses, the patriarchal family, church, schools, prisons, the modern state, class division, and the social relations of production, against all other practical consciousnesses, African polygamous tribalism, homosexuality, etc., arrived at through drives of the body, impulses of subatomic particles, and the deferment of meaning in ego-centered communicative discourse, for their embourgeoisement. From the late seventeenth century to the present, the ideology and ideological apparatuses of the modern state, family, church, and education, class division, and the social relations of production enframed by the Protestant ethic and spirit of capitalism of rich, white, heterosexual, Protestant, men would be the structure, language, ideology, ideological apparatuses, and communicative discourse within which social identities were constituted, subjectified, differentiated, discriminated against, and marginalized.

This theoretical framework differs from both Marxist and non-Marxist structural interpretations of the constitution of modern society in that it begins with the socioreligious cultural (ideal) conceptions, Protestant enchantment of the world, that initially structured the social integrative practices that gave rise to the society, while the Marxist and neo-Marxist schools derive the terms from which they begin their analysis from the (material) social relations of production. These two viewpoints, systems and social integration, as my phenomenological structural approach implies, are inextricably linked, however, and represents the relational structural-cultural framework organized around social relations of production, class division, and the modern state and its ideology and ideological apparatuses, i.e., nuclear family, education, prisons, etc., which determined social identity and practices in modern societies. In other words, although philosophically we are able to think these two approaches apart as idealism and materialism, they are not necessarily entirely separable in reality in my phenomenological structural logic.

Weber defines a capitalistic economic action,

> as one which rests on the expectation of profit by the utilization of opportunities for exchange, that is on (formally) peaceful chances of profit. Acquisition by force (formally and actually) follows its own particular laws, and it is not expedient, however little one can forbid this, to place it in the same category with action which is, in the last analysis, oriented to profits from exchange. Where capitalist acquisition is rationally pursued, the corresponding action is adjusted to calculations in terms of capital. This means that the action is adapted to a systematic utilization of goods or personal services as means of acquisition in such a way that, at

the close of a business period, the balance of the enterprise in money assets (or, in the case of a continuous enterprise, the periodically estimated money value of assets) exceeds the capital, i.e. [,] the estimated value of the material means of production used for acquisition in exchange (Weber, 1958, pg. 17-18).

Although this relationship appears paradoxical, since protestant beliefs did not embrace the idea of economic gain for its own sake,

Weber's argument is that the rational pursuit of the ultimate values of the ascetic Protestantism characteristic of sixteenth-and seventeenth-century Europe led people to engage in disciplined work; and that disciplined and rational organization of work as a duty is the characteristic feature of modern capitalism—its unique ethos or spirit (Marshall, 1998, pg. 534).

Thus,

The crucial link to Protestantism comes through the latter's notion of the calling of the faithful to fulfil their duty to God in the methodical conduct of their everyday lives. This theme is common to the beliefs of the Calvinist and neoCalvinist churches of the Reformation. Predestination is also an important belief, but since humans cannot know who is saved (elect) and who is damned, this creates a deep inner loneliness in the believer. In order therefore to create assurance of salvation, which is itself a sure sign (or proof) of election, diligence in one's calling (hard work, systematic use of time, and a strict asceticism with respect to worldly pleasures and goods) is highly recommended—so-called 'this-worldly asceticism'. In general terms, however, the most important contribution of Protestantism to capitalism was the spirit of rationalization that it encouraged. The relationship between the two is deemed by Weber to be one of elective affinity (Marshall, 1998, pg. 535).

The affinity between the Protestantism of a sect and their purposive-rational actions, as I understand Weber to be saying, gave rise to the *economic* organization of modern society, systems integration, as the social psychological practices and ego-ideals (rationally calculating individuals attempting to prove their predestination reflected in their economic gains) of a form of Protestantism, social integration, were rationally and purposively incorporated into the physical world through the bureaucratic organization of the material resource framework around language, ideology, ideological apparatuses, the patriarchal family, church, schools, state, prisons, and economy, social relations of production, in order to direct and constitute the identity and practices of social actors and societies for economic gain, status, and upward social mobility. (In some instances, as in the attempt of the Puritans to usurp power and takeover the

English nation-state of the seventeenth century under Oliver Cromwell, bureaucratic means or structural practices—purposive-formal-rational action to organize the lived world—were established around already existing material elements which were re-conceptualized by the sect of rich, white, Protestant, men to foster a society based on wealth, economic gain or capital accumulation as a sign of their salvation in the eyes of God and others).

Thus, the sociohistorical logic here is that following the Protestant Reformations of the fifteenth and sixteenth centuries, as rich, white, heterosexual Protestant men and their ethos encountered social problems in their attempt to reconfigure or reconstitute sixteenth and seventeenth century European catholic feudal governments, mode of production, ideology, and ideological apparatuses, along the lines of their social class language game, Protestantism and social relations of production, they became a discriminated against "other" (Puritans, Pilgrims, Calvinists, Lutherans, etc.) minority in the Feudal (catholic) social structure of Europe of the middle ages. Subsequently, these newly created and marginalized "others" left Europe and reformulated society, in the form of the American social structure by recursively reorganizing and reproducing their "other" Protestant form of being-in-the-world, i.e. Protestantism and the spirit of capitalism, via the organization of the state and its ideological apparatuses, family, church, and schools, class division, and social relations of production, i.e., mercantile, agricultural, industrial, and subsequently postindustrial beginning in the 1970s.

The rules of conduct and ideological apparatuses of the new American society, in other words, were formulated to facilitate the relational logic, ends (substantive rationality), of their, rich, white, heterosexual Protestant men, form of Protestantism, individualism, humanitarianism, rationalism, economic gain, or loss, as a sign of one's election or "damned-ness" in a particular "calling," mercantile, agricultural, industrial, and postindustrial capital, which "embedded" social or cultural relations in what became the modern American political-economic (liberal/neoliberal) system. With this sociohistorical conversion, within the Westphalian nation-state system, of Western society in general and American society in particular, from a catholic feudal social order to a Protestant capitalist social order through the purposive-rationality or social class language game of rich, white, heterosexual Protestant men against all other forms of being-in-the-world, the Protestant ethic became an allowed religion of the society, and thus the "metaphysical" ideas of the Protestant Church became joined with the power and discursive practices of the American Protestant nation-state government as organized around ideological apparatuses, i.e., prisons, the family, church, school, state, class division, and work or the social relations of production to facilitate economic gain, status, and upward mobility through the acquisition of money, private property, and luxury commodities. This "invisible" marriage of church and state led to the formation of the "visible" universal ideals/ideologies (liberalism, democracy, individualism, bourgeois classism, and nationalism) of the American nation-state under god to direct the material economic practices of all social actors, and over time caused the American nation-state/government to refine its doctrine and develop its structure in a way that best served its purposive-rational end, economic gain as a sign of the country and its citizens' salvation and predestination in mercantile, agricultural, industrial, and postindustrial social relations of production, within the emerging global (colonial) economic world-system, which they would gain control of following World War II through transnational ideological apparatuses such as the World Bank (WB), International Monetary Fund (IMF), United Nations (UN), etc.

In materialist terms, the endless accumulation of economic gain, capital, or profit by rich white heterosexual Protestant men became "the defining characteristic and *raison d' être* of this [social] system," which over time pushed "towards the commodification of everything, the absolute increase of world production, and a complex and sophisticated social division of labor based on class" or the amount of capital (economic gain) one had accumulated (Balibar and Wallerstein, 1991, pg. 107). As Jürgen Habermas concludes of this process by which the integrative substantive-rationality of a form of Protestantism, "the spirit of capitalism," came to dominate modern times by the systemic purposive-rational action of its power agents:

> ...economic production is organized in a capitalist manner, with rationally calculating entrepreneurs [(the predestined prosper)]; public administration is organized in a bureaucratic manner, with juristically trained, specialized officials—that is, they are organized in the form of private enterprises and public bureaucracies. The relevant means for carrying out their tasks are concentrated in the hands of owners and leaders; membership in these organizations is made independent of ascriptive properties [(today, maybe, but not the case for this type of society's early formation)]. By these means, organizations gain a high degree of internal flexibility and external autonomy. In virtue of their efficiency, the organizational forms of the capitalist economy and the modern state administration establish themselves in other action systems to such an extent that modern societies fit the picture of "a society of organizations," even from the standpoint of lay members (Habermas, 1987 [1981], pg. 306).

In this understanding of the origins and organizational basis of modernity and its paragon modern American capitalist society, where "the cultural struggle for distinction is intricately connected to the economic distribution of material goods, which it both legitimates and reproduces" (Gartman, 2002, pg. 257), Weber's explanation, as Jürgen Habermas points out,

> ...refers in the first instance not to the establishment of the labor markets that turned abstract labor power into an expense in business calculations, but to the "spirit of capitalism," that is, to the mentality characteristic of the purposive-rational economic action of the early capitalist entrepreneurs. Whereas Marx took the mode of production to be the phenomenon in need of explanation, and investigated capital accumulation as the new mechanism of system integration, Weber's view of the problem turns the investigation in another direction. For him the explanans is the conversion of the economy and state administration over to purposive-rational action orientations; the changes fall in the domain of forms of social integration. At the same time, this new form of social integration made it possible to institutionalize the money mechanism, and thereby new mechanisms of system integration (Habermas, 1987 [1981], pg. 313).

These two analytic levels, systems and social integration, are not separate if the understanding of the constitution of modernity is understood through my phenomenological structural and organizational logic. The argument from this Althusserian structural position is that the "predestined" white Protestant entrepreneurial males, a once marginalized group in pre-modern or feudal (catholic) Europe, by re-conceptualizing and maintaining, "present-at-hand," the control of the then feudal market and state within the mythical realities or social class language game of their heterosexual bourgeois male Protestantism, reified their Protestant "practical consciousness" with the state and its ideological apparatuses, prisons, family, church, schools, etc. This Protestant metaphysical cultural value or ideology (enchantment of the world), in other words, they rationalized with reality and existence as such, in institutions or ideological apparatuses, prisons, the family, church, schools, capitalist global market economy and bourgeois state, operating "through materialized metaphors beyond logical or empirical proof, on ungroundable premises, on nonobservable substances" (Friedland, 2002, pg. 384), in order to mechanically and systemically interpellate, constitute, and direct (embourgeois) the identity and agential moments or purposive-rationality of all social actors of the world for the sole purpose of accumulating economic gain (Marx's "capital accumulation") as a sign of their election or progress in the world against those who either were damned as revealed by their poverty in the social relations of production of the society, or conceived of other practical consciousnesses arrived at through the deferment of meaning in ego-centered communicative action and other processes.

Class division and the organization of work, mercantile, agricultural, industrial, and postindustrial, for economic gain or profit in modern society was mechanically constituted as white Protestant heterosexual males believing themselves to be "predestined" came as a social class to militarily dominate and control the ontological security of the world and its people of color, who, within their social class language game, they interpellated, subjugated, and embourgeoised as the irrational damned or laborers working in the aforementioned social relations of production, through subsequently global institutions or ideological apparatuses like the Protestant churches, schools, the IMF, World Bank, United Nations, etc., in order to (re) produce economic gain for those (predestined) who owned the means and modes of work or production. To put the matter simply, the logic here is that "the spirit of capitalism," which is characteristic of modernity in general and American society in particular, is the socioreligious discursive practice or purposive rationality (mythopraxis) of a form of cultural Protestantism that gave rise to the class identity of social actors, who became differentiated by class, race, and sexual divisions and their social behavioral (methodical) relation to the means and mode of work in modern societies.

The metaphysics of the Protestant Ethic as initially interpreted by rich, white, Protestant men, in other words, structured, through their bodies, languages, ideologies (Protestantism, liberalism, racism, etc.) and ideological apparatuses, the physical material world wherein individual social relations and actions were constituted and (re) produced through the organization of work, the modern state, class division, and the praxis of capitalist relations of production.

Thus, the Enlightenment project or attempt to constitute society based on democratically arrived at rational rules of conduct which are sanctioned which began in the seventeenth century with philosophers and artists never materialized as rich, white, heterosexual, bourgeois Protestant males, the emerging power elites of the seventeenth century, incorporated the products of scientific reason and rationality itself into their Protestant metaphysics or social class language game so as to facilitate their purposive socioreligious rationale of economic gain via capitalist relations of production. So it is not that modernity and the organization of the contemporary social world under the hegemony of the American nation-state represents the ever-increasing, present-at-hand, rationalization of the world, which dates from the Enlightenment. Instead, it represents the ever-increasing mystification (enchantment) of the world around the discursive practices, "mythopraxis" (Marshall Sahlins' term), or social class language game of the Protestant Ethic and the spirit of capitalism. The reason and rationality of the scientific method, which comes out of the Enlightenment project, was not constituted as a distinct social class language game to direct society under the leadership of scientists and philosophers; instead, the rational-empiricism that would come to dominate the seventeenth century became a facilitator for promoting the ethos of an emerging Protestantism and the spirit of capitalism reified in the discourse and discursive practices of the nation-state and its ideological apparatuses, i.e., education, church, family, etc., and organization of work or social relations of production under the leadership and social class language games of rich, white, Protestant, heterosexual men.

Hence, the Americentric dominated form of modernity, neoliberalism with its emphasis on family life, individualism, education, class division, entrepreneurialism, free markets, free trade, political and economic liberalism, outsourcing of jobs, privatization, austerity, non-profit organizations, non-governmental organizations, etc., which contemporarily dominates the world in and through the discourse of globalization represents the continual attempt to homogenize and universalize social identities and social practices the world over to fit within the metaphysical discourse and discursive practices of agents of the Protestant Ethic who purposively rationalized the discourse of their metaphysic into the laws and practices of their society and global institutions against the metaphysics of adherents of the Enlightenment, the poor, and other metaphysics. Hence, the mythical realities of rich, white, Protestant, heterosexual bourgeois males canonized in laws and social institutions determined their praxis, and relationally attempted to determine the praxis of all "others" they encountered in their quest to prove their predestination. It should also be mentioned that modern societies in the global economic world-system, as all became interpellated as owners and workers, itself became a dialectical totality that underwent reproduction and transformation based on internal contradictions and class differentiation based upon capital accumulation motivated by the desire to acquire capital or economic gain for its own sake as prescribed by the substantive-rationality or social class language game of the Protestant Ethic and the spirit of capitalism (Balibar and Wallerstein, 1991; Smith, 1996). In fact, the modern political and economic ideologies of liberalism, conservatism, and radicalism are grounded in, and can be deduced from, the metaphysics of "the Protestant Ethic and the spirit of capitalism": radicalism representing a revolutionary response against the ideals and practices of liberal bourgeois heterosexual white male Protestantism that included bourgeois technical rationality, individualism, class inequality, racialism, and heterosexism; conservatism, representing strict commitment to its ideologies of individualism, class inequality, heterosexism, religiosity, and racialism; and liberalism was deduced from the Christian (Protestant) ethic of individual humanism, rationalism, anti-dogmatism, classism, and the liberal democratic capitalist state's ability to foster that ethic. In contemporary postindustrial times in America, (neo) liberalism is ingrained in the ideologies of both the Republican and Democratic parties: the former, espouses the ideas of personal responsibility, individualism, private property, etc., which the latter embraces via the narcissism of the self, sexual liberation, and identity politics in a postindustrial economic framework intent on the cultural as the site for capital accumulation.

Globalization and Neoliberalism

From the sixteenth century to the present, the Protestant Ethic and the spirit of capitalism social class language game under the leadership of rich, white, Protestant, heterosexual men became the dialectical structural framework (enchantment of the world) within which all peoples of the world were interpellated, subjectified, embourgeoised, and differentiated via European languages, white male/female bodies, ideology, ideological apparatuses of the nation-state, and modes of production. The contemporary phenomenon of globalization under American hegemony is the continuing attempt, under the leadership of an embourgeoised hybrid, multiracial, multisexual, multinational, etc., upper-class of owners and high-level executives, who, unready-to-hand (because of the discriminatory effects of their societies, which prevented them from participating in it), in the 1960s dialectically sought equality of opportunity, recognition, and distribution with their white counterparts, to structure the world within the structural metaphysics or social class language game of the Protestant Ethic and the spirit of capitalism against other practices and organizations of realities arrived at through the drives of the body, impulses of subatomic particles, and the deferment of meaning in ego-centered communicative discourse. Albeit the Protestant Ethic and the spirit of capitalism social class language game under American hegemony, unlike when Weber was writing when the emphasis in the agricultural and industrial modes of producing that wealth was simply capital accumulation, is today defined by economic gain for its own sake and material (personal) wealth as a sign of God's grace and blessings in America's postindustrial economy with its neoliberal overemphasis on deregulation, privatization, etc.[2]

Contemporarily, "culture of globalization" and the "globalization as culture" metaphors represent two sociological approaches to understanding the contemporary post-modern phenomenon we call globalization, the current configuration of the Protestant Ethic and the spirit of capitalism, under American hegemony (1970s-2000s). These two sociopolitical understandings regarding the origins and nature of globalization, as Kevin Archer et al (2007) points out, have "set off a vigorous and at times rancorous debate within the social sciences" (2007, pg. 2). On one side of the debate you have theorists who emphasize the "culture of globalization" and argue the idea that "the constitutive role of culture is critical for grasping the continued hegemony of capitalism in the form of globalization...Culture, they assert is increasingly being co-opted and deployed as a new accumulation strategy to broaden and deepen the frontiers of capitalism and to displace its inherent crisis tendencies" (Archer, 2007, pg. 2-3). In a word, in the continual hegemonic quest of capitalism to equalize the conditions of the world to serve capital, globalization, in the eyes of "culture of globalization" theorists, represents a stage of capitalism's development highlighted by the commodification of culture as a means for accumulating profits from the purchasing and consuming power of a transnational class of administrative bourgeoisies and professional cosmopolitan elites in core, semi-periphery, and periphery nation-states who subscribe to the social integrative norms of liberal bourgeois Protestantism (hard work, economic gain, political and economic liberalism, consumption, etc.).

In other words, the material and symbolic cultural elements of the cultures of the world are commodified by the upper class of owners and high-level executives of core countries—where finance capital and service jobs predominate—to make a profit or produce surplus-value—given the declining significance of profit from industrial production that have been shipped or outsourced to semi-periphery and periphery nations giving rise to their national bourgeoisies whose cultural practices and tastes have been nationalized—by fulfilling the consumption tastes of the financiers, administrative bourgeoisies, professional classes, and cosmopolitan elites of nation-states throughout the world who control their masses as a surplus labor force and cultural producers for global capital. Globalization, therefore, is the integration of the cultural realm and individual experiences into the commodity chains of the capitalist elites, who homogenize, through the media and other "ideological state apparatuses," the behavior and tastes of global social actors as consumers thereby homogenizing the cultural practices and tastes of the middle and under class peoples of the world in order to generate profit in postindustrial economies such as the US and UK.

This "culture-of-globalization" understanding of globalization or the postmodern condition in late capitalist development is a well-supported position, which highlights, in the twenty-first century, the continued hegemony of capitalism or capitalist relations of production in the form of globalization (Hardt and Negri, 2000; Kellner, 1988; Giddens, 1991; Harvey, 1989, 1990; Jameson, 1984, 1991). This line of thinking, in which theorists point to the underlining drive of globalization as the continuing historical push to socially, economically, and politically (under) develop the rest of the world along the lines, or as a simulacrum, of Western American and European Societies to facilitate capital accumulation, began with European colonialism, continued through the "development project" of the Cold-war era, and now is embodied in the globalization process. This historical process is highlighted in modernization, development, dependent development, world-systems theories, and contemporarily it is a trend outlined in the theoretical works of postmodern theorists such as David Harvey (1989, 1990) and Fredric Jameson (1984, 1991) who view globalization as postmodern or the cultural logic of capitalist development in core or developed countries. "Culture of globalization" theorists, such as Harvey and Jameson, therefore, view globalization as the new initiative, with the same intentions, replacing the accumulation and modernization project of colonialism and development.

The homogenization, accumulation, and "modernization" project in European colonialism operated through the establishment of either colonies of settlement, "which often eliminate[d] indigenous people," or rule, where colonial administrators reorganize[d] existing cultures by imposing new inequalities [(around class, gender, race, and caste)] to facilitate their exploitation, wherein an unequal division of agricultural (monoculture) labor was physically and psychologically forced upon the peoples of color the world over to sustain the industrial and manufacturing cultural life of Europeans, while simultaneously disrupting, destroying, and reconfiguring the cultural practices and tastes of the colonized peoples within the binary (structural) logic of the (European) colonizer (McMichael, 2008 pg. 27). As Philip McMichael (2008, pg. 31) observed of the European colonization process,

> From the sixteenth century, European colonists and traders traveled along African coasts to the New World and across the Indian Ocean and the China seas seeking fur, precious metals, slave labor, spices, tobacco, cacao, potatoes, sugar, and cotton. The principal European colonial powers—

Spain, Portugal, Holland, France, and Britain—and their merchant companies exchanged manufactured goods such as cloth, guns, and implements for these products and for Africans taken into slavery and transported to the Americas. In the process, they reorganized the world.

The basic pattern was to establish in the colonies specialized extraction and production of raw materials and primary products that were unavailable in Europe. In turn, these products fueled European manufacturing as industrial inputs and foodstuffs for its industrial labor force. On a world scale, this specialization between European economies and their colonies came to be termed the colonial division of labor.

While the colonial division of labor stimulated European industrialization, it forced non-Europeans into primary commodity production. Specialization at each end of the exchange set in motion a transformation of social and environmental relationships, fueled by a dynamic relocation of resources and energy from colony to metropolis: an unequal ecological exchange. Not only were the colonies converted into exporters of raw materials and foodstuffs, but also they became "exporters of sustainability."

The sociocultural outcome of this exploitative and oppressive socioeconomic military system was a racialized social structural relationship relationally constituted based on the "unequal" colonial division of labor and "unequal" ecological exchanges, which divided the social actors of the world between white, Christian, civilized, and "developed" European colonizers (masters) whose "burden" was to civilize and (under) develop the "undeveloped," "backward," non-European, colonized, colored, other, "heathens" (slaves) of the world. This European civilizing of the non-European colored "heathens" of the world initially took place through the Christian churches of the West, whose biblical tenets and metaphysics were used to justify the master/slave relationship of colonialism as well as teach its work ethic, which eventually homogenized the social actions of social actors to benefit the white male power elites of an emerging gendered, racialized, and religious global capitalist world-system that developed the white colonizer, while simultaneously underdeveloping the colored colonized who were systematically forced to become agents of the Protestant ethic in agricultural production. A hybrid administrative bourgeoisie, and the poor seeking to be like them, emerged among the colonizers.

The end of the socioeconomic military colonial system in the form of decolonization in the twentieth century did not end the colonizer/colonized relational relationship, but gave rise to a new nation-state system of civilizing, domination, and exploitation within the hegemony of this emerging gendered, racialized, and religious global capitalism. Decolonization gave birth to what Philip McMichael calls, "the development project."

According to McMichael, "[t]he mid-twentieth century development project (1940s-1970s), an internationally orchestrated program of national economic growth, with foreign financial, technological, and military assistance under the conditions of the Cold War, managed the aftermath of collapsing European and Japanese empires within the idealistic terms of the United nations and its focus on [national-state] governments implementing a human rights-based social contract with their citizens…to equalize conditions across the world in laying the foundations of a global market that progressively overshadowed the states charged with development in the initial post-World War II era" (McMichael, 2008, pg. 21). Hence, the development project from the postcolonial era to the 1970s emphasized and continued the "unequal" colonial division of labor and "unequal" ecological exchanges within an Americentric dominated capitalist world-system subdivided into three geopolitical segments to benefit capitalist accumulation: the First World, the developed (postindustrial) capitalist Western countries plus Japan with America the model for development; the (industrial) Second World comprised of Communist Soviet blocs; and the (agricultural) Third World comprised of postcolonial bloc of nations.

Whereas under colonialism, as McMichael notes, "[t]he basic pattern was to establish in the colonies specialized extraction and production of raw materials and primary products that were unavailable in Europe. In turn, these products fueled European manufacturing as industrial inputs and foodstuffs for its industrial labor force" (31), in the development phase of postcolonial capitalism, the process was reversed as the First World sought to take advantage of the desire of the postcolonial elites, the administrative bourgeoisie, of the Third World to develop their nation-states along the lines of the industrial First World. The basic global pattern was to establish in the emerging postcolonial "Third-World" nation-states specialized manufacturing and industrial production sites that were outsourced from the First World. In turn, the outsourcing of these manufacturing and industrial jobs by the First World to take advantage of the urban underemployment and low-wage economy caused by the de-agriculturalization of Third World countries fueled First World, especially American, agribusinesses that channeled food surpluses, under a "food-aid-regime," to Third World countries. "In agriculture, the Third World's share of world agricultural exports fell from 53 to 31 percent between 1950 and 1980, while the American granary consolidated its critical role in world agricultural trade. By the 1980s, the United States was producing 17 percent of the world's wheat, 63 percent of its corn, and 63 percent of its soybean; its share of world exports was 36 percent in wheat, 70 percent in corn, and 59 percent in soybeans" (McMichael, 2008, pgs. 67-68). What developed from this global economic relationship was that Third World industrialization outlined by W.W. Rostow's stages of development fueled First world economic growth agriculturally and technologically, while underdeveloping some Third World countries, and dependently developing others within the capitalist global world-system, hence recolonizing the Third World as they became indebted given their need to import food to feed their populous.

The postcolonial nations had no say in this new "unequal" development paradigm as "decisions about postcolonial political arrangements were made in London and Paris where the colonial powers, looking to sustain spheres of influence, insisted on the nation-state as the only appropriate political outcome of decolonization" (McMichael, 2008, pg. 47). Be that as it may, "[t]his new paradigm inscribed First World power and privilege in the new institutional structure of the postwar international economy. In the context of the Cold War between First and Second Worlds (for the hearts and resources of the ex-colonial world), "development" was simultaneously the restoration of a capitalist world market to sustain First World wealth, through access to strategic natural resources, and the opportunity for Third World countries to emulate First World civilization and living standards" (McMichael, 2008, pg. 45). The "development project," in this way, as McMichael further observed, continued the hegemony of capitalism, which started with colonialism, through the universalization of a global market system driven by the nation-state and economic growth through agricultural and industrial productions (2008, pg. 46). Globalization (1970s-2000s) is a continuation of this hegemonic capitalist process in a post-communist world under the guidelines of neoliberalism.

Globalization under American capitalist hegemony seeks to dismantle the state-centered exploitation of colonial and development capitalism via the invisible hand of economic (neo) liberalism, deregulation, privatization, education, class division, and social relations of global production. "The globalization project (1970s-2000s)," as McMichael observes, "liberalizing trade and investment rules, and privatizing public goods and services, has privileged corporate rights over the social contract and redefined development as a private undertaking" (2008, pg. 21). That is to say, in reestablishing a global capitalist economy through the development project that followed colonialism, the First World was able to indebt Third World countries through an export-oriented industrialization that fueled the wealth of First World agribusinesses, transnational corporations, and their citizens who became consumers of inexpensive manufactured goods from the Third World. Hence, "[e]xport-oriented industrialization fueled rapid economic growth, legitimizing a new 'free market' model of development, and in the 1980s this was represented as the solution to the debt crisis [of Third World countries]. Development, which had been defined as nationally managed economic growth, was redefined in the World Bank's *World Development Report 1980* as 'participation in the world market'" (McMichael, 2008, pg. 117). This global market is controlled and directed by multinational and transnational corporations operating in First World postindustrial cities where high finance banking jobs and low-end service jobs predominate over manufacturing and industrial jobs that have been outsourced to semi-periphery or developing nations. What has developed in turn is a continuation of the tripartite system of the development phase. In the globalization phase, however, what has developed is a tripartite system in which the global economic system parallels Immanuel Wallerstein's world-systems conception: a periphery group of poor nations whose comparative advantage are raw materials, agricultural production, and tourism; a semi-periphery group of industrial based nations, i.e., India, Mexico, Brazil, South Africa, Russia, and China; and a postindustrial group of core or developed nations led by the United States of America who generate profit by servicing the cultural consumptive needs of a multicultural and multiethnic transnational capitalist class who control and monitor their (US and other core countries) investments in periphery and semi-periphery nations.

In other words, the contemporary (1970 to the present) post-industrial mode of production in developed (core) states like the US is no longer characterized or driven by the industrial means for accumulating capital, which dominated the social relations of production of the last one hundred years in core or developed nations. Instead, the present globalization condition is driven-by, post-industrialism (consumerism)—the new means for accumulating capital—, and in such "developed" societies like the U.S., is characterized not by the industrial organization of labor, which have been outsourced overseas, but rather by capitalist finance and service occupations catering to the consumerist demands of a dwindling (transnational, transcultural, transracial, etc.) middle class the world over. In short, the rate of economic gain for its own sake or profit has fallen in industrial production due to labor laws (products of the welfare state) and ecological cost in developed countries like the US; hence the practice now among investors operating out of the US and other developed nations is on financial expansion "in which 'over-accumulated' capital switches from investments in production and trade, to investments in finance, property titles, and other claims on future income" (Trichur, 2005, pg. 165).

On a global scale, the bifurcation defining this current conjuncture is characterized on the one hand by an expansion of industrial production into some (others remain agricultural producers) developing or periphery countries, i.e., the semi-periphery, where the rate of labor exploitation has risen given their lack of environmental and labor laws, devalued labor, and the dismantling of the welfare state; and on the other hand, consumerism of cheaply produced goods and high-end service occupations has come to dominate developed and developing societies as capital in the developed world seeks to allow and incorporate, through the commodification of their cultural identities, the transnational class of elite "others" who administer the assets of capital into their consumption patterns. Archer et al (2007) sum up the nature of this position brilliantly,

> since the mid-1990s, the application of GATS ([General Agreement on Trade in Services)] has slowly but surely led to a redefinition of culture primarily if not exclusively within the parameters of neo-liberal capitalism. The presumption is that flourishing cultures go hand-in-glove with flourishing capitalism….[t]his strategic articulation and subordination of culture to the requirements of capitalism is what has been called 'cultural capitalism'….This line of thinking is best exemplified by David Harvey…and to a lesser extent by Fredric Jameson…himself. These theorists have launched an unrelenting critique of cultural capitalism as a 'carnival for the elite' which enables politicians and policymakers to conceal growing socio-spatial inequalities, polarizations, and distributional conflicts between the haves and the have-nots. This critique is further underscored by their dismissal of culture as nothing more than a tool for economic regeneration through the 'mobilization of the spectacle'…, because the tourist and entertainment city requires the urban spectacle to reinforce place-marketing and residential development….In short, for this group, culture is just another commodity available for consumption in the world's supermarkets (3).

"Globalization-as-culture" theorists out rightly reject this socioeconomic position or interpretation underlying the processes of globalization. They believe "that globalization is marked by the hollowing out of national cultural spaces either consequent upon the retrenchment of the nation state or because culture continues to be a relatively autonomous sphere" (Archer et al, 2007, pg. 2). That is, "[f]or the "globalization-as-culture" group…culture is not that easily enjoined due to its inherent counter-hegemonic properties vis-à-vis neo-liberal globalization. Rather, for this group…, contemporary globalization is not merely economic, but a system of multiple cultural articulations which are shaped by disjunctive space-time coordinates. In other words, globalization is as much if not more the product of inexorable and accelerated migratory cultural flows and electronic mass mediations beyond the space-time envelopes of the nation-state system and the successive socio-spatial fixes of global capitalism"

(Archer et al, 2007, pg. 4). In fact, culture, in many instances, serves as a counter-hegemonic movement to (neo) liberal capitalism as a governing "rational" system. This line of thinking is best exemplified in the works of Stuart Hall (1992), John Tomlinson (1999), Homi Bhabha (1994), and Edward Said (1993) among many (postcolonial) others. For these theorists cultural exchanges are never one-dimensional, and hybridization of culture in many instances serves as a counter-hegemonic force to the homogenization processes of global capital.

Theoretically, this debate between the advocates of the "globalization-as-culture" and the "culture-of-globalization" hypotheses is a fruitless debate grounded in a false ontological and epistemological understanding regarding the origins and nature of the (neo) liberal capitalist system that gives rise to the processes of globalization. Both groups ontologically and epistemologically assume that the origins of capitalism and its discursive practice is grounded in reason and rationality, thus drawing on the liberal distinction between capitalism as a public and neutral system of rationality that stands apart from the understanding of it as a private sphere or lifeworld cultural form grounded in the social ontology of the Protestant ethic as argued by Max Weber. The latter position, if assumed by both schools, is a point of convergence that resolves their opposition, and gives a better understanding of the origins and nature of the processes of globalization and counter movements to what are in fact metaphysical cultural forces/social class language games.

Both schools of thought are putting forth the same convergence argument, the culture of globalization position from a Marxian systems integration perspective and the globalization as culture position from a Weberian social integration perspective. For the culture of globalization position cultural practices are homogenized to be integrated within the rational rules or systemicity/social class language game of capitalist relations of production and consumption at the world-system level so as to generate surplus-value from the consumption of cultural products as commodities in core postindustrial nations, industrial production in semi-periphery nations, and agricultural production in periphery nations.

The globalization as cultural group suggests that in the process of acculturating social actors to the organization of work within the capitalist world-system, homogenization does not take place. Instead, in the process of integration within the world-system, cultural groups, present-at-hand, intersubjectively defer meaning in ego-centered communicative discourse to hybridize the lexicons of significations coming out the globalization process thereby maintaining their cultural forms not in a commodified form but as a class-for-itself seeking to partake in the global community as hybrid social actors governed by the liberal rational logic of the marketplace.

The two positions are not mutually exclusive, however. Within my phenomenological structural logic, globalization contemporarily represents the homogenization of social discourse and action via hybridization. That is globalization represents the discursive practice, "spirit of capitalism," social class language game of agents of the Protestant Ethic seeking to allow for and homogenize "other" human behaviors, cultures, around the globe within the logic of their metaphysical discourse, "The Protestant Ethic and the spirit of capitalism social class language game," so as to accumulate profit, via agricultural, industrial, and post-industrial/consumerist production, for the predestined from the damned on a global scale. That is, via neoliberal globalization social actors around the globe are interpellated and socialized or embourgeoised via ideological apparatuses, churches, education, prisons, class division, and social relations of production, to become agents of the Protestant ethic so as to fulfill their labor and consumption roles in the organization of work, agricultural, industrial, or postindustrial production, required by their states in the global capitalist world-system under American hegemony since World War II. Proper socialization in the contemporary capitalist American dominated world-system is tantamount to hybridization, i.e., a liberal bourgeois Protestant *other* working for those who own, via the privatization of everything, the means and forces of production so as they themselves can become bourgeois as profit trickles down from capital operating in the first world or developed countries to the rest of the world, in order to consume the cultural and individual products found in postindustrial world-cities throughout the globe. Hence, hybridization of other cultures, via the homogenization process of globalization, is a simulacrum of white agents of the Protestant ethic, which enables the latter (whites) to make social actors of other cultures known for two reasons, to socialize them to the work ethic of the globalizing process and to accumulate surplus-value as the former service the others of their community for what has become since the 1960s a multicultural, multisexual, multiracial, etc., global capitalist world-system dominated by whites and hybrid others, who unready-to-hand (because the discriminatory effects of the society prevented them from doing so under slavery, colonial, etc.) sought during colonization to partake in the Protestant capitalist social structure for equality of opportunity, recognition, and distribution with their white counterparts. The créolité, hybridity, ambivalence, etc., language of postmodern, post-structural, and postcolonial discourses represents the concepts, pathologies, etc., of the once-discriminated against "other" as they seek equality of opportunity, recognition, and distribution with their former slavemasters and colonizers by recursively reorganizing and reproducing their ideas and ideals as an "other."

Be that as it may, like other blacks in Africa and the diaspora, Haiti, as the first black republic in the world and the only successful slave revolution in recorded history, would become constituted as a republic between the hybrid mulatto elites and educated petit-bourgeois blacks (collectively known here as the Affranchis), dialectically, seeking, unready-to-hand, to be agents of the Catholic/Protestant Ethic and the spirit of capitalism for equality of opportunity, recognition, and distribution with whites, and the Haitian masses who were and are not a structurally differentiated other, i.e., poor black underclass interpellated as laborers and consumers. On the contrary, they were and are, unlike other blacks in America and the diaspora, structuralized or interpellated and ounganified/manboified within the language, ideology, ideological apparatuses, and communicative discourse of *oungan yo, manbo yo, gangan yo*, and *granmoun yo* who recursively reorganized and reproduced a different form of system and social integration, the Vodou Ethic and the spirit of communism, on the island against the former, the Catholic/Protestant Ethic and the spirit of capitalism social class language of the whites and Affranchis. However, the adoption of economic policies, corvée system, export processing zones, neoliberal policies, wage-labor, privatization, by the Affranchis class to reproduce Haitian society as a simulacrum of the Protestant capitalist West has produced a structurally differentiated Haitian "my nigga" identity in Haiti and the US diaspora, which parallels the practical consciousness of the black American underclass in the US.

Notes

[1] Here, once again, I am using the African/Taino/Haitian Kreyol language for priests, priestesses, healers, and elders.

[2] The prosperity gospels of the Protestant churches in contemporary America go hand in hand with the conspicuous consumptive logic of its postindustrial mode of production. Whereas frugality and accumulative wealth once dominated the Protestant Ethic, today the emphasis is on hard work and material wealth as a sign of God's grace and blessings, which feeds the consumptive logic of postindustrial finance capital.

CHAPTER IV

THE CONSTITUTION OF BLACK AMERICA WITHIN THE PROTESTANT ETHIC AND THE SPIRIT OF CAPITALISM

Haiti would become constituted as a republic between the hybrid mulatto elites and educated petit-bourgeois blacks (collectively known here as the Affranchis), dialectically, seeking, unready-to-hand, to be agents of the Catholic/Protestant Ethic and the spirit of capitalism for equality of opportunity, recognition, and distribution with whites, and the Haitian masses who were and are not a structurally differentiated other, i.e., poor black underclass interpellated as laborers and consumers. On the contrary, they were and are, unlike other blacks in America and the diaspora, structuralized or interpellated and ounganified/manboified within the language, ideology, ideological apparatuses, and communicative discourse of *oungan yo, manbo yo, gangan yo*, and *granmoun yo* who recursively reorganized and reproduced a different form of system and social integration, the Vodou Ethic and the spirit of communism, on the island against the former, the Catholic/Protestant Ethic and the spirit of capitalism social class language of the whites and Affranchis. However, the adoption of economic policies, corvée system, export processing zones, neoliberal policies, wage-labor, privatization, by the Affranchis class to reproduce Haitian society as a simulacrum of the Protestant capitalist West has produced a structurally differentiated Haitian "my nigga" identity in Haiti and the US diaspora, which parallels the practical consciousness of the black American underclass in the US.

Africans (an estimated 430,000 imported to North America during the whole period of the Atlantic Slave trade)[1] were like Native Americans and many poor whites had "other" forms of orientation in the world distinct from the Protestant form of the American social structure and its agents. The Africans encountered or were brought (1619-1808), ready-to-hand, unready-to-hand, and present-at-hand, into this once marginalized, unready-to-hand, Protestant worldview as marginalized forced laborers and indentured servants in order to satisfy the idea and practice of "economic gain" in agricultural production expropriated from the "damned" for the benefit of the industrially developed "predestined" in urban centers that the new Protestant—global economic—order ("slave-based plantation" agricultural capitalism)[2] proffered. In this ideologically economic driven new symbolic colonial world where the peoples of color of the world were commodified, present-at-hand, as ignorant agricultural workers to sustain the white urbane industrial labor force of Europe and America, however, individual property rights were reconceptualized and elevated to a position sanctioned by divine authority and considered superior to all other rights, including the human rights and life of indigenous peoples, bonded laborers, and those who would eventually be bought as slaves (Smedley, 1999: 53; McMichael, 2008, pg., 21). Thus, the institutional regulators (rich, white, Protestant, male landowners), given the need to maintain and reproduce the then bifurcated agriculturally/industrially based economic stratified order of things among those "others" who did not subscribe to it in order to sustain and maintain the labor force of white industrial workers, rationalized the labor requirements within what was already understood, the purposive-rationality of the Protestant Ethic and the spirit of capitalism. By the time America became a nation-state in the late eighteenth-century this stratification or class differentiation had already been established through the commodification of the African. In the bifurcated colonial order of bureaucratic social structural relations of white Protestantism and agricultural capitalism, Africans became the structurally differentiated undeveloped perpetual "black," non-Protestant, damned agricultural worker (commodity) who worked (as their property) *freely* for the industrially developed predestined white Protestants in order to maximize the rate of profit or economic gain in the colonial global economic system of the seventeenth, eighteenth, and nineteenth centuries.[3]

As the black radical nationalist thinker Maulana Karenga (1993) observed, several material factors made the enslavement of Africans for the increase of the rate of profit or economic gain in agricultural production to sustain the industrial labor force of Europe and America more feasible and permanent than that of other marginalized "damned" groups such as Native Americans and poor white indentured-servants:

The first factor was Africa's closeness to the Caribbean where plantations were set up early and where Africans were "seasoned," i.e., made manageable, and then re-exported. Secondly, Africans already had experience in large-scale agriculture with their own fields and European plantations in Africa, unlike the Native Americans who mainly hunted and gathered their food. Thirdly, Africans had relative immunity to European diseases due to long-term contact, whereas the Native Americans did not and were decimated at first by this.

Fourthly, the practicality of African enslavement rested in their low escape possibilities as opposed to Native Americans and whites due to unfamiliarity with the land, high social visibility and lack of a nearby home base. Fifthly, there were no major political repercussions for the enslavement of Africans, unlike the Native Americans who had people here to retaliate and the whites whose enslavement would challenge the tenets of Christianity and the age of enlightenment and reason on which Europe prided itself.

Finally, the basis of the American system of enslavement was in its justifiability in European racist thought. Although the enslavement of Africans was based in economic reasons, it also rested in racism as an ideology.... Racism as an ideology became a justification and encouragement for African enslavement (Karenga, 1993, pgs., 121-122).

These factors, however, were not perceived or conceived from a transcendental Enlightenment vantage point as Karenga's scientized material perspective implied. But their conjunctures were reasoned within what was already understood by those rich, white, Protestant, men in power positions in the society.[4] Their rationalization through the prism of their Protestant ideology or substantive-rationality, social class language game, would come to relationally explain the social organization of the society and the structural framework by which African American practical consciousness was constituted.

The ever-increasing purposive-rationalization of the Protestant Ethic and spirit of capitalism by rich, white, Protestant men progressively elaborated and expanded on ideological themes of Christian brotherhood, human rights, and the elevation of the good of the many over the privileges of the few, which were recursively organized and reproduced through the "secular" practice or purposive-rationality of bourgeois racial, gender, and patriarchal capitalism that would come to constitute American society. The ideas of predestination through economic gain (as a sign of one's election or progress) justified the privileging of the good of the many (who were predestined to succeed—success being reflected in their economic gains or rate of profit) to have dominion over those who were not predestined and who were based on the structural (relational) logic of the former, undeveloped, ungodly, backward, and damned. Within the structural logic and differentiation of this worldview, those Protestants and non-Protestants, who were not predestined, like their predestined counterparts, were uncertain of their plight. They had to work hard in a particular calling for economic gain "as a sign." The enslaved, "damned"

Africans, given their physical and behavioral differences, were rationalized in relation to the symbolic signifiers of white Protestantism. Interpellated and embourgeoised in the white Protestant new world order, the Africans were not quite human to the white Protestants given the differences in African pigmentation, irrationalism, promiscuity, barbarity, carelessness, etc., created by their material conditions, and were therefore made to work for the whites. Class, and status position, and one's predestination were reflected in the rate of profit or economic gain obtained from the production of the "damned" and racial typology in class reinforced the belief in predestination.

Rich, Protestant, white, male factory and land owners (the power elites of the society), the "enlightened" and "progressive" predestined, institutionalized or rationalized, present-at-hand, their biblical, cultural, and entrepreneurial values and mysticism into laws and practices, slave codes, miscegenation laws, systematic labor, capitalism, the individualism of civil rights and liberties, patriarchal family, and republicanism. Their values and ideals were embedded in laws, treaties, pacts, agreements, the US and state constitutions and came to bureaucratically structure the political economy of the material resource framework within which the society became ensconced. At the same time structural or relational "blackness" and economic "class" developed as social categories (among others) for identity construction. More than anything else, this process of class and "racial"/national differentiation, counterposed as it was by equalization between predestined rich, white, Protestant, men, was responsible for the dialectical totality that gave rise to the black practical consciousnesses that would come to constitute and dominate modern American society embedded in the social class language game of heterosexual black male bourgeois liberalism.

Hence, the structural position assumed here is that the purposive-rationality of these Protestant laws and practices were utilized in the social institutions ("ideological apparatuses") of family, church, schools, organization of work (indentured servitude and slavery initially, consumerism and wage-labor, presently), etc., to condition or socialize (integrate) the masses—the constituting unit of the social structure—for the sole purpose of work or the reproduction of the American social relations of production, i.e. agricultural production in the South and industry in North. The, ready-to-hand, acceptance and embodiment of these laws and practices gave the masses and the power elites or institutional regulators their practical consciousness or purposive-rationality, while all other forms of social action, arrived at through the deferment of meaning in ego-centered communicative action, drives of the body, impulses of neuronal energies, and the structurally differentiated were marginalized and discriminated against as unequal and "other" by rich, white, Protestant, heterosexual men.

So in this case, the Africans, ninety percent of whom could not read, were introduced (in 1619), ready-to-hand, as a marginalized unit of the structure and "seasoned" in the Protestant doctrines through slave codes, the Protestant churches (initially by white ministers, later on by native-born slaves), slavery, individual civil rights and liberties, etc. Unlike literate non-Protestant and Protestant whites who could work hard and eventually—if predestined—become masters or what amounted to the same thing institutional regulators, the structurally differentiated group of Africans had to accept their prescribed lowly conditions (slaves) given the fact that their physical difference and perpetual "otherness," in relation to white bourgeois (patriarchal) Protestantism, did not allow for their predestination or equality.

The relationship of Africans with the white, heterosexual, Protestant, power elites, therefore, operated along a master/slave relationship where the rich, white, Protestant males (masters) worked and re-worked the ideas and practices of the Protestant Ethic on the one hand and on the other their terms and representations for the Africans' forms (soul-less, blacks, poor, savages and barbarous, less intelligent and human than their white counterparts, ungodly, promiscuous, undeveloped, etc.) of being in the world. The rich, white, Protestant, heterosexual males used the African representations to delimit their own form (godly, pious, urban, obedient, pure, civilized, diligent, intelligent, industrial, etc.) of being in the world and reproduced the colonial social relations of production through agricultural slavery and industrialism.

The Africans initially transported into this global "mechanical solidarity" or social class language game and its differentiating affects in the seventeenth and early part of the eighteenth centuries were different and heterogeneous "others" with distinct practical consciousnesses. As a "ready-to-hand" dominated deployable unit of the white Protestant economic social relations of American society they became a homogeneous group or social class language game, blacks (later differentially stratified along class lines and their adaptive responses to enslavement) prepared for one facet of life in the American social structure, "systematic [agricultural slave] labor" (Blassingame, 1972, pg. 3), conditioned by the obedient work ethic of Protestantism, which was juxtaposed against the industrial urban life and work of whites.

Africans came from all over Africa[5] and embodied different structurally determined subjective forms of being-in-the-world, which ranged from rigid patriarchy and traditional Islamic practices to matrilineal polygamous tribalism, by which they recursively organized and reproduced their practical consciousness. By the nineteenth-century (1808), which marks the discontinuation of the African slave trade to the United States, these "other" forms of being-in-the-world were discriminated against and marginalized within the American Protestant social structure. Native-born classified blacks, "the best of the house servants, mulattoes, artisans, and the educated free Negro from the [(industrial)] North," due to their intimacy with whites, freedom, and privileges, served as a reference group for the larger black community. They accepted, embodied, and recursively reorganized and reproduced the Protestant socioreligious cultural work ethos of the society in their material practices and purposive-rationality. Black identity or practical consciousness for them became, in keeping with the ethos of their white counterparts, synonymous with Standard English, Protestantism, development, education, freedom, equality, hard work, wage-labor, and monogamous patriarchal family against the material condition or pathologies, Black English Vernacular, poverty, single female-headed households, emotionalism, promiscuity, etc., of agricultural Southern (poor) black field slaves. However, given the discriminatory effects of the society against them, they became, as the European Protestant whites were under Catholic feudalism, "unready-to-hand" seeking equality of opportunity, recognition, and distribution either in a national position of their own or via integration and assimilation.

Given these "unready-to-hand" response amongst the more free and powerful majority of the descendants of African slaves, who constituted the black bourgeoisie but were barred from reorganizing and reproducing their African institutions within the material resource framework of the American Protestant bifurcated social and economic order, it is in terms of the structural variables (class and status, given the economic basis for the social relations of the society) of the Protestant American society, not other factors, that black consciousnesses in America became, can be, and has been assessed and determined. Other practical consciousnesses amongst blacks within American society were defined and relationally delimited, present-at-hand, as "other" by whites and these blacks, the "best" of the house servants, mulattoes, artisans, and the educated free Negro from the North, who, when they became institutional regulators within the American social structure, delimited or represented, present-at-hand, the "proper" and "pure" way of being-in-the-world for all blacks in terms of Protestant liberal heterosexual bourgeois practical consciousness, interests, ideals, habitus, etc., against the language game and material conditions of the black poor in the Deep South who operated ready-to-hand, unready-to-hand, and present-at-hand within the systemicity of the Protestant Ethic and the spirit of capitalism.

Thus, "after the end of the [(slave)] trade in America in the latter half of the eighteenth and early part of the nineteenth centuries [Africanisms] importance as an explanation of slave personality declines: only about 400,000 native-born Africans had been brought to the United States before 1807 [(the slave trade, as sanctioned by the US Constitution, legally ended in 1808)]. Since an overwhelming percentage of nineteenth-century Southern slaves were native Americans" (Blassingame, 1972, pg., 39), they, about 3,953,760 of the black population at the outbreak of the Civil War, had to construct their identity or consciousness as a deployable unit of the American social structure in relation to and led by the social class language game of "the best of the house servants, who were freed by their masters, [and] the educated free Negro from the North" who together numbered about 500, 000, twelve percent of the total black population, "at the outbreak of the Civil War," against the social class language game of the black poor in agricultural slavery, and sought equality of opportunity, recognition, and distribution with their white counterparts[6] (See Table 4.1).

So it was not "in the process of acculturation the slaves made European forms serve African functions" (Blassingame, 1972: 17) as many scholars contend (Allen, 2001; Asante, 1988, 1990; Billingsley, 1968, 1970, 1993; Blassingame, 1972; Early, 1993; Gilroy, 1993; Gutman, 1976; Herskovits, 1958 [1941]; Holloway, 1990a; Karenga, 1993; Levine, 1977; Lewis, 1993; Lincoln and Mamiya, 1990; Nobles, 1987; Staples, 1978; Stack, 1974; West and Gates, 1997; West, 1993). On the contrary, the majority of slaves had to relationally define and choose, for their ontological security within the American social structure, between the European forms prescribed, present-at-hand, by power (whites and the best of the house servants, mulattoes, artisans, and the educated free Negro from the North) or the continual practice of their ontologically insecure "other" (African) forms of being-in-the-world or any "other" fully visible, albeit discriminated against, "alternatives," which delimited the social structure.

This does not mean that nothing of Africa survived slavery because of the African's need to forsake African forms in order to move from being "other" in American Protestant liberal bourgeois society. The suggestion here is that different alternative categorical boundaries or social class language groups existed, ready-to-hand, unready-to-hand, and present-at-hand, in the African community, and it was the "practical consciousness" of "the best of the house servants, mulattoes, artisans, and the educated free Negro from the North" that, to a large extent rejected African forms in order to be recognized by their white masters, which became dominant. Rejection of African forms would come to represent and define black identity/practical consciousness as these blacks became institutional regulators and the bearers of ideological and linguistic domination within the "class racism" of the dominant Protestant American society where they, unready-to-hand and present-at-hand, sought equality of opportunity, recognition, and distribution with their white counterparts against the material conditions and practices of the black poor in the Deep South (Reed, 1997; Winant, 2001).

Table 4.1: *Growth of the Slave and Free Negro Population in the United States 1790-1860*

| CENSUS YEAR | NEGRO POPULATION | | | |
| | Total | Free | | Slave |
		Number	Per Cent	
1860	4,441,830	488,070	11	3,953,760
1850	3,638,808	134,495	11.9	3,204,313
1840	2,873,648	386,293	13.4	2,487,355
1830	2,328,642	319,599	13.7	2,009,043
1820	1,771,656	233,634	13.2	1,538,022
1810	1,377,808	186,446	13.5	1,191,362
1800	1,002,037	108,435	10.8	893,602
1790	757,181	59,557	7.9	697,624

Note. Adapted from *The American Negro: His History and Literature* (p. 5), by E. Franklin Frazier, 1968, New York: Arno Press and The New York Times. Copyright 1968 by Arno Press, Inc.

Thus, in terms of the structural logic and differentiation presented here the idea is that in the development of American society within an emerging global economic colonial world-system, white, Protestant males developed, present-at-hand, a series of laws and judicial rulings, "enframed" (Heidegger's term) by the cultural metaphysical ideology of their protestant ethic, to define and represent the African (black cursed son of Ham, ungodly, licentious, emotional, undeveloped, irrational, uncivilized and barbaric, soul-less, etc.) situation in relation to whites (white, godly, pious, obedient, pure, civilized, diligent, rational, industrial, developed, etc.) within the class division and social relations of production of a Protestant global capitalism. Whites' morally justified (given the internal contradiction between slavery and Christian brotherhood, human rights, etc.) reproduced the integrative economic (Protestant) social relations of agricultural production (slavery) proffered by them as the predestined or power elites of the society via ideology and ideological apparatuses to sustain their industrial developed base and bring about civilization to the black backward undeveloped "damned" African. As the historian Vincent D. Harding (1981) highlights,

> Beginning in Virginia at the end of the 1630s, laws establishing lifelong [(*durante vita*)] African slavery were instituted.[7] They were followed by laws prohibiting black-white intermarriage, laws against the ownership of property by Africans, laws denying blacks all basic political rights (limited as they were among whites at the time). In addition, there were laws against the education of Africans, laws against the assembling of Africans, laws against the ownership of weapons by Africans, laws perpetuating the slavery of their parents to African children, laws forbidding Africans to raise their hands against whites even in self-defense.
>
> Then, besides setting up legal barriers against the entry of black people as self-determining participants into the developing American society, the laws struck another cruel blow of a different kind: they outlawed many rituals connected with African religious practices [(which were deemed heathenistic, lewd, licentious, etc.)], including dancing and the use of the drums. In many places they also banned African languages. Thus they attempted to shut black people out from both cultures, to make them wholly dependent neuters.
>
> Finally, because the religious and legal systems were so closely intertwined, everywhere in the colonies a crucial legislative decision declared that the Africans' conversion to Christianity [(the Protestant type)] did not affect their enslavement.... Again, Virginia led the way: in 1667 its Assembly passed an act declaring that "the conferring of baptism doth not alter the condition of the person as to his bondage or freedome." Such laws freed many whites to do their Christian duty of evangelization and to reap the profit and the social standing of slave ownership at the same time (27).

Africans who began arriving on the North American mainland "over more than a century preceding the War of Independence" (Gutman, 1976, pg., 328) did not initially subscribe to this racial, class, gendered, patriarchal ideological foundation. They resisted enslavement and its institutionalization through ship mutinies prior to their arrival to the "New World;" guerilla wars; rebellions, the New York City Revolt in 1712, the Stono, South Carolina revolt in 1739, Gabriel Prosser revolt in 1800, Denmark Vesey conspiracy in 1822, the Nat Turner revolt in 1831, etc.—

over 250 revolts are recorded in the US; suicide and infanticide; flights; and sabotage, i.e., breaking tools and destroying crops, shamming illness or ignorance, taking property, spontaneous, and planned strikes, work slow-downs, self-mutilation, arson, attacks on whites and poisoning of slaveholders and their families (Karenga, 1993; Bennett, 1982; Harding, 1981; Blassingame, 1972; Gutman, 1976; Aptheker, 1964; Franklin and Moss, 2000). These efforts, however, proved to be counter productive to resisting subjugation, as they were incorporated, "present-at-hand," in the ideologies and ideological apparatuses of the white masters as evidence of the African's barbaric or savage disposition. The image of the African as unruly, rebellious, irrational, stupid, prone to thievery, destructive, sophomoric, licentious, were in turn used, relationally, to demonstrate to the slaves—during the "seasoning" process where the African learned Protestantism and its systematic work ethic—what was unacceptable behavior of a barbaric black slave without religion.

As the historian John Blassingame (1972) points out in *The Slave Community*, "white ministers taught the slaves that they did not deserve freedom, that it was God's will that they were enslaved, that the devil was creating those desires for liberty in their breasts, and that runaways would be expelled from the church. Then followed the slave beatitudes: blessed are the patient, blessed are the faithful, blessed are the cheerful, blessed are the submissive, blessed are the hardworking, and above all, blessed are the obedient" (Blassingame, 1972, pgs., 62-63).[8] During the "seasoning" process, where the newly arrived Africans were forcefully taught by slave masters, over-seers and native-born slaves the language, religion, and work ethic (purposive-rationality) of the Protestant American social structure. The majority of the early slaves, Stanley Elkins's (1959) Sambo, who worked intimately with their white masters, for their ontological security, incorporated, ready-to-hand, these beliefs and practices, which they recursively organized and reproduced in their own material practices, and they became the structural terms of "good moral character, Standard English, economic accumulation, temperance, industry, thrift, and learning," by which the larger slave community, which either maintained some element of their Africanisms in their material practices or developed a pathological-pathogenic form of the structural terms of the society given their relative isolation and poverty, was assessed, present-at-hand by the former, Sambos (Elkins, 1959; Frazier, 1939, 1957; Stampp, 1956; Genovese, 1974).

With their very survival dependent upon following rules of sanctioned conduct, many Africans accepted and acculturated or accommodated, ready-to-hand, to the institution of slavery and incorporated the Protestant ethos (its work ethic, family organization, "white standards of morality", godliness, obedience, rationalism, etc.), as defined, present-at-hand, by white and black agents of the Protestant Ethic and the spirit of capitalism, into their way of being-in-the-world or what amounted to the same thing the social structure (Elkins, 1959; Frazier, 1939, 1957; Stampp, 1956; Genovese, 1974). They and the dominant whites, as bearers of ideological and linguistic domination, used that Protestant socioreligious work ethos and the language game of their masters to assess and determine the proper rules of conduct for the larger slave community.[9] Those who did not accommodate were for the most part killed or brutally tortured until they complied. As a deployable unit, black slaves of the social structure, the social organization of family and cultural life in the majority of the African slave quarters became based on the ethical rules of the Protestant Ethic against fully visible African ways of being-in-the-world, as demonstrated in the practices of newly arrived Africans or those who, through the constitution of alternative meanings and behaviors through ego-centered communicative discourse, drives of the body, etc., either rejected the substantive and purposive-rationality of the American social structure or sought to exercise them in "a national position"[10] of their own. This latter group of blacks included maroon communities of runaway slaves who attempted to exercise their African agential moments in the new world order, and nationalist and conservative literate black leaders such as Booker T. Washington, David Walker, Gabriel Prosser, Denmark Vesey, Nat Turner, Martin Delany, Henry Highland Garnet, etc., who, although they embodied the Protestantism of the social structure, sought not integration, like the majority of their liberal bourgeois male counterparts, but separation and black nationalism (Meier, 1963, 1966; Stuckey, 1987).

Consequently, the agential moments of those blacks who failed to exercise the substantive and purposive-rationality of the society, or rejected it in order to exercise them in "a national position" of their own, were discriminated against and marginalized. Slave owners, white overseers, and native-born acculturated liberal blacks, "the best of the house servants, mulattoes, artisans, and the educated free Negro from the North," recursively organized and reproduced the purposive-rationality of the social structure, "the standard of good society," i.e., "Standard English, temperance, industry, thrift, and learning", in their own material practices, for the sole purpose of integration in order to obtain equality of opportunity, distribution, and recognition in the society with their white counterparts against the language and material conditions of the black poor and other groups, feminists, homosexuals, etc. (Meier and Rudwick, 1966 [1976], pg., 127).[11]

What developed from all this was a class-color-caste system, i.e. a "racial caste in class," superordinate industrial whites and subordinate agricultural blacks, perpetually subordinate, each dominated by the "predestined" class. Blacks in relation to whites, in other words, emerged in the social structure of the "spirit of colonial capitalism" as a caste (a racial class-in-itself as a result of "racial" structural differentiation) defined by their inherent fitness for slave agricultural labor to produce economic gain for their white masters, to a "caste in class" defined in relation to whites by those good obedient slaves (Stanley Elkins' Sambo, resulting from "class" structural differentiation), who embodied the language game and Protestant work ethic of the society for the sole purpose of integration or proving their predestination and those who did not because of their lack of "class" or need for separation.

This racial class social system became "reinforced" by the sociopolitical, religious, economic "legal system" (slavery and Jim Crow segregation) in which the majority of the Africans followed the rules of conduct which were sanctioned by the master for the slave and himself (Drake, 1965, pg. 3).[12] The majority of the slaves, given their "seasoning" in the American Protestant solidarity as a structurally differentiated racial class-in-itself, black slaves,[13] recursively reorganized and reproduced the rules and language of their masters, against the reproduced negative images (unruly, barbaric, savages, etc.) of themselves by these same masters. To demonstrate their "predestination", or a sense of self-worth, blacks acculturated European and Protestant practices within the social structure among themselves: speaking Standard English; jumping over the broomstick to legalize marriages, an old English tradition commonly used instead of church weddings, which were illegal for slaves; establishing traditional patriarchal nuclear families based on monogamy; establishing, as a result of segregation, Masonic lodges, churches, and mutual aid societies patterned after their white counterparts; demonstrating diligence in their work; instilling in their children a sense of Christian values;[14] black hymns; penning petitions for their liberation—the idea "that God granted temporal freedom, which man, without God's consent, had stolen away" (Blassingame,1972, pg. 63),—based on reason and revelation as their white masters did against England; and a developing class distinction (also based on color, lighter blacks v, darker ones) between house, "mixed-bloods," Negroes and field slaves, the former, given their close ties to the slave owner and quasi-freedom, better off then the latter (Franklin, 1957; Karenga, 1993; Bennett, 1982; Harding, 1981; Blassingame, 1972; Gutman, 1976; Aptheker, 1964; Franklin and Moss, 2000).[15]

This acculturation for survival in essence eventually turned African consciousness among a *few* blacks, "favored" slaves, house slaves, artisans, "mixed-bloods", free colored population, who together numbered about 500, 000 at the outbreak of the Civil War, into an American, black heterosexual liberal bourgeois Protestant type. A practical consciousness amongst many blacks defined (by black heterosexual men), unready-to-hand and present-at-hand, by their struggle for freedom, to exercise the purposive-rationality of the social structure and obtain class and status "based upon possession of money, education, and family background as reflected in distinctive styles of behavior" (Drake, 1965, pg. 3), against the claim of "their inherent fitness for slavery and backwardness" as highlighted amongst the language game of the black underclass, which delimited the social structure and barred them from achieving economic gain and recognition. This social psychological identity, represented most dynamically in the figure W.E.B. Du Bois and his double consciousness construct, stood in contradistinction to the social class language games of black heterosexual male conservatism, black nationalism, the ethos of black folk culture, and the material conditions and so-called pathologies, Black English Vernacular, emotionalism, promiscuity, poverty, single-headed households, etc., of the black underclass. In fact, heterosexual black male bourgeois Protestant liberalism would come to dominate as the dominant social psychological identity and player in the black quest for freedom, paradoxically, from the vagaries and contradictions of liberal bourgeois heterosexual white male Protestantism. Following the American Civil War and the black migrations from the rural agricultural South to the urban industrial North and Midwest, the nuclear family, the Protestant Ethic, Standard American English, education, and wealth, as defined, present-at-hand, by "favored" slaves, house slaves, artisans, "mixed-bloods", free colored population, who together numbered about 500, 000 at the outbreak of the Civil War constituted the practical consciousness of the black bourgeoisie and as a result the bearers of ideological and linguistic domination in black America against the purposive-rationality, female-headed households, promiscuity, Black/African American English Vernacular (BEV/AAEV), illiteracy, poverty, etc., of Southern agricultural blacks and the urban segregated black poor, whose bodies, language, practices, etc., were a result of racial-class divisions and social relations of agricultural and industrial production. The former sought, unready-to-hand and present-at-hand, equality of opportunity, recognition, and distribution for the latter. Double consciousness, hybridity, intersectionality, etc., represent their concepts, psychological pathologies, and practical consciousnesses amidst the continual discriminatory effects of the society.

Black America Today

Although, contemporarily, the postindustrial service occupations by which American capitalist society seeks economic gain, with its emphasis on consumerism and material wealth, conceal the Puritanical Protestantism that "enframes" or structure the society (albeit, contemporarily, material wealth as opposed to frugality is seen as a sign of God's grace, blessings, and salvation in the prosperity gospel that would emerge in neoliberal globalization). The purposive-rationality of the society's ideology and ideological apparatuses/institutions are still grounded in the mysticism of the Protestant ethic and spirit of capitalism through what Weber calls the ever-increasing, purposive, rationalization of the world. That is, the purposive-rational intent, through the contemporary process of (neoliberal) globalization, continues to be to integrate all peoples the world over into the class division and social relations of production of the Protestant mysticism, hard work, economic gain, etc., of the American nation which is presented in its educational apparatuses as the rational nature of the world as such, so as to obtain economic gain or capital accumulation and material wealth via agricultural, industrial, and postindustrial work as a sign of God's grace, blessings, and salvation.

Contemporarily, American blacks, as interpellated (workers) and embourgeoised agents of the American dominated global capitalist social structure of inequality, represent the most modern (i.e. embourgeoised and socialized) people of color, in terms of their "practical consciousness," in this process of homogenizing social actors as agents of the protestant ethic or disciplined workers working for owners of production in order to obtain economic gain, status, and upward mobility in the larger American society (Frazier, 1957; Wilson, 1978; Glazer and Moynihan, 1963). Whereas, they once occupied the social space as agricultural and industrial workers, the former less educated than the latter, which were much wealthier because of their education and industrial work and therefore made education and industry the means to economic gain and upward economic mobility. Today, they continue to constitute the social space and their practical consciousness in terms of their relation to the consumerist means of production in post-industrial capitalist America, which differentiates black America for the most part into two status groups, a dwindling middle and upper class (living in suburbia) that numbers about 25 percent of their population (13 percent) and obtain their status as doctors, athletes, entertainers, lawyers, teachers, and other high-end professional service occupations; and a growing segregated "black underclass" of unemployed and under-employed wage-earners occupying poor inner-city communities and schools focused solely on technical skills, multicultural education, athletics, and test-taking for social promotion given the relocation of industrial and manufacturing jobs to poor periphery and semi-periphery countries and the introduction of low-end post-industrial service jobs and a growing informal economy in American urban-cities. Consequently, the poor performance of black American students, vis-à-vis whites, in education as an ideological apparatus for this post-industrial capitalist sociolinguistic worldview leaves them disproportionately in this growing underclass at the bottom of the American class social structure of inequality unable to either transform their world as they encounter it, or truly exercise their embourgeoisement given their lack of, what sociologist Pierre Bourdieu (1973, 1984) refers to as, capital (cultural, social, economic, and political).[16]

Ironically, contrary to John Ogbu's (1986) burden of acting white hypothesis, it is due to their indigent (pathological-pathogenic) class structural position within the American dominated global capitalist social structure of inequality, as opposed to a differing or oppositional cultural ethos from that of the latter, as to the reason why black American school children achieve and paradoxically underachieve vis-à-vis their white counterparts. The majority of black school children underachieve in school in general and on standardized test in particular, vis-à-vis their white counterparts, not because they possess or are taught (by their peers) at an early age distinct normative values from that of the dominant classes in the social structure that transfer into cultural and political conflict in the classroom as an ideological apparatus for capitalists. To the contrary, black students underachieve in school because in acquiring the "verbal behavior" of the dominant social structure in segregated "poor" gentrified inner-city communities which lack good legal industrial jobs and affordable resources that have been outsourced by capital to the Third World or developing countries, the majority, who happen to be less educated in the "Standard English" of the society, have reinforced a linguistic community or status group, the black underclass, financed by the upper-class of owners and high-level executives, as the bearers of ideological and linguistic domination for black America in particular and blacks all over the world in general (Mocombe, 2006, 2011; Mocombe and Tomlin, 2012).

That is, industrial work, which once dominated the American urban landscape, has disappeared or been outsourced to developing countries in favor of high finance postindustrial service work and an informal economy, which requires language skills and a level of education suitable to service consumers and investors. America's transition to a postindustrial, financialized service, economy beginning in the 1970s, decentered black bourgeois identity with its emphasis on economic gain, status, and upward mobility via the church and education, and reified and positioned black American underclass ideology and language, hip-hop culture and athletics, as a viable means for black American youth to achieve economic gain, status, and upward economic mobility in the society over education. Finance capital in the US beginning in the 1970s began investing in entertainment and other service industries where the inner-city language, entertainment and athletic culture of black (underclass) America became both a commodity and the means to economic gain for the black poor in America's postindustrial (consumerist) economy, which subsequently outsourced its industrial work to semi-periphery nations thereby blighting the inner-city communities. Blacks, many of whom migrated to the northern cities from the agricultural south looking for industrial work in the north following the Civil War (1861-1865), became concentrated in blighted communities where work began to disappear, schools were underfunded, and poverty increased. The black migrants, which migrated North with their BEV/AAEV from the agricultural South, became segregated sociolinguistic underclass communities, ghettoes, of unemployed laborers looking to illegal, athletic, and entertainment activities (running numbers, pimping, prostitution, drug dealing, robbing, participating in sports, music, etc.) for economic success, status, and upward mobility. Educated in the poorly funded schools of the urban ghettoes, given the process of deindustrialization and the flight of capital to the suburbs, with no work prospects, many black Americans became part of a permanent, (African American English Vernacular) AAEV speaking and poorly educated underclass looking to other activities for economic gain, status, and upward economic mobility in the emerging individualism and diversified consumerism of postindustrial capitalism. Those who were educated became a part of the social class language game of the Standard-English-speaking black middle class of professionals, i.e., teachers, doctors, lawyers, etc. (the black bourgeoisie), living in the suburbs, while the uneducated or poorly educated constituted the social class language game of the black underclass of the urban ghettoes. Beginning in the late 1980s, finance capital began commodifying and distributing (via the media industrial complex) the social class language game of the underclass black culture for entertainment in the emerging postindustrial (consumerist) economy of the US over the ideology and language, social class language game, of the black bourgeoisie. Be that as it may, efforts to succeed academically among black Americans, which constituted the ideology and language of the black bourgeoisie, paled in comparison to their efforts to succeed as speakers of Black English, athletes, "gangstas", "playas", and entertainers, which became the ideology and language of the black underclass living in the inner-cities of America. Authentic black American identity became synonymous with black underclass hip-hop ideology and language.

Hence, contemporarily, black American students have a peer status group in the American dominated global capitalist social structure of inequality with its own language, style of dress, music, etc. Contemporarily, the group is institutionalized or occupies a status position in the American postindustrial class social structure of inequality based for the most part on their academic (under) achievement and social relation to the means of production, and not their race. The poor academic achievement of black American students, which initially results from their "linguistic structure," disproportionately leaves them at the bottom of the educational system, which leads to poor or no jobs in the American post-industrial labor market, which has transferred its industrial jobs overseas for higher paying financial jobs. As such, the status group is constituted as a class of poorly educated and unemployed or poorly employed laborers, living in predominantly inner-cities where low technical work has disappeared for low paying service and higher paying financial jobs. They, the black underclass, are unable to achieve a better life chance compared to those well educated and employed in high paying service occupations and therefore turn to other activities (drug dealing, sports, hustling, music, etc.) in the formal and informal economy that are more likely to payoff in the society given their poor linguistic skills and education, and the outsource of industrial jobs overseas by capital.

Subsequently, the material conditions and practices of this black underclass social psychologically have given rise to celebrated ideological and linguistic structures (Hip-Hop culture and Black/African-American English Vernacular), which appear to stand in contradistinction to the ideology and language (Standard English) of middle class black bourgeois and white America. This "mismatch of linguistic social class function" as constituted through and by the commodification of hip-hop culture is an appearance because the practical consciousness of this black underclass is no different from middle and upper middle-class black folks. Their purposive-rational end within the class division and social relations of production of American capitalism remains economic gain, status, and upward mobility in the society just like that of middle and upper middle-class black folks. Only the ideological apparatuses by which they are interpellated and embourgeoised and the means to those ends, economic gain, status, and upward mobility, have changed in a jobless postindustrial American material condition: poor schools, the streets, and prisons became the dominant ideological apparatuses by which they are interpellated and embourgeoised; and athletics, music, entertaining, hustling, etc. serve as means to achieving economic gain, status, and upward mobility over the educational avenues paved by the social class language game of the black and white middle and upper class suburban America. That is, given the commodification by finance capital of black American underclass practices as hip-hop culture and the predominance of the entertainment industry, media, etc., as the medium for its mass dissemination in the American post-industrial landscape, presently, they, the black American underclass of poorly educated and poorly (un) employed laborers, have become the bearers of ideological and linguistic domination in black America to the chagrin of their working, middle, and upper-middle class brethrens living in the suburbs and obtaining economic gain from their education based professions. Many black students growing up in inner-cities around the world no longer identify with academic achievement and success as means to obtaining economic gain as previously outlined by the social class language game of the black middle and upper classes, but instead they identify with the material practices of the black American underclass, which is over-represented and glorified in the media through hip-hop and athletic cultures, and seek to have their "blackness" as defined by that status group pay-off for them at the expense of achieving academically as defined by the black professional class working in high-end service occupations.

This is the social structural and social psychological manifestation of John Ogbu's the burden of acting white hypothesis within an American dominated post-industrial capitalist social structure of inequality that predominantly differentiates along class lines, and has institutionalized Black English, athletics, the entertainment industry, hustling, etc., financed by capital, as viable means or social functional roles to economic gain, status, and upward mobility in the larger American society for black America over more academically oriented careers. It is this economic payoff associated with hustling, sports, entertainment, etc., for underachieving blacks in the larger American society, which perpetuates the achievement gap, and prevents all effective corrective measures implemented by school systems from achieving complete success to reorient black functional roles in the society to more academically oriented careers (Mocombe, 2001, 2006, 2011; Mocombe and Tomlin, 2010).

As black youth become adolescents they are disadvantaged in school by the social functions the black American underclass and the larger mainstream society reinforces. That is, success or economic gain amongst the "black underclass," who speak or adopt Black/African American English Vernacular, listen to hip-hop music, participate in sports, is not measured by status obtained through education as in the case of black bourgeois middle class standards; on the contrary, athletics, music, and other activities (illegal ones) not typically "associated" with educational attainment, but which they are rewarded for by finance capital if they work hard, etc., serve as the means to success or economic gain, status, and upward mobility. Thus effort in school, in terms of academics, in general suffers, and as a result test scores and grades are further impacted. That is, for these youth, especially the black male in the society, there is no logical and obvious connection between academics and economics in their poor and blighted cities; instead, sports, music, drugs, etc., appear to be more accessible and viable means for improving their life goal of economic gain as opposed to the education promulgated by the "black bourgeoisie," which has expanded, contemporarily, to include athletes, rap-stars, hustlers, and other black entertainers (Frazier, 1957). This has led to a retention and expulsion rate in black America for example that is doubled that of whites, 33 and 18 percent respectively; an ever-increasing criminalization of black urban America, 43.9 percent of the state and federal prison populations; the ever-increasing proletarianization of the black masses; and an ever-increasing academic achievement gap that has the black bourgeois professional class clamoring that there is a conspiracy in the capitalist social system to destroy black boys.

It is this "mismatch of linguistic social class function," the ideals of middle class black bourgeois (standardized) America against the so-called "pathologies" (functions) of the black underclass, Ogbu and other post-segregationist black middle-class scholars inappropriately label, "acting-white" or culture of poverty.

The black underclass in America's ghettoes has slowly become, since the 1980s, replacing their middle-class brethren in suburbia, the bearers of ideological and linguistic domination for the black community in America and the world over. Their language (Ebonics or Black English Vernacular) and worldview as commodified through hip hop culture and financed by capital have become the means by which black youth (and youth throughout the world) attempt to recursively organize and reproduce their material resource framework against the means or social roles of black bourgeois middle class America. The aim, in an American post-industrial landscape that has commodified black hip-hop and athletic culture as (diversified consumerism) means to economic gain, status, and upward economic mobility is no longer to seek status and economic gain through a Protestant Ethic that stresses hard work, diligence, differed gratification, and education; on the contrary, sports, music, instant gratification, illegal activities (drug dealing), and skimming are the dominant means portrayed.

Schools, with their emphasis in the postindustrial society on celebrating diversity, throughout urban inner cities are no longer means to a professional end in order to obtain economic gain, status, and upward mobility, but obstacles to that end. That is, schools in urban American centers are no longer means to achieving economic success, status, or prestige in the society for young blacks, males in particular; instead, the focus on cooperative group works, cultural sensitivity training, and dialogical processes become the acculturative means of training blacks on how to market their underclass linguistic community and social roles as athletes and entertainers to others in both the American postindustrial economy and the global marketplace under American hegemony (Mocombe, 2007). Hence black youth are not "acting white" when education no longer becomes a priority or the means to economic status as they get older; they are attempting to be white and achieve bourgeois economic status in the society by being "black" in a racialized post-industrial capitalist social structure wherein the economic status of "blackness" is (over) determined by white capitalists and the black proletariats of the West, the black underclass, whose way of life, language, and image ("athletes and hip-hopsters") has been commodified (by white and black capitalists) and distributed throughout the world (via the black entertainment television network BET) for entertainment, (black) status, and economic purposes. Paul Gilroy's and Cornel West's, "present-at-hand," usurpation of Du Boisian double consciousness to define black bourgeois consciousness in relation to the material conditions of the urban black underclass ideologically attempts to do for this shift in the social relations of production, from agricultural to industrial to post-industrial, what Du Bois attempted to do in defining black bourgeois consciousness in relation to the material conditions of blacks in the agricultural deep south following the end of the Civil War. Just the same, the theory of intersectionality among black bourgeois academics highlight the discourse by which variant subjective positions (standpoint theories) have been marginalized and prevented from achieving equality of opportunity, recognition, and distribution within the global (postindustrial) capitalist social structure of class inequality and differentiation of the US, UK, and the diaspora. Be that as it may, by no means can double consciousness and intersectionality be viewed, against the discourse of the pathological-pathogenic, adaptive-vitality, anti-essentialist, and anti-anti-essentialist positions, as the universal mechanism by which black consciousness and communities were constituted as their rhetoric, like black consciousness and black communities in the US, UK, and the diaspora are the unready-to-hand and present-at-hand by-product (bourgeois ideology) of the global (industrial and postindustrial) capitalist social structure of class inequality and differentiation, which attempts to structure the practices of subjective experiences within class differentiation and thereby control diversity and meaning constitution for capital accumulation. So it is within the racial class division and social relations of production that black American and diasporic identity must be understood. Contemporarily, the two dominant social class language games of black America are heavily influencing the diaspora via the material wealth of black preachers, educators, athletes, and entertainers giving rise to the "my nigga" identity of the black underclass as the dominant bearer of ideological and linguistic domination for blacks in the global capitalist world-system. The case of the "my nigga" Haitian identity in the US and Haiti is a case in point.

Notes

1. See Philip D. Curtin, *The Atlantic Slave Trade: A Census* (Madison, 1969), Pp.72-87.
2. See William Julius Wilson's *The Declining Significance of Race: Blacks and Changing American Institutions* (1978) for the economic and political dynamics involved in shaping Southern institutions.
3. Whether on large plantations or small ones, all enslaved Africans in interaction with whites developed their practical consciousness by warring against the ways of the slave master and what they said the slaves were based on the fully visible behavior of newly arrived Africans.
4. In my structural understanding, the origins of American slavery, and its relation to the ideology of racism, are social structural. Slavery in America was not an autonomous system which developed out "of the condition and status of seventeenth-century labor" (Elkins, 1968 [1972]), but, as Oscar and Mary F. Handlin imply (albeit for the Handlins their position was also in reference to economic conditions whereas I am taking their reference to encompass a structuring ontology that gives rise to institutions), slavery "emerged rather from the adjustment to American conditions of traditional European institutions" (Handlins, 1950 [1972], pg. 23), which gave rise to the necessary conditions for the ever-increasing need for cheaper labor-power, which was in-turn rationalized or justified within the order of things, i.e., the Protestant ethic and the spirit of capitalism.
This synthesizing position, in the debate among historians of slavery as to the origins of racism in the United States, sides with Winthrop Jordan (1962 [1972]) who sees "both slavery and prejudice as species of a general debasement of the Negro", which stemmed, as Carl Degler (1959 [1972]) points out, from a stratifying, and discriminatory worldview bent on oppressing and exploiting (since

the aim was extracting the most value out of labor for economic gain) the means it deemed necessary to meet or live out its end or ontology, i.e., economic gain for its own sake. In my view, accordingly, it is not enough to look at the material conditions, but on the contrary the structuring ontology by which the material condition is structured or recursively organized and reproduced.

5. See Joseph E. Holloway, "The Origins of African-American Culture," in *Africanisms in American Culture* (1990). Bloomington and Indianapolis: Indiana University Press, Pp. 2.

6. See E. Franklin Frazier's *Black Bourgeoisie* (1957), Pp. 15.

7. Massachusetts, founded by the Pilgrims, a Protestant sect, became the first colony (1641) to pass any enslavement laws.

8. It is no surprise that the seven major historic black denominations—the African Methodist Episcopal (A.M.E.) Church; the African Methodist Episcopal Zion (A.M.E.Z.) Church; the Christian Methodist Episcopal (C.M.E.) Church; the National Baptist Convention, U.S.A., Incorporated (NBC); the National Baptist Convention of America, Unincorporated (NBCA); the Progressive National Baptist Convention (PNBC); and the Church of God in Christ (COGIC)—that account for more than 80 percent of black religious affiliation in the United States are of the Baptist, Methodist, and Pentecostal Protestant variety. These Protestant churches with their high emotionalism, fervor, enthusiasm, and excitement, their revivalism, their excesses of sinning and high-voltage confessing (Bell, 1960, pg. 103), have provided—for an illiterate mass prevented for a long time, on account of their immorality, lasciviousness, and heathenism, from partaking in the "thisworldly" affairs of the Protestant American social structure, derived from the intellectualism of traditional Protestantism—the means for access, via what is required for "otherworldly" existence, into the "thisworldly" affairs of the social structure.

In other words, for blacks, the Christianity of Methodism and Baptism served as a means to the Protestant ethic and the spirit of capitalism, the structuring structure of the culture that is American society. The "Christianity that was spread among slaves during the First and Second Awakenings was an evangelical Christianity that stressed personal conversion through a deep regenerating experience, being born again. The spiritual journey began with an acknowledgement of personal sinfulness and unworthiness and ended in an emotional experience of salvation by God through the Holy Spirit. The rebirth meant a change, a fundamental reorientation in the approach to life" (Lincoln and Mamiya, 1990, pg. 6)—becoming moral agents of the Protestant ethic in "this world" in order to have access to the "other world."

9. Some historians argue that the period prior to the cessation of the slave trade was more brutal and harsh than the period after the ban when slave masters relied almost completely on natural increase to reproduce the labor force. In my view, this distinction underestimates the degree to which the enslaved blacks' ontological security (the degree of brutality and oppressiveness) was attached to following plantation rules of conduct. In essence, my position is whether benign or brutal the general intent of the institution of slavery, as an ideological institution, was to inhibit the general autonomy and determine the agential moments of blacks. Just

like the general intent of the organization of work in contemporary times is to maintain the capitalist social relations of production and determine the agential moments of all wage laborers.

10. Martin Robinson Delany quoted in August Meier and Elliott Rudwick, *From Plantation to Ghetto* (New York, 1976), Pp. 151.

11. As August Meier and Elliott Rudwick (1966 [1976]) point out, this was the platform of the "Negro Convention Movement," which began in 1830 and met annually until the end of the century. A predominantly Northern phenomenon, "led and attended by the most distinguished leaders of the race—prominent ministers, physicians, lawyers, businessmen, and, after the Civil War, politicians...the conventions provide illuminating insight into the thinking of articulate blacks on the problems facing the race" such as slavery and the discrimination and "indignities" of the free colored folks (126).

12. To practice their traditional African ways would bring about cruel and unusual punishments, even death, considering that the African was, for the most part, under twenty-four hour surveillance in order to prevent insurrections. There is a debate amongst historians of slavery, who argue over the extent to which blacks within slavery had some form of autonomy. As can logically be deduced, the historians of the adaptive-vitality school (Blassingame, Gutman, Franklin, etc.) maintain that blacks were able to retain some of their African cultural heritage because they were to some extent autonomous. The historians of the pathological-pathogenic school (Elkins, Stampp, Genovese, etc.) argue to the contrary.

13. It should be noted that a debate lingers regarding the origins of African spirituality. Given that the Africans were prevented from establishing any institutions to reproduce their ethos in the colonies, I rather agree with E. Franklin Frazier's (1957) understanding:

The most important institution which the Negro has built in the United States is the Negro church. Contrary to the claim of some students of the Negro that the Negro church was an African survival resurrected on American soil, the Negro church is a product of the American environment. The form of its organization and the character of its religious services were the result of the proselyting of Protestant missionaries, especially the Baptist and the Methodist missionaries. This does not mean that the Negro's peculiar experience in America did not contribute to the shaping of the institution. The influence of the Negro's experience in the building of his church is seen in the variations in the character of the Negro church, which reflect the extent of the Negro's education and isolation in American life and his economic and social status (87).

14. The character of the black family during slavery was so patterned after the institutional regulators of the American social structure that today there is talk of its disintegration resulting not from slavery, as E. Franklin Frazier (1939) proclaimed, but from the post-World War II public policies of welfare and job relocations out of urban, which has fostered female-headed households, teenage pregnancy, promiscuity, welfare dependency, out-of-wedlock births, etc. See William Julius Wilson's (1987) *The Truly Disadvantaged* and Herbert Gutman's (1976) *The Black Family in Slavery and Freedom*.

15. "As long as the slaves communed with whites [(and remained illiterate)], their religious instruction was circumscribed. The planters, in spite of their piety, insisted that their slaves not learn any of the potentially subversive tenets [(which whites themselves had used against their former masters, the English crown)] of Christianity (the brotherhood of all men, for instance)" (Blassingame, 1972, pg. 61). Once the slaves learned these tenets, their quest for freedom became a fight for their "God" given rights.

16. Pierre Bourdieu's (1984) theory of social reproduction refers to several forms of "capital" (cultural, economic, symbolic, and social). I will not go into details about Bourdieu's social reproduction theory, what I will say, however, is that the "capital" references refer to the institutional norms, resources, connections, etc. that one needs in their respective societies' to participate in its cultural, economic, symbolic, and social life. Bourdieu posits that the possession of, for the most part, middle class "capital" is assumed by the educational system in contemporary society, but is not taught. Thus, education theorists (i.e., James Coleman), who have operationalized Bourdieu's concept, conclude, poor students enter school at a disadvantage (i.e., they lack "middle class capital), which leads to their "poor" achievement. The solution from this perspective is to teach and orient these poor students to more middle class values and norms so that they can achieve like their white counterparts. In the postindustrial economies of the US and UK, where the lack of capital is commodified and celebrated for capital accumulation, Bourdieu's theory is problematic in that to speak of the lack of capital, social, cultural, political, etc. as a barrier to upward economic mobility and status in the societies is no longer the case, and politically incorrect. Hence this need to develop a cultural realm to explain agency within capitalist relations of production as Bourdieu has done with his theory of praxis negates the agential moments of the actors through the commodification of their structural position, which brings Bourdieu's theory and the actions of those who lack capital back to the structural realm of analysis. This is why I refrain from using Bourdieu's cultural notions to outline the constitution of black American practical consciousness.

CHAPTER V

THE CONSTITUTION OF HAITIAN IDENTITY WITHIN THE PROTESTANT ETHIC AND THE SPIRIT OF CAPITALISM: THE CHILDREN OF SANS SOUCI, DESSALINES/TOUSSAINT, AND PÉTION

If the African and diasporic experience as encapsulated in slavery, colonization, abolitionism, and decolonization dialectically represents the intent of former slaves to be like their masters amidst racism, slavery, colonization, and their structural differentiation, the Africans of Haiti who met at Bois Caïman, August 14ᵗʰ, 1791, and other congresses to commence the Haitian Revolution attempted to do the contrary. That is, they, anti-dialectically, rejected not only their slave status, racism, and colonization, but the very practical consciousness of their former slavemasters for their own structuring structure or form of system and social integration, i.e., lakouism and the Vodou Ethic and the spirit of communism social class language game, respectively. Their discourse and discursive practices would eventually be supplanted by the practical consciousness or language game of the *Affranchis*, free (creole) blacks and mulatto, *gens de couleur*, bourgeoisies, seeking, like their liberal bourgeois black counterparts in America and the diaspora (the black Atlantic), equality of opportunity, distribution, and recognition with their *blanc* counterparts within the capitalist world-system via the Haitian state and its ideological apparatuses. Prior to this usurpation, however, the Vodou and Kreyol ceremony or congress at Bois Caïman under the leadership of Dutty Boukman, Edaïse, Cecile Fatima, the Vodou manbo priestess, is a rejection of both slave status and European civilization, and cannot be, contrary to Susan Buck-Morss's (2009) work, *Hegel, Haiti, and Universal History*, and others, conceptualized within the framework of Hegel's master/slave dialectic, postmodern, post-structural, or postcolonial theories. Whereas the purposive-rationality of the two bourgeoisies, free landowning blacks and mulatto elites, can be conceptualized within a Hegelian dialectical, postmodern, post-structural, and postcolonial struggle, that of *oungan yo, manbo yo, gangan yo*, and *granmoun yo* of Bois Caiman, who would assume the leadership of the masses of the provinces and mountains, cannot. The purposive-rationality of the latter was not a structurally differentiated identity as found amongst the creole blacks and mulatto elites. Oungan yo, manbo yo, gangan yo, and granmoun yo, the leadership or power elites of the Africans, of Bois Caiman offered an alternative structuring structure (form of system and social integration) for organizing the material resource framework and the agential initiatives of social actors, and must not be enframed within the structurally differentiating dialectical, postmodern, post-structural, and postcolonial logic of the West and the Affranchis (today's Haitian mulatto, Arab oligarchy, and petit-bourgeois blacks) (Mocombe, 2016).

Essentially, when the Haitian Revolution commences in 1791, there are three distinct groups vying for control of the island, the whites (*blancs*); free people of color and mulattoes (*Affranchis*), and the enslaved and escaped (maroon) Africans of the island. The latter, over sixty-seven percent of the population, were not a structurally differentiated other. They had their own practical consciousness, what Paul C. Mocombe (2016) calls the "Vodou Ethic and the spirit of communism," by which they went about recursively (re)organizing and reproducing the material resource framework via the lakou system (Lakouism). The former two, free blacks and *gens de couleur* (Affranchis), were interpellated, embourgeoised, and differentiated by the language, communicative discourse, mode of production, ideology, and ideological apparatuses of the West and shared the same European practical consciousness, the Catholic/Protestant Ethic and the spirit of capitalism social class language game, as the whites. The latter social class language game stood against the Vodou Ethic and the spirit of communism social class language game of the majority of the Africans who were interpellated and ounganified/manboified by the language, communicative discourse, mode of production, ideology, and ideological apparatuses of *oungan yo, manbo yo, gangan yo*, and *granmoun yo* (James, 1986; Fick, 1990; Du Bois, 2004, 2012; Ramsey, 2014).[1]

Be that as it may, four distinct Revolutions would come to constitute the Haitian Revolution: The Revolutions of the whites; mulattoes; creole blacks; and the Africans. The whites, were divided between large plantation owners, *grand blanc*, and *petit-blancs*, i.e., managers, slave drivers, artisans, merchants, and teachers. The former, *grand blanc*, were independent-minded, and like the American colonists wanted political and economic independence from their mother-country, France, where their rights and economic interests were not represented in the National Assembly. The *petit-blancs* were more racist and feared the alliance between the larger landowners and the Affranchis. The Affranchis were free people of color and mulatto, *gens de couleur*, property and slave owners on the island who shared the religion, culture, language, and ideology of their white counterparts and wanted then Saint-Domingue to remain a French colony. Although internal antagonism based on race (color) and class existed between the free (creole) blacks and *gens de couleur*, I group them together under the nomenclature, Affranchis, to highlight the fact that their interpellation and embourgeoisement via the ideological apparatuses of the West rendered their practical consciousnesses identical even though there were racial/color (based on phenotype, not ideology) tensions between them (racial tensions, which still plaques Haiti today). Unlike the majority of white large plantation owners, however, the Affranchis, like Vincent Ogé, André Rigaud, Alexandre Pétion, Pierre Pinchinat, Toussaint Louverture, for examples, did not want independence from France. In the case of the mulattoes, who after independence would come to be referred to as the children of Alexandre Pétion, the first president of the Haitian Republic, they simply wanted their social, political, and economic rights recognized by France within the colony, not an independent nation-state or the end to slavery. In regards, to the children of Dessalines/Toussaint, creole slave drivers and free blacks, they sought equality of opportunity, recognition, and distribution vis-à-vis the whites and mulattoes. The enslaved and escaped Africans, the children of Sans Souci, of the island were divided between field slaves, domestic slaves, and maroons. The domestic slaves, like their African-American counterparts, "house slaves," more so identified with their slavemasters. However, for the most part, the field slaves and maroons, because of their relative isolation from whites, domestic slaves, *gens de couleur*, and free blacks, were interpellated and ounganified/manboified by the modes of production, language, ideology, ideological apparatuses, and communicative discourse of the Vodou Ethic and the spirit of communism, and many sought to reproduce their African ways of life in a national position of their own. In the end, the Revolution would come down to a struggle between the *Affranchis* and the enslaved and maroon Africans of the island, the latter of whom commenced the Haitian Revolution on August 14th, 1791 at Bois Caiman and other congresses (Genovese, 1979; James, 1986; Fick, 1990; Du Bois, 2004, 2012; Mocombe, 2016).

Following the Revolution, between 1804 and 1806, the purposive-rationality of the enslaved and maroon Africans would become a part of the *modus operandi* of the Haitian nation-state until October 17, 1806 when Jean-Jacques Dessalines was assassinated by Alexandre Pétion and Henri Christophe. At which point, the purposive-rationality of the *Affranchis* with their emphasis on integration into the global capitalist world-system, capitalist wealth, French culture, religion, and language became dominant at the expense of the African linguistic system, Kreyol; Vodou ideology; its ideological apparatuses; and modes of production, subsistence agriculture, husbandry, and *komes*, of the African masses on the island who took to the mountains and provinces following the death of Dessalines (Fick, 1990; Nicholls, 1979; Du Bois, 2004, 2012). This is not to say that Dessalines completely sided with the purposive-rationality or practical consciousness of the African masses who sought to recursively reproduce their Vodou Ethic and spirit of communism, i.e., subsistence agriculture, husbandry, and komes (commerce), practical consciousness on the island via the lakou system. The argument here is that he attempted to balance the purposive-rationality of his *grandon* class of former generals and slave drivers, i.e., the creole blacks, who yearned to become wealthy landowners and masters like the whites and racist mulatto elites amidst the desires of the African masses seeking to reproduce their subsistence agriculture, husbandry, and komes. Be that as it may, the internal struggles between the two bourgeoisies within the Affranchis, the mulatto elites who controlled the export/import trade and the free blacks who controlled the land and agribusinesses where the African masses toiled as cultivators, over control of the state and its ideological apparatuses would dominate the political and economic conditions of post-revolution Haiti to the present at the expense of the practical consciousness of the African masses (James, 1986; Dupuy, 1989; Fick, 1990; Nicholls, 1979; Du Bois, 2004, 2012; Buck-Morss, 2009). Both groups would arm the youth and peasants of the island to achieve their initiatives, i.e., control of the state and its ideological apparatuses. Today, the latter, *grandon* class, composed of educated professionals, former drug dealers, entertainers, and police officers attack the former Affranchis class, which is now a comprador bourgeoisie seeking to build, own, and manage hotels and assembly factories producing electronics and clothing for the US market, under the moniker the children of Jean-Jacques Dessalines against the children of Alexandre Pétion in the name of the African masses of the island, the majority of whom are peasant farmers (the children of Sans Souci and Macaya, i.e., Congolese leaders of the Revolution who wanted no part of the capitalist world-system).

Pre-Revolutionary Haiti

Contemporarily, the island which Haiti occupies in the Caribbean is inhabited by two independent nation-states: The Republic of Haiti and the Dominican Republic. Initially, the island was occupied by the Taino indigenous people. In 1492 Christopher Columbus, seeking a Western passage to the East Indies, claimed the island for Spain. The Spanish occupied the island and renamed it *La Española* (written in English as Hispaniola). They exploited the island's gold mines and reduced the Taino natives to slavery. After fifty-years of Spanish rule the Taino natives, who numbered between 3,000,000 to 4,000,000 prior to the advent of the Spanish, were decimated through the hardship of their condition as slaves, organized massacres, and diseases they contracted from the Spaniards (James, 1986; Fick, 1990; Nicholls, 1979; Du Bois, 2004, 2012; Buck-Morss, 2009).

The genocide of the Taino natives on the island was one of the most brutal in recorded history. As a result, Bartholomew de Las Casas, a Spanish priest, protested against the massacre of the so-called "Indians" and demanded the cessation of the injustices committed against them. He advocated for the importation of blacks from Africa to work in the mines and on the plantations as a means of ending Indian slavery on the island. Thus, in 1503, the first Africans landed on the island. These initial Africans were indentured servants from Spain. Eventually, by 1697 Africans and the French would subsequently displace the Spanish on the western side of the island of Hispaniola.

In 1625, the first French adventurers landed on the island of La Tortue (Tortuga Island) in the northern coast of what is today the Republic of Haiti. Later, they began exploring and settling on the main land to eventually displace the Spanish from the western part of the island through warfare. Tired of French attacks, and also because of the results of war in Europe, Spain signed with France the Treaty of Ryswick in 1697, ceding to the latter the western part of the island. The French renamed their possession Saint-Domingue. The French developed Saint-Domingue/Haiti into the richest colony in the world at the time through an export-oriented agricultural (plantation) economy based on enslaved Africans imported from West and Central Africa (Senegambia, Bight of Benin, and the Kongo). To build this wealth, France imported thousands of slaves from Africa who, under France's *Code Noir*, or black codes, were submitted to virtually the same abuses and mistreatments imposed on the Taino natives by the Spanish.

Subsequently, the importation of Africans in large numbers would change the demographics of Saint-Domingue/Haiti. Under French rule,

Saint-Domingue's population, as previously mentioned, was divided into three main social groups or racial-classes, the whites or "Blancs", the "Affranchis", a group composed of free blacks and mulattoes, and the great masses of imported enslaved Africans who constituted 75 percent of the population. By 1789, the colony's population comprised between 400,000 and 500,000 Africans, compared to about 40,000 whites and 30,000 mulattoes and free blacks or Affranchis (Fick, 1990; Du Bois, 2012). A great number of mulattoes were the offsprings of the union between "Blancs" and African women who were raped by their slavemasters. In many instances, slavemasters married the women, adopted these children, and provided them with the necessities of life. These offsprings, mulattoes, would in-turn inherit the wealth of their fathers and serve in the colony's police force, *maréchaussée*, which was in place to protect the colony against the enslaved Africans. Thus, by the end of the 18th century, the mulattoes would own around 25 to 30 percent of the colony's plantations and wealth, while most of them went to France to get a higher education (Fick, 1990; Nicholls, 1979; Du Bois, 2004). Yet, despite their wealth and Western interpellation, subjectification, and embourgeoisement via the Catholic Church and French education, the mulattoes, because of their color, were considered inferior to the blancs or whites by law and were discriminated against. For example, they could not enter certain professions, i.e., law, medicine, etc., wear European clothes, or sit among the whites in church. They were reduced to a land and slave-owning, educated, merchant class who exported indigo, coffee, and other cash crops while simultaneously serving as the police force, *maréchaussée,* of the colony against slave insurrection (Fick, 1990; Du Bois, 2004).

Because of these discriminatory practices under the *Code Noir* of the colony, conflict arose between the *Affranchis*, particularly the *gens de couleur*, and the whites throughout the 18th century with the former claiming civil and political equality with the latter who wanted to maintain the status quo. Simultaneously, the whites on the island were demanding from France the right to participate in the running of the colony. They wanted to make of Saint-Domingue a country that would be autonomous from France. Both groups would voice their grievances at the time of the French revolution in 1789, which proclaimed the principles of liberty, equality, and fraternity (James, 1986; Dupuy, 1989; Fick, 1990; Nicholls, 1979; Du Bois, 2004, 2012). In many instances, the *gens de couleur*, through their French supporters in Paris, *Société des Amis des Noirs*, did so at the expense of the free blacks, a majority of creole slave-owning blacks seeking equality of opportunity, recognition, and distribution with the mulattoes and whites, whom they looked down upon on account of their race (color).

The enslaved Africans and maroon communities of Africans in the mountainsides, contrary to popular beliefs, were neither a part of the dialectical conflict between the *Affranchis* and the whites, nor this claim for liberty, equality, and fraternity proclaimed by them. The Africans of Saint-Domingue/Haiti, for the most part, came from three regions of Africa: The Congo, Dahomey/Benin, and the Nago regions of the continent (James, 1986; Fick, 1990; Desmangles, 1992; Du Bois, 2004, 2012). Although from different tribes of Africa what united the Africans together was the Vodou worldview, its ideological apparatuses, Lakous, peristyles, etc., and modes of production, husbandry, subsistence agriculture, and *komes*.[2] Unlike the British and Spanish colonies where Africans were bred like animals upon their arrival to the Americas, the French did not breed their enslaved Africans. Instead, upon illness, disability, and or death, they simply imported more Africans to replace the labor supply in the colonies. In the mind of the White landowners, it was actually less expensive to import enslave Africans than to breed them (Du Bois, 2004). Be that as it may, given the importation policy of the French planters coupled with the relative isolation of the newly arrived Africans on the island from the whites and Affranchis, the Africans imported to Saint-Domingue by the French were able to maintain and recursively reorganize and reproduce their African Vodou ideology, ideological apparatuses, practical consciousnesses, and social relations of production without any discontinuity in spite of the orders of the *Code Noirs*, which they tirelessly fought against.

The enslaved Africans who were imported to the French colonies manifested their rejection of their condition through different forms of resistance. Enslaved Africans poisoned their masters; others committed infanticide to save their offsprings from the hellish conditions of slavery (Genovese, 1979; Fick, 1990; Karenga, 1993; Du Bois, 2004). The most successful and persistent form of slave protest was marronage. Marronage consisted of slaves running away from plantations to hide in the mountains of the island or in its forests where they reconstituted their African ways of life (Genovese, 1979; Fick, 1990; Desmangles, 1992; Karenga, 1993). From their retreat, the maroons also conducted raids on the plantations and often would come out at night to poison or kill their masters. One of the most famous Haitian maroons was François Makandal. Makandal was an *oungan*, or Vodou priest, from Guinea. At night, he would attack plantations, burning them and killing their owners. During his six-year rebellion, he and his followers poisoned and killed as many as 6000 whites. In 1758, however, the French captured him and publicly executed him on the public square of Cap Francais, present-day Cap-Haitian (Fick, 1990; Desmangles, 1992). So in essence, unlike the Affranchis, who, dialectically, sought equality of opportunity, recognition, and distribution with whites within the Protestant/Catholic capitalist world-system, the majority of Africans sought simply freedom and liberty to recursively organize and reproduce their lakou and Vodou form of system and social integration in a national position of their own (Fick, 1990; Mocombe, 2016).

Race and Class in Revolutionary Haiti

Hence given the Africans' desires to reproduce their form of system and social integration amidst the desires of the creole blacks, mulattoes, and whites to enslave them as wage-earners within the emerging Protestant capitalist world-system, the French Revolution of 1789 in France was not the spark that lit the Haitian Revolution of 1791 as many theorists propose (James, 1986; Du Bois, 2004, 2012). It sparked the Revolution for the mulatto and petit-bourgeois black classes seeking equality of opportunity, recognition, and distribution with their white counterparts, not the mass of Africans and their leadership imported into the colony. As previously highlighted, the revolution began the minute the Africans arrived on the island. However, the interests of the Africans were not the same as the interests of the other economic racial groups on the island, which created some very strange alliances and movements. Within the emerging Protestant capitalist world-system, France enforced a system called the "exclusif" on Saint-Domingue/Haiti. Similar to the capitalist world-system in globalization under American hegemony, this "exclusive" (mercantilist) system required that Saint-Domingue sell 100 percent of her agricultural and raw material exports to France, and purchase 100 percent of her manufactured imports from them as well. The French merchants and crown set the prices for both imports and exports, and the prices were extraordinarily favorable to France and in no way competitive with world markets. This "exclusive" system was virtually the same as the one which England had forced on its North American colonies. Like the North Americans, the white and landowning *Affranchis* Saint-Domingueans did not abide strictly by this system. A contraband trade grew with the British in Jamaica and North America, and after its successful revolution, the United States. The Americans wanted molasses from Saint- Domingue for their burgeoning rum distilleries, and Saint-Domingue imported huge quantities of low quality dried fish to feed to the slaves. The planters (both white and free people of color) chafed under the oppression of France's "exclusif." There was a growing independence movement, and in this movement the white planters were united with the free people of color. It was a curious alliance, since the whites continued to oppress the free people of color in their social life, but formed a coalition with them on the political and economic front (Fick, 1990; Du Bois, 2004). Conversely, the petit-blancs remained outside of this coalition, primarily because they were unwilling to form any sort of alliance with any persons of color, free or not. The petit-blancs were avowed racists and were especially offended and threaten by the elevated economic status of most of the free people of color. It is important to note that this economic independence movement did not include the majority of the enslaved Africans, *bossales*, in any way whatsoever, who were enslaved by both the *Affranchis* and whites. Those who were a party to the movement were avowed slave owners and their vision of a free Saint-Domingue was liked that of the United States, a slave owning nation.

As such, the Africans, such as Armand, Martial, Macaya, Sans Souci, and others on the island, fought against the whites, mulattoes, and free persons of color, i.e., creoles (Fick, 1990). The slave owners, both white and people of color, i.e., free blacks and mulattoes, feared the Africans and knew that the incredible concentration of enslaved Africans (the slaves outnumbered the free people 10-1) required exceptional control. The owners tried to keep slaves of the same tribes apart; they forbade any meetings of slaves; and they tied slaves rigorously to their own plantations under the *Code Noir*. The Africans rebelled against these conditions. The African slave rebellions were without allies among the whites, mulattoes, or free people of color. They were not even fully united among themselves, and the domestic slaves, like their American counterparts, especially tended to be more loyal to their masters than the field slaves or maroon Africans. The maroons, in the meantime, were in contact with rebellious slaves, but they had few firm alliances. Nonetheless, their hatred of slavery, their fear of being re-enslaved, and their desire to be free and safe in their own country, made them ready allies were a serious slave revolution to begin. In the mountains they practiced their Vodou religions, reproduced its ideological apparatuses, and modes of production, i.e., subsistence agriculture, husbandry, and *komes* in order to reconstitute their societies in the Americas (Genovese, 1979; Fick, 1990; Du Bois, 2012).

So by 1790 one year before the official commencement of the Revolution, the colony was divided between French bureaucrats, white planters, petit-blancs, mulatto elites, free (creole) people of color, enslaved Africans, and maroons each with their own agendas, alliances, and worldviews or structuring structures (Genovese, 1979; Fick, 1990; Du Bois, 2004). The split between the two colonial white groups gave strength to the French government officials who had lost effective control of the colony. The mulatto elites despised the free persons of color based solely on race and class, while at the same time forming a strange alliance with the white elites, who in alliance with the petit-blancs discriminated against them. Meanwhile, the maroons distrusted all the groups including the enslaved (house and field) Africans who were left to their own devices on the plantations. Each of these forces were poised to strike against the other. Yet, in the crazy contradictions of this whole situation, the petit-blancs and white planters each carried on their own private war of terror against the mulattoes, free people of color, and the enslaved Africans. These divisions among maroon and enslaved Africans, slave owners, the divisions among the whites, free persons of color, and mulattoes, were not only racial and economic, they were sociocultural as well, European (an emerging Protestant Ethic and the spirit of capitalism) on the one hand, and African (The Vodou Ethic and the spirit of communism) on the other (Genovese, 1979; Mocombe, 2016). Many scholars (James, 1986; Dupuy, 1989; DuBois, 2012) overlook this sociocultural component or sweep it in the literature by referring to the Africans as masses, peasants, maroons, or blacks. As though, outside of the dominant European worldview and practical consciousness, which the Affranchis internalized and sought to reproduce, the Africans had no other worldview to recursively reorganize or reproduce in the material world (Genovese, 1979; Mocombe, 2016).

Revolutionary Haiti

Typically, historians date the beginnings of the Haitian Revolution with the uprising of the slaves on the night of August 14th, 1791. On August 14th, 1791, as the whites and the Affranchis continued on their war for greater participation in the running of the colony and for equality of opportunity, recognition, and distribution, the African maroons entered into a full-fledge rebellion that would ultimately result in the creation of the nation-state of Haiti and the abolition of slavery on the island. Boukman Dutty, another oungan following the path of Makandal (who led a rebellion in 1758), organized a meeting with the diverse African tribes/nations of the island in the mountains of the Northern corridors of the island. This meeting, referred to as *minokan* in the Vodou tradition, took the form of a spiritual Petwo Vodou ceremony. According to Haitian folklore and oral history, it was raining and the sky was raging with clouds. The elders and representatives of the African tribes began the ceremony by confessing their resentment for their condition. A woman, Cecile Fatiman, a Vodou manbo priestess, started dancing languorously in the crowd, taken by the spirits of the lwa, African lunar Goddess, Erzulie Danthor. With a knife in her hand, she cut the throat of a black pig (according to Max Beauvoir, an actual person was sacrificed that night. Black pig, *Kochon noir*, refers to the nomenclature given to maroon Africans by the French.), a sacrifice to Danthor, and distributed the blood to all the participants of the meeting who swore to unite, kill all of the whites and mulattoes on the island with the aid of Manbo Danthor, and constitute a new equitable society based on the principles of Bon-dye. Manbo Fatima/Danthor proceeded to layout the leadership of the rebellion, naming Georges Biassou, Jeannot, Jean Francois, Macaya, etc. On August 22, 1791, the blacks of the North entered into a rebellion, killing all the whites and mulattoes they met and setting the plantations of the colony on fire.

The French quickly captured the leader of the enslaved Africans, Boukman, and beheaded him, bringing the rebellion under control. Just like Francois Makandal, however, Boukman had managed to instill in the Africans the idea of his invincibility. Thus, the French exposed his head on Cap's (present-day Cap-Haitian) square to convince the slaves that their leader was really dead. The death of Boukman, although it had temporarily stopped the rebellion of the North, it failed, however, to restrain the rest of the Africans from revolting against their condition. Toussaint Louverture, a free literate black *Affranchis*, and Jean-Jacques Dessalines, an enslaved first generation Saint-Dominguean/Haitian (creole field slave) whose parents were directly from Africa, among many others (George Biassou, Jean Francois, etc.), would assume the leadership of the revolt after the death of Boukman.

Unlike Boukman, who was a charismatic leader that incorporated the maroon West African slaves', sixty-seven percent of whom were directly from Africa when the Revolution commenced, Vodou spiritualism, and culture to organize the rebellion at Bois Caïman and other places against the *blancs* and *Affranchis*, Toussaint Louverture, a creole black excluded from the African Vodou leadership, proved to be a military genius and a formidable leader in the tradition of the West. Toussaint, a literate free creole black who was treated well by his slavemaster and interpellated and embourgeoised by the church and his slavemaster, who taught him to read, did not exclude the *Affranchis* from the revolution. He organized the maroons, masses of slaves, and a few *Affranchis* free slaves and mulattoes into an organized army. With political manipulation, and military campaigns, he would gain notoriety in the colony. During the period of

1791 to 1800, Toussaint outmaneuvered the French, the Spaniards, and the English. He managed to eliminate all his enemies on the island until he was the only power left in Saint-Domingue/Haiti. By 1801, he governed the entire island, and proclaimed himself governor-general of the colony. A constitution was soon drawn-up that same year by the white planter class under Toussaint's directives declaring Saint-Domingue an autonomous French black possession where slavery was abolished.

Although Toussaint abolished slavery on the island, he maintained the export-oriented agricultural system of slavery under a new share-cropping partnership, *corvée* system, between the Africans and their former slavemasters who became cultivators. Many of the maroons and mulatto elites (Andre Rigaud, Alexander Pétion, Jean-Pierre Boyer, etc.) rebelled against Toussaint's position and continued their fight against his army of free blacks, whites, and mulattoes. The former, maroon Africans, did so because they were against anything that resembled slavery, and the latter, mulatto elites, due to the emergence of the new free black *grandon* property classes composed of the black generals in Toussaint's army and the continuing economic role of the white planters. Defeated in what is famously referred to as "the war of knives" by Jean-Jacques Dessalines, the mulattoes André Rigaud, Alexandre Pétion, and Jean-Pierre Boyer would leave for France, while Macaya, Sans Souci, and many of the African maroons either became landowners or returned to the mountains leaving Toussaint in control of the plantation system. Hence the pre-1791 status-quo was re-instituted under Toussaint without slavery.

Following his European campaign, Napoleon Bonaparte wary of Toussaint's great power in the colony sent 82,000 of his battle proven troops commanded by the mulattoes Alexandre Pétion, Jean-Pierre Boyer, and his brother-in-law, General Charles Leclerc, a fleet of warships, canons, munitions and dogs in order to quell the rebellion and recapture Haiti as a slave colony. Whereas the *Affranchis* surrendered, the Africans under the leadership of Sans Souci and Macaya continued their warfare against the French and Affranchis from the mountains. Two years of war ended in a stalemate; however, the French treacherously arrested Toussaint Louverture during a meeting in June 1802. He was exiled to France and died in the *Fort de Joux* prison high in the cold Alpine mountains of Jura in April 1803.

With the arrest, and eventual death, of Toussaint, Jean-Jacques Dessalines, a trained oungan in the traditions of Makandal and Boukman, whose dislike for the whites and mulatto *Affranchis* was not shared by Louverture, formed a shaky alliance with the maroon Africans, free blacks, and mulattoes (under the leadership of Alexandre Pétion who was sent back under Leclerc's army to reclaim the island for France) and emerged as the new leader of the Haitian Revolution, bringing it, with the aid of Henri Christophe, Francois Capois-la-Mort, and the maroon Africans to its ultimate climax, the first black independent nation in the world on January 1, 1804, and the only successful slave rebellion in recorded history.

Unlike Toussaint, Dessalines was a creole field slave interpellated and ounganified/manboified by the Vodou ideology and ideological apparatuses of the Africans. He had no formal Western education and disagreed with Toussaint over the roles of the mulattoes and whites in the revolution. Nonetheless, in his eventual move to liberate Haiti, he united with the maroon Africans (Macaya, Sans Souci, etc.), free blacks, and mulatto elites led by Alexandre Pétion. Haiti's revolution against colonialism and slavery was the first successful black movement resulting in an independent state headed by so-called blacks. On January 1, 1804, Dessalines, to honor the Taino natives who had been massacred by the Spanish, renamed the island its original Tainoian name, Haiti or Ayi-ti (mountainous land). Since these glorious events, Haiti has been the pariah of the West bearing the mark of the poorest country in the Hemisphere. This distinction is a product of the racial-class divisions and struggle for power between the mulattoes, free blacks, and the Africans, which would continue in Haiti during and following the Revolution and the death of Jean-Jacques Dessalines.

Following the Revolution, Haiti was marginalized by all the European powers of the time, and fighting amongst the three remaining groups, the mulatto elites, the free black generals and creole blacks, and the African maroons, emerged over the constitution of the new nation-state. The mulatto elites desired the land of their white fathers, the free black generals wanted to maintain their land they had obtained from Toussaint during the early parts of the war, and the African maroons wanted no parts of anything that resembled the old system of slavery or Toussaint's *corvée* system. The former two, interpellated, subjectified, and embourgeoised by the ideology and ideological apparatuses of the West, sought to reproduce the same export-oriented colonial system as their former colonial slavemasters, while the latter and the majority of the population interpellated and ounganified/manboified by the leadership of the Vodou Ethic and the spirit of communism did not. Instead, they went about practicing their religion, husbandry, subsistence agriculture, and komes as enframed by the Vodou Ethic and the spirit of communism in order to reconstitute the society in a national position of their own. Dessalines, who essentially sided with the *grandons*, sought to constitute the new nation-state within these two opposing structuring structures. As such in his 1805 constitution he proceeded to divide the land equitably among all those who fought in the Revolution; renounced everything that was French for systems grounded in the experiences of the African people of the island; and renounced white supremacy for a Pan-African discourse that would have Haiti become the land for and of blacks (Fick, 1990; Nicholls, 1979; Du Bois, 2012).

This constitution of Haiti did not sit well with the *Affranchis* who desired their pre-war status and wealth, which tied them to the global capitalist world-system. Instead of focusing on fortification of the island, national production, food security, and agricultural production for local consumption as Dessalines attempted to do with his equitable redistribution of land among the population, the *Affranchis* assassinated him over his land reform and the masses of Africans fled to the mountainsides and provinces of the island where they organized and reproduce their "being-in-the-world via the Vodou Ethic and the spirit of communism and the lakou system. With the death of Dessalines, the majority of the productive land was divided among the mulatto elites, who took over their fathers' land and estates, and the black commanding officers of the revolution. They kept intact the export based economic arrangements which existed under colonialism and Toussaint's regime with the mulatto elites—because of their status as mulattoes—serving as the middle persons between the nation-state and outside merchants. What emerged in Haiti, following the Revolution, was the same colonial (mercantilist) class structure under the leadership of the Affranchis and their adversarial partnership with an emerging foreign white merchant class, which assisted in the acquisition of manufactured goods, petit-bourgeois blacks who converted their plantations into agribusinesses, and the Africans in the provinces and mountains whose products were heavily taxed by the emerging nation-state under the leadership of the Affranchis (Pierre-Louis, 2000; Du Bois, 2012). As Francois Pierre-Louis (2000) brilliantly highlights of the emerging Haitian racial-class structure following the Revolution,

> The ostracism of Haiti by the major powers also affected inter-class relationships. In order to obtain cash, the revolutionary governments kept intact the export based economic arrangements which existed under colonialism. The most productive lands in the country were divided between the generals and their families for the cultivation of cash crops. Most of the slaves who fought in the independence war had to resign themselves to working small parcels of land in the mountains for their subsistence. As a result of this arrangement, the class structure of Haiti

evolved into three categories: The vast landowners (made up primarily of generals and relatives of the fleeing colonists who moved up the ranks under revolutionary governments), the merchant class and the landless peasants. The large landowners encouraged the production of cash crops on their plantation through a system of share cropping.... Soon after the revolution the government attempted to restore a forced labor system called *corvée* on the plantations in order to restore Haiti's pre-independence level of productivity in commodities such as coffee and sugar. The leaders had a tough time enforcing the forced labor system due to massive resistance from the former slaves. Instead, a system of share cropping was instituted through which they succeeded in obtaining a substantial labor from the peasant population.

After the large landowners came the merchant class. This class was composed primarily of descendants of the colonists and foreigners. The merchant class acted as an intermediary between the landowners and the external market. A symbiotic relationship developed between the landowning-class and the merchant class. This symbiotic relationship manifested itself in the property relations, the labor relations, and the mechanism of distribution that they both depended on to maintain their economic status. The only way the landowners could obtain manufactured goods was through the merchant class who in turn would sell Haiti's commodities in the international market. The primary role of the merchant class...was to sell the cash crops in the international market and buy manufactured goods for the local economy. Therefore, the landowning class depended on the merchant class for its manufactured goods while, the merchant class could not survive without the landowning class. Even though in some cases there were a few members of the merchant class who had large tracts of land, their main activities were in the import-export sector (pp. 6-7).

Haiti Since 1804

I do not completely share in the urban-rural and peasant-landowner-merchant dichotomy of Pierre-Louis. Such a Marxian position negates the agential initiatives of the Africans, who, had a different structuring structure (form of system and social integration) from the mulatto elites and petit-bourgeois black landowners looking to the West, for equality of opportunity, recognition, and distribution. My phenomenological structural approach is more Weberian than Marxian, in other words, and can be summed up as such. That is, unlike Pierre-louis, I view the peasant class as implementing their form of system and social integration, i.e., lakouism and the Vodou Ethic and the spirit of communism, in the mountains and provinces as a counter-balance/counter-hegemonic force to the emerging

Protestant/Catholic Ethic and spirit of capitalism of the landowning and merchant classes (Mocombe, 2016).

Following the Haitian Revolution, the majority of the Africans, given their refusal to work on plantations or agribusinesses (*corvée system*), migrated to the provinces and the mountains, abodes of formerly established "maroon republics," and established a "counter-plantation system" (Jean Casimir's term) based on husbandry, subsistence agriculture, and *komes*, i.e., the trade and sell of agricultural goods for income to purchase manufactured products and services. The mulatto elites and petit-bourgeois free blacks, a Francophile neocolonial oligarchy, countered this counter-plantation/lakou system through their control of the ports, export trade, and the political apparatuses of the state, which increased their wealth through the taxation of the goods of the African peasants. As Laurent Du Bois (2012) observed of the process, the former enslaved Africans,

> [t]ook over the land they had once worked as slaves, creating small farms where they raised livestock and grew crops to feed themselves and sell in local markets. On these small farms, they did all the things that had been denied to them under slavery: they built families, practiced their religion, and worked for themselves.... Haiti's rural population effectively undid the plantation model. By combining subsistence agriculture with the production of some crops for export, [*komes*,] they created a system that guaranteed them a better life, materially and socially, than that available to most other people of African descent in the Americas throughout the nineteenth and early twentieth centuries. But they did not succeed in establishing that system in the country as a whole. In the face of most Haitians' unwillingness to work the plantations, Haiti's ruling groups retreated but did not surrender. Ceding, to some extent, control of the land, they took charge of the ports and the export trade. And they took control of the state, heavily taxing the goods produced by the small-scale farmers and thereby reinforcing the economic divisions between the haves and the have-nots (pg. 6).

This counter-plantation/lakou system the African majority established against the spirit of capitalism social class language game, i.e., economic gain for its own sake, individualism, personal wealth, private property, labor exploitation, etc., of the *Affranchis*, mulatto elites and petit-bourgeois free blacks, who were interpellated, embourgeoised, and differentiated by the mode of production, ideology, and ideological apparatuses of the West was not a reaction to slavery or the material resource framework of the island as presented by Du Bois and Casimir. Instead, it was and is a product of the enchantment of the world around the ideology (*konesans*) of Vodou and its Ethic of communal living or social collectivism, democracy, individuality, egalitarianism, cosmopolitanism, spirit of social justice, xenophilia, balance, harmony, and gentleness, which united the majority of the African tribes shipped to the island during the slave trade (Mocombe, 2016). What I am calling the Vodou Ethic and the spirit of communism social class language game of the Africans was, and is, reified and recursively reorganized and reproduced via the ideology of Vodou; its modes of production, *komes*, husbandry, and subsistence agricultural; and ideological apparatuses, lakous or *lakou yo* in Kreyol (*yo* in Kreyol is used to pluralize terms and concepts), *lwa yo*, *ounfo* (temples) peristyles, *sosyete sekré* (secret societies), *vévés*, herbal medicine, proverbs, songs, dances, musical instruments, Vodou magic and rituals, and ancestor worship (Mocombe, 2016). Haiti, since 1804, has been marked by this struggle between agents of these two forms of system and social integration, the Protestant/Catholic Ethic and the spirit of capitalism and the Vodou Ethic and the spirit of communism, with the merchant and landowning classes (agents of the former) constantly seeking to supplant the Vodou Ethic and spirit of communism of the African majority via what Karl Polanyi calls the fictitious commodities (land, labor, and money) of capitalism: the commodification of the land of the island, the labor of the African masses, and money, which ties Haiti to the global Protestant capitalist world-system of the Europeans and Americans.

The Vodou Ethic and the Spirit of Communism

Two structuring structures (system/social integration) emerged in Haiti prior to, during, and following the Revolution, the former, the Catholic/Protestant Ethic and the spirit of capitalism social class language game, in the urban centers, internalized and recursively organized and reproduced by the Affranchis. The latter, the Vodou Ethic and the spirit of communism social class language game, in the maroon republics of the provinces and mountains. That is, the constitution of Haitian society in the provinces and mountains is the by-product of the structuralizing and differentiating effects of the Vodou ethic and the spirit of communism— via subsistence agricultural mode of production, husbandry, commerce (*komes*); the Kreyol language; Vodou ideology (*konesans*); and its ideological apparatuses, i.e., Lakous (Vodou family compounds), peristyles (Vodou temples), communal living (communism), *lwa yo*, herbal medicine, healers, songs, dance, etc., initially—under the leadership of religious African men and women, *oungan yo* (priests), *Bokor yo* (sorcerers), *gangan yo/dokté fey* (healers), and *Manbo yo* (priestesses), of Bois Caiman, "maroon republics," who institutionalized it both as a form of system and social integration. They rejected the class division and social relations of production of the Catholic feudal and Protestant capitalist orders established by the French, Americans, and the *Affranchis* on the island because of its discriminatory effects. In its place, *Oungan yo* (priests), *Bokor yo* (sorcerers), *Manbo yo* (priestesses), *gangan yo* (healers), and *granmoun yo* (elders) recursively reorganized and reproduced their linguistic systems, Vodou ideology, its ideological apparatuses, mode of production, and communicative discourse in a national position of their own in order to interpellate and socialize or ounganified/manboified the masses as agents/subjects of the Vodou Ethic and the spirit of communism worldview in the material world against the Catholic/Protestant bourgeois liberalism of the *Affranchis* and their European counterparts.

As previously observed, I am not suggesting that the Africans who met at Bois Caiman syncretized their African Vodou practical consciousness with that of the Europeans, and the ambiguity, hybridity, and liminality of that syncretism provided them the space to speak as subalterns. This latter perspective is the position of the Affranchis, contemporarily, who, ambivalently, seek to creolize, hybridize, etc., the African worldview not as a form of system/social integration but as a commodity form to generate economic gain and equality of opportunity, recognition, and distribution with whites within the capitalist world-system under American hegemony. Conversely, what I am suggesting is that at Bois Caiman, the representatives of the African "maroon republics" rejected the European worldview or social class language game and their leadership or power elites, *oungan yo, manbo yo, bokor yo, gangan yo*, and *granmoun yo* (elders), syncretized their African worldviews with native Taino traditions, which paralleled the Congo African traditions. They reified and sought to institutionalize it in the material world via the language of Kreyol; the ideology and ethic (*konesans*) of Vodou; its ideological apparatuses, Lakous, peristyles, herbal medicine, *lwa yo*, songs, dance, musical instruments, magic and rituals, and proverbs, against that of the European worldview or language game; and modes of production, subsistence agriculture, husbandry, and komes. The European worldview operated within but beneath the *les mysteres* of the Vodou Ethic and spirit of communism social class language game as prescribed by the power elites, *oungan yo, manbo yo, Bokor yo, gangan yo*, and *granmoun yo* (elders) of the communities.

Hence whereas priests, pastors, merchants, educated professionals, and landowners served as the power elites of the Catholic/Protestant Ethic and the spirit of capitalism, *oungan yo, Manbo yo, Bokor yo, gangan yo*, and *granmoun yo* of Haiti served as the power elites of the Vodou Ethic and the spirit of communism social class language game in the maroon republics of the provinces and the mountains. Through the subsistence agricultural mode of production, husbandry, and commerce (*komes*); the Kreyol language; the ideology of Vodou; and the ideological apparatuses of the Lakous (village and family compounds) as its form of system integration, peristyles (Vodou temples), herbal medicine, Vodou ceremonies, magic and rituals, secret societies, zombification, etc., they recursively (re)organized and reproduced Haitian society in the provinces and mountains around the African and Taino practical consciousness or language game of Vodou and communal living, i.e., the Vodou Ethic and the spirit of communism and the lakou system. This latter worldview and its parishes or regions of influence was juxtaposed against the French language, liberal bourgeois ideology, and ideological apparatuses (Catholic church, so-called modern medicine, Haitian police force) of the Haitian state under the *Affranchis* and merchant classes, the comprador bourgeoisie of Haiti, which exploited and marginalized the majority of the Haitian masses as a peasant and underclass, in order to achieve equality of opportunity, recognition, and distribution with whites (in their factories, agribusinesses, and tourism) within the global capitalist world-system. It is incorrect to assume because in many instances the Africans used images of Catholic saints to represent the *lwas/lwaes* (*lwa yo* in Kreyol) of Vodou that this was and is a syncretism or hybridization between Vodou and Catholicism (Métraux, 1958; Deren, 1972; Fick, 1990; Desmangles, 1992; Bellegarde-Smith and Michel, 2006). The images were Africanized and incorporated, present-at-hand, into Vodou by oungan yo, manbo yo, gangan yo, and granmoun yo to interpellate and ounganify/manboify the African masses leaving the plantations into the Vodou Ethic and the spirit of communism social class language game (Desmangles, 1992).

Haitians who serve *lwa yo, serviteurs of Vodou* and Haitian Catholics are cognizant of the differences between themselves. For example, the annual July 16th pilgrimage performed by Serviteurs and Catholics to *Saut D'eau/Sodo* (Kreyol form), which is a commune and sacred waterfall located in the central department of Haiti, is a case in point. Both serviteurs and Catholics make the pilgrimage in honor of Erzulie Danthor in Vodou and the Virgin Mary in Catholicism. In many instances the same image represents both entities. But the serviteur will testify to the fact that they are going to serve manbo Erzulie Danthor, recognized as the goddess of the Haitian nation by Vodou serviteurs, and Catholics will tell you they are going to honor the Virgin Mary, who appeared at the site in the nineteenth century.

What was established in Haiti by *oungan yo, manbo yo, bokor yo, gangan yo*, and *granmoun yo* prior to, during, and following the Revolution was the Vodou Ethic and the spirit of communism language game as the supreme mystery system, which governs the universe and all social relations, including the practices of the whites which operated beneath, but within the mystery system of Vodou, which they rationalized as the nature of reality as such against the Catholic/Protestant Ethic and the spirit of capitalism of the whites and *Affranchis*. The latter, like their white counterparts before them, attempted (through their anti-superstitious campaigns), with the aid of the French clergy, Protestant Churches, and American occupying forces, to marginalize and eradicate (*dechoukaj*) the Vodou Ethic and the spirit of communism in an effort to constitute the Haitian nation-state as a so-called black Republic within the global capitalist world-system (Métraux, 1958; Deren, 1972; Fick, 1990; Desmangles, 1992; Bellegarde-Smith and Michel, 2006; Du Bois, 2004, 2012; Ramsey, 2014). However, thus far they have failed. Instead, as their economic policies, adopted from their former colonizers, forced many Africans off of their lands into the cities where they recursively reorganized and reproduced the Vodou Ethic and the spirit of communism in the urban slums, the Affranchis had no choice but to co-opt and incorporate it into their nation-building efforts as a commodity form to entertain tourists as opposed to a form of system and social integration.

Hence, the argument here is that the African metaphysical system of Vodou gave rise to its epistemology, Haitian/Vilokan Idealism, which in-turn gave rise to the form of system and social integration, The Vodou Ethic and the spirit of communism and lakouism, which their leadership or power elites utilized to interpellate and socialize human actors.

Vodou Metaphysics

Like the Europeans who migrated out of Africa and experienced, ready-to-hand, a brutal existence in the barren environment of Europe, where they constituted and reified, unready-to-hand and present-at-hand, an overarching worldview via the Protestant Ethic and the spirit of capitalism that juxtaposed the world as an object that stands against their subjective existence, which it threatened. Africans, prior to their enslavement, also reified, present-at-hand, a worldview based on their initial ready-to-hand experiences of the earth. However, unlike the Europeans, the Africans encountered a bountiful environment that provided everything they needed for their physical survival in the material world. Be that as it may, they reified and constituted their being-in-the-world under an overarching worldview/language game, the Vodou Ethic and the spirit of communism social class language game, which emphasized their existence as sacred, communal, and an extension or manifestation of Bon-dye, i.e., the world-spirit, which is everywhere and in everything. The earth, which is a manifestation of Bon-dye, and its tilling and cultivation, through agricultural production, became a means of uniting with the spiritual world, which is good (*Bon-dye Bon*).

As such, for the Africans, Vodou/Vilokan became a monotheistic religion in which the one God, *Bon-dye*, or *Gran-Mèt* (I am using the language of Haitian/African Vodou as opposed to switching back and forth to different African tribal nomenclatures for the name of God), the primeval pan-psychic field, is an energy force that gave rise to a sacred, cosmic, and geometrical world out of itself. Everything that is the world, universe, galaxies, animate and inanimate objects, etc. are a manifestation of *Bon-dye*, and are sacred. Thus, unlike the jealous and barbaric God of Judaism, Christianity, and Islam, which stands outside of spacetime and makes human beings, the fallen, the superior creation of its design, i.e., the earth, which is to be exploited and dominated for human happiness and wealth. The God of Vodou has no such place for the human being. *Bon-dye* is spacetime, and the human being is no different from any other creation that is a part of this being. The aim of the human individual is to maintain balance, harmony, and perfection between nature/God, the geometric laws of creation, the cosmic forces (which aided Bon-dye in creating the multiverse), the community, and the individual.

Out of Bon-dye, the geometric laws of creation and the cosmic forces (lwa Legba, Gede, Zaka, Damballah, and Ezili) were created to assist Bon-dye in creating the multiverse and habitable worlds. According to Vodou mythology, one of Bondye's first creations when he fashioned the world was the sun (identified with the lwa Legba in Haitian Vodou metaphysics). Without its existence, lwa yo, human beings, and all the multiplicity of things could not exist. All derive from this primordial light. In Vodou, the sun with which Legba is identified is a regenerative life-force whose rays cause the vegetation to grow and ensure the maturation and sustenance of human life. Legba is the patron of the universe, the link between the Godhead and the universe, the umbilical cord that connects the universe to its origin. Bondye fashioned the universe; Legba has nurtured it, has fostered its growth, and has sustained it. Legba is also said to be androgynous; hence, his vévé contains the symbol of his sexual completeness, and he is invoked in matters related to sex. He is the cosmic phallus. Both as phallus and as umbilical cord, Legba is the guarantor of the continuity of human generations. Just as Legba initiates time, so Gede ends time, for he is the master of Ginen who rules over death. In a sense, Gede is Legba's opponent, for whereas Legba as the sun is omnipresent during the day, Gede is lord of the night and is symbolized by the moon. Whatever, Legba conceives, Gede aborts; and whatever Legba sustains Gede destroys, for he is the lord of death, the master of destruction of things. Although these two divine forces appear to have opposite functions, and indeed are inversions of each other, they nevertheless are similar in many ways, for both participate in the creative forces at opposite ends of the spectrum of life. Damballah, the gentle snake of the primal seas is identified with eternal motion in the universe. This motion is characterized by the passage of all physical phenomena from birth to decay, and produces the physical displacement of objects in space and in time, manifests itself in the incessant motion of the waves of the ocean, the waters of springs and rivers, ensures the alternation of day and night, and impels the cyclical motion of the astral bodies. In short, Damballah is a living quality expressed in all dynamic motion in the cosmos, in all things that are flexible, sinuous, and moist, in all things that fold, and unfold, coil and recoil. In humans, this energy-force is the giver of children. It is identified not only with the eternal motion of human bodies but also with motion as seen in the cycle of life and death and in the passing of human generations. If motion is ensured by Damballah, and if, as generating principle, the phallus is symbolized by Legba and Gede, Ezili represents the cosmic womb in which divinity and humanity are conceived. She is the symbol of fecundity, the mother of the world who participates with the masculine forces in the creation and maintenance of the universe. As mother, Ezili/Erzulie cooperates with the sun lwa Legba, who ensures the florescence and nurture of all living things. When she cooperates with Gede, she symbolizes Ginen's cosmic womb from which the released ancestral gwo-bon-anjs are reclaimed. In combination with Damballah, Ezili guarantees the flow of human generations. Vodou mythology conceives her as the mother of the lwas and of humanity. She is believed to have given birth to the first human beings after Bondye created the world, and since that time her powers of provision have continued to grant children to the human community, a community reliant on Gede's cousin, Zaka, the cosmic lord of agriculture, who is docile, gentle, and kind (Desmangles, 1992, pgs. 108-132).

Ideologically in Vodou, therefore, as in all other West African and Native American beliefs, the human being and all that is the universe is a manifestation of *Bon-dye*. Within this Spinozaian pantheism, balance, harmony, perfection, and subsistence living with this Being as revealed in nature and it's tilling, cultivation, and husbandry is the *modus operandi* for human existence. This one good God is an energy force that manifests itself in the human plane of existence via the ancestors and four hundred and one *lwa yo* (concepts, cosmic forces, and animistic spirits materialized), which humans can access as a material energy force and concepts to assist them in being-in-the-world in order to maintain the aforementioned balance, harmony, perfection, and subsistence living of Bondye. Hence, like the God of Judaism, the Good God, *Bon-dye Bon*, of Vodou is active in history and in current political events, via ancestors, *lwa yo*, and humans, rather than in the primordial sacred time of myth. Unlike the God of Judaism, however, in Vodou human beings are not distinct, fallen, from that great energy force due to sin and must, therefore, seek to reunite with it by exercising good moral conduct on earth. In the pantheistic worldview of Vodou, the human being, like all other beings, whether sentient or not, are a manifestation of the energy force of *Bon-dye*. In other words, the human being is a spirit or energy force living in a material body or physical temple. We are constituted energy, which is recycled or reincarnated sixteen times, eight times as a male and eight times as a female, on the planet earth in order to achieve perfection (Beauvoir, 2006). There is no moral right or wrong in Vodou. "Followers define moral principles for themselves and are guided by life's lessons, the wisdom of ancestors, and communication with spirits" (Michel, 2006, pg. 34). The aim is the manifestation of the power of Bon-dye amongst the plane of human existence. As such, the energy, which constitutes the human being, is not punished for acts done in the material world through the descent into animal embodiment as highlighted in the reincarnation logic of Buddhism and Jainism. The emphasis in Vodou is on experiencing the lived-world, subsistence living, and perfection. The closer the human being gets to their sixteenth experiences on earth and perfection, the wiser and less materialist they are (which is different from the Protestant ethic which emphasizes material wealth as a sign of god's grace and predestination). At the end of their sixteenth life cycles the energy that constitutes the human being is reabsorbed with the original energy force, *Bon-dye*, the primeval pan-psychic field, which manifested them as life.

In sum, Vodou is a manifestation of the Egyptian/Ethiopian mystery system, *les mystere*. "The entire hieroglyphic system of Egypt is based upon the symbolic connection which exists between the various beings [of the world] and the cosmic forces, between the beings and the *lois* [(lwa in Kreyol)] (laws of creation)" (Rigaud, 1985, pg. 11). The Vodou belief system posits that *Bon-dye*, God, is the architect of the universe, which was created via geometric laws of creation and cosmic forces. The "laws of creation" create the cosmic forces and other *lwa yo* in visible manifestations such as the planets, suns, plants, animals, and human beings within geometric spacetime. The Vodou rites are derived from the cosmic forces of the planets and suns created by the geometric laws of creation, which are recreated in the phenomenal world of human action via the ideological apparatuses, i.e., peristyles, dances, songs, musical instruments, magic and rituals, vévés, alters, etc., of human beings. From the cosmic forces of the planets and suns, plants, animals, and human beings were created within geometric spacetime. So out of the perfect world of Vilokan/Vodou, a parallel mirrored world was created where embodied humans act so as to achieve balance and harmony between the Vilokanic world and the phenomenal mirrored one. Nature, the ideological apparatuses, i.e., symbols, musical instruments, lakous, peristyles, and ounfo of human beings, and their practical consciousness must correspond to these geometric laws of creation and the cosmic forces, which stems from the noumenal world of Vilokan/Vodou.

As such, human beings recreate this creation via the lakous, ounfo, peristyles, vévés, magic and rituals, personal alters (*pe*) to the cosmic forces and ancestors, agricultural production, husbandry, and komes, which in total capture that creation and how humans are to live within it. As Gerdés Fleurant (2006) highlights,

> [t]he primary unit of Vodun social organization is the *lakou* (compound), and extended family and socioeconomic system whose center is the *ounfo* (temple), to which is attached the *peristyle* (the public dancing space). Vodun, a danced religion, acknowledges the unity of the universe in the continuity of Bondye, or God; the Lwa, or mediating spiritual entities; humans, animals; plants; and minerals. Vodun is also a family religion in the sense that its teachings, belief systems, and rituals are transmitted mainly through the structure of the family. It has a sacerdotal hierarchy comprised of the *oungan* (male) and the *manbo* (female) and their assistants, the *laplas* (sword bearer), *ounsi kanzo* (spouses of the spirits), *oungenikon* (chorus leader), and *ountó* (drummers). In the absence of priests, the head of the family, much like a traditional paterfamilias, conducts the service. Most ceremonies take place in the *peristyle*, whose *potomitan* (center post) is believed to incarnate ancestral and spiritual forces of family and community. The people dance around the *potomitan*, which is the point of genesis of essential segments of the ritual process (pgs. 46-47).

The center post or *potomitan* of the peristyle is the solar support of the community which unites lwa yo, the earth, nature, sun, humans, plants, animals, etc. within one geometric spacetime:

> the peristyle forms geometrically the following 1) the mitan, or center— the non-dimensional point; 2) the rectangle, or lengthened square; 3) the circle; 4) the triangle; 5) the straight, horizontal line; 6) the spiral; 7) the

curved, horizontal line; 8) the round, vertical line; 9) the square, vertical line; 10) the perfect square; 11) the cross, or intersecting straight lines; 12) the equilateral and the isosceles triangle, formed by the beams which secure the post to the roof (Rigaud, 1985, pg. 17).

As Leslie G. Desmangles further highlights,

> The principle of inversion and retrogression is fundamental to Vodou theology as well as to its rituals.... In Vodou the relationship between the cosmic mirror and the profane reality that it represents takes the cosmographic form of the cross. In the cross, Vodouisants see not only the earth's surface as comprehended by the four cardinal points of the universe, but also the intersection of the two world, the profane world as symbolized by the horizontal line, and Vilokan as represented by the vertical line.... The foot of this vertical line "plunges into the waters of the abyss" to the cosmic mirror where the lwas reside; there, in this sacred subtelluric city, is Africa (or Vilokan), the mythical home of Vodouisants, the place of the lwas' origin, and Ginen, the abode of the living dead.... The point at which the two lines intersect is the pivotal "zero-point" [(non-dimensional point)] in the crossing of the two worlds. It is a point of contact at which profane existence, including time, stops, and sacred beings from Vilokan invade the peristil through the body of their possessed devotees (pgs. 104-105).

As such the peristyle is a mirror reflection and ideological constitution of the universe and all of its forces from the moment of creation to the presence:

> The four poles sustaining the structure symbolize mythologically the four cardinal points of the universe, covered by an overarching roof that represents the cosmic vault above the earth. Like the horizontal lines of the cross, the floor of the peristil symbolizes the profane world, while the vertical pole (potomitan) in the center of the peristil represents the axis mundi, the avenue of communication between the two worlds. Although the downward reach of the potomitan appears to be limited by the peristil's floor, mythologically its foot is conceived to plunge into Vilokan, the cosmic mirror. The point at which the potomitan enters the peristil's floor symbolizes the zero-point. During the ceremonies, the potomitan becomes charged with or "polluted" by the power of the lwas. Hence, before tracing the geometrical symbols of the lwas (vévés), the oungan or mambo may touch the pole, a ritual act that empowers him or her to summon the lwas into the peristil. Thereafter, like the potomitan, the oungan's (or mambo's) body becomes in itself the source of power, a repetition of the microcosmic symbol, a moving embodiment of the vertical axis around which the universe revolves (Desmangles, 1992, pg. 105).

Within the knowledge and functions of the cosmic forces and the geometric laws of creation *oungan yo, manbo yo, bokor yo,* and *gangan yo/dokté féy,* can access *lwa yo* (animistic and cosmic spirits) for wealth, healing, luck, etc. in a community based on living in harmony with nature and its laws and products of creation, which is expressed through music, dance, husbandry, tilling and cultivating the land (for medicinal and agricultural purposes), and *komes* for human sustenance and well-being. The rites and ceremonies of Vodou, "which can be seen as the reliving of the first act of creation when Bondye fashioned the world," ensure the delicate balance and harmony between Bon-dye, the cosmic forces, the geometric laws of creation, and human actions (Desmangles, 1992, pg., 152). Within this metaphysical social system, the aim of individual existence is not economic gain as a sign of God's grace and predestination, but balance, harmony, perfection, and subsistence living.

From Egypt/Ethiopia this Worldview would spread throughout the continent and the world as human beings migrated out of Africa ((Métraux, 1958; Deren, 1972; Rigaud, 1985; Diop, 1981, 1988, 1989; Desmangles, 1992; Bellegarde-Smith and Michel, 2006). As such, Vodou united all of the African tribes/nations taken to the Americas, and with their encounter with the Amerindians who emigrated out of Africa tens of thousands of years prior to the slave trade the Africans recognized their mystery system (Diop, 1988, 1989; Karenga, 1993; Van Sertima, (1976 [2003]). The power elites of the different tribes/nations (Ibo, Yoruba, Congo, Nago, Mandingo, Arada, etc.) brought to Haiti during the slave trade would, present-at-hand, assemble and unite *lwa yo* into various *nanchon* (nations) grouped into two dominant *nanchon*/nations, *Rada* and *Petwo.*

Haitian Epistemology

Normally referred to as "animism," "fetishism," "paganism," "heathenism," and "black magic" in the Western academic literature, Vodou (spelled Vodun, Voodoo, Vodu, Vaudou, or Vodoun) is the oldest monotheistic religion in the world. Commonly interpreted as "Spirits" or "introspection into the unknown," Vodou is the structuring structure (metaphysics) of the Fon people of Dahomey and other tribes of the continent who would arrive on the island of Haiti/Ayiti as named by the Taino natives (Métraux, 1958; Deren, 1972; Rigaud, 1985; Desmangles, 1992; Bellegarde-Smith and Michel, 2006). Unlike German Idealism whose intellectual development from Kant to Schopenhauer, Hegel, Marx, Nietzsche, Husserl, Heidegger, and the Frankfurt school produced the dialectic, Marxist materialism, Nietzschean antidialectics, phenomenology, and deontological ethics. Haitian Vodou, epistemologically, i.e., Haitian/Vilokan Idealism, produces a hermeneutical phenomenology, materialism, and an antidialectical process to history enframed by a reciprocal justice as its normative ethics, which is constantly being invoked by individual social actors to reconcile the noumenal (sacred—ideational) and phenomenal (profane—material) subjective world in order to maintain balance and harmony between the two so that the human actor can live freely and happy with all of being without distinctions or masters. As such, Haitian epistemology as a form of transcendental realism and idealism is phenomenological, in the Heideggerian sense (i.e., hermeneutical), material in the Marxian sense, and antidialectical. It refutes Hegel's claims for the importance of historical formations and other people to the development of self-consciousness. Instead, Haitian/Vilokan idealism, phenomenologically, emphasizes the things in the consciousness (lwa or concepts, ideas, ideals) of the individual as they stem from the noumenal/Vilokan world, and get interpreted according to their level of learning, development, capacity for knowledge, and modality, i.e., the way they know more profoundly—kinesthetically, visually, etc., as they antidialectically seek to reproduce them in the phenomenal world as their practical consciousness against other interpretive formations of these same concepts in the material world.

Haitian Epistemology, i.e., Haitian/Vilokan Idealism

The Haitian epistemological position that would emerge out of the metaphysical worldview, Vodou, of the African people of Haiti and their form of system and social integration it would produce is a strong form of Kantian transcendental idealism and realism, which would be institutionalized throughout the provinces and mountains of the island (Desmangles, 1992; Author, 2016). This position suggests that Haitian epistemology is not a synthesis between modernity and Vodou magic and spiritualism as proposed by many scholars such as Susan Buck-Morss (2009), for example. On the contrary, my argument is that the process of demystification and rationalization of Vodou metaphysics, and only Vodou metaphysics, reveals an epistemological position, Haitian/Vilokan Idealism, which parallels Kantian transcendental idealism coupled with a transcendental realism found in Haitian Vodou with its emphasis on the knowability of the noumenal world via trances, revelations, and extrasensory perceptions.

Kantian transcendental idealism "attempts to combine empirical realism, preserving the ordinary independence and reality of objects of the world, with transcendental idealism, which allows that in some sense the objects have their ordinary properties (their causal powers, and their spatial and temporal position) only because our minds are so structured that these are the categories we impose upon the manifold of experience" (Blackburn, 2008, pg. 356). Haitian epistemological transcendental idealism, Haitian Idealism or Vilokan Idealism, is a form of transcendental idealism in the Kantian sense in that it attempts to synthesize empiricism, idealism (rationalism), and realism via synthetic a priori concepts/ideals the Haitians believe can be applied not only to the phenomenal but also the noumenal (Vilokanic) world in order to ascertain the latter's transcendentally real absolute knowledges they call, *lwa*, gods/goddesses (401 concepts, ideas, and ideals represented as gods/goddesses), of Vilokan/Vodou. So like Kant, Haitian epistemological transcendental idealism, holds on to analytic truths, truths of reasons or definitions, as outlined in their proverbs (*pwoveb*); a posteriori truth, truths of experience or experiments, also embedded in their proverbs, geometry (*veves*), rituals, magic, sorcery, and herbal medicine; and synthetic a priori concepts (categories in Kantian epistemology supplemented with trances, dream-states, extrasensory perceptions), truths stemming from the form of the understanding and sensibility of the mind and apparatuses of experience embedded not only in their proverbs and Vodou rituals, beliefs, and magic, but also their understanding of trances, dream-states, and extrasensory perceptions as categories of the mind applicable to the noumenal or Vilokanic realm where transcendental real concepts, lwa yo, exist (as Platonic forms) which they must ascertain in order to live life happily in the phenomenal world without masters or owners of production. The latter (trances, dream-states, and extrasensory perceptions) they believe, in other words, can be applied to the noumenal or Vilokanic world in order to know gods/goddesses, *lwa yo*, which are immutable/absolute concepts, ideas, and ideals God has created and imposed upon and in the material world, from the mirrored world of the earth (Vilokan), which the people, who embody these concepts, ideas, and ideals, should utilize to recursively reorganize and reproduce their being-in-and-as-the-world in order to achieve perfection over sixteen life cycles (Desmangles, 1992; Beauvoir, 2006; Author, 2016). Hence, unlike Kantian transcendental idealism, which removes God out of the equation via the categories, which imposes the order we see in the phenomenal world, Haitian epistemological transcendental idealism and realism, Haitian/Vilokan Idealism, holds on to the concept of God, supernatural, and the paranormal to continue to make sense of the plural tensions between the natural (material) world, i.e., the world of phenomenon, and the world as such, ideational, noumena, i.e., the supernatural and paranormal world, transcendental real world, which is knowable as truth-claims, knowledge, and beliefs, through dreams, divinations, revelations, experience, reason and rationality, and the synthetic a priori, for pure (development of science, i.e., herbal medicine, etc.) and practical reason (i.e., morals and values). Thus Haitian/Vilokan Idealism, unlike Kantian Transcendental Idealism, implies that the objects, concepts, ideals, ideas, etc., of the (ideational) noumenal world are transcendentally real and the form of sensibilities and understandings, which include dream states, trances, and extrasensory perceptions are other categories of the understanding, which can be applied beyond the phenomenal world, where the objects are really subjective (interpretive) ideas, in order to ascertain the nature of the absolute concepts of the Vilokanic/noumenal world in order to achieve balance and harmony with it in the phenomenal.

Within this pantheistic (Spinozaian) conception of the multiverse and material world, knowledge, truth-claims, and beliefs arise from transcendentally real ideational concepts (lwa yo) of bondye/God as embedded in the earth's mirrored world (Vilokan) and gets deposited in our *nanm* (souls) intuitively, in dreams, revelations, divinations, extrasensory perceptions, reason, rituals, and or experiences which in turn constitutes and structures the form of the understanding of our minds and bodies (senses) so that we can experience the material world according to our interpretations of these concepts in consciousness and developmental track over sixteen reincarnated life cycles (Beauvoir, 2006; Mocombe, 2016). The human being recursively (re) organize and reproduce these (Platonic) transcendentally real ideational concepts as their practical consciousness in the phenomenal material world not always in its absolute form as defined noumenally (the sacred mirrored world of Vilokan), but according to their level of learning, development, capacity for knowledge, and modality, i.e., the way they know more profoundly—kinesthetically, visually, etc.

As defined, Haitian epistemology is an epistemological transcendental idealism and realism, Haitian Idealism or Vilokan Idealism, which posits that both phenomena (the profane world) and noumena (its mirror image where wisdom, ideals, and ancestors reside) are knowable through experience and the form of human sensibility and understanding (the categories of Kantian epistemology supplemented with, dreams, divinations, extrasensory perceptions, and trance states), which stems from the energy force of a God, which constitutes our nanm (a material thing), and used to recursively organize and reproduce their being-in-and-as-the-world. Ontologically speaking, within the Haitian metaphysical worldview, Vilokan/Vodou, the world is a unitary (energy) material world created out of Bondye. The world is a creation of a good God, *Bondye Bon*, which created the world and humanity out of itself composed of two intersecting spheres, the profane (the phenomenal world) and sacred (noumenal/Vilokanic, mirrored world of the profane). Embedded in that pantheistic material world are concepts, *lwa yo* in Haitian metaphysics, from the parallel mirrored (Vilokanic) world, that humanity can ascertain via experience and the structure of its being, form of understanding and sensibility (dreams, reason and rationality, extrasensory perceptions), to help make sense of their experience and live in the world, which is Bondye, and therefore sacred, as they (via their nanm) seek perfection and reunification (reintegration) with God, the energy force/source.

That is to say, it, Bondye, provided humanity with objects, concepts, ideas, ideals, and practices, i.e., *lwa yo* of Vodou, proverbs, rituals, dance, geometry, knowledge of herbal medicine, trades, and skills, by which they ought to know, interpret, and make sense of the external (phenomenal profane) world and live in it comfortably. These transcendentally real objects, concepts, ideas, ideals, and practices can either be known through dreams, divinations, experience or rationality, and becomes the structure (once reified and institutionalized as proverbs, husbandry, dance, rituals, institutions, etc.), form of sensibility and understanding, through which humanity come to know, hold beliefs and truth-claims. So Bondye, a powerful energy force that always existed created the world and humanity out of itself using four hundred and one transcendentally real concepts (God and four-hundred lwa), ideas, and ideals (geometric principles, mathematics, etc.). Humanity and the world around it is an aggregation of bondye's material energy, the energy of God, which constitutes its existence. In humanity this existence is composed of three distinct aggregation of energy (*ti bon anj*; *gwo bon anj*; *ko*, the body), all of which are material stuff, which constitute our *nanm* (souls) where personality, truth-claims, knowledge, and beliefs are deposited, via dreams, revelations, extrasensory perceptions, divinations, experience, reason, the energy source of a God as manifested via a lwa, and can be examined and explored as the synthetic a priori of the human agent.

For humanity to constitute its existence and be in the world according to the will of God or Bondye, in other words, transcendentally real concepts stemming from God's will (the mirrored world of the profane, Vilokan) are embedded in the material world, which is God, and can be ascertain and embodied by humanity via their constituted being as a material being with extrasensory perceptions, reason and rationality, and or through experience. As these transcendentally real concepts are ascertain, they are constituted and institutionalized, and passed on through humanity via priests/priestesses and early ancestors who institutionalized (reify)/ institutionalize them in the natural world via religious ceremonies, dance, rituals, herbal medicine, trades, concepts, and proverbs. These trades, ideals, proverbs, and or concepts are truisms, mechanisms to ascertain and constitute knowledge, which although they are deduced from the constituted make-up (i.e., consciousness) of the human being, in Haitian metaphysics they are attributed to God and the ancestors who institutionalized (reified) them in order to be applied in the material world so that their descendants can live freely in the world, satisfy their needs, be happy, and achieve perfection in order to reunite with God after their sixteen life cycles.

So on top of the twelve Kantian schematized categories of the understanding, divided into four groups of three (1. The axioms of intuition, i.e., unity, plurality, and totality; 2. The anticipations of perception, i.e., reality, limitation, and negation; 3. The postulates of empirical thought, i.e., necessary, actual, and possible; 4. The analogies, i.e., substance, cause, and reciprocity), necessary for experience by making objective space and time possible, Vilokanic/Haitian idealism adds dream states, trances, and extrasensory perceptions as a fifth group of three to make known the concepts, lwa, of the Vilokanic world knowable so that human actors can achieve balance between the phenomenal world and the former (Vilokanic/noumenal).

For Kant experience requires both the senses, the a priori forms of sensibility, i.e., space and time, and the understanding, i.e. the twelve categories. A unified consciousness (not a self or the Cartesian "I"), which is a structural feature of experience necessary to provide the unity to our experience, what Kant calls, "the transcendental unity of apperception," rule-governed and connected by the categories, experiences real objects that we perceive and exist independently of our perception of them. Thus, the spatio-temporal objects are necessarily relative to and subject to the a priori forms of experience, i.e., forms of sensibility and the understanding. In this sense, Kant does away with the noumenal world of absolutes, which is unknowable as the independent objects are phenomenal, relative to the a priori forms of experience. Unlike Kant, however, Haitian/Vilokan Idealism posits that the nanm, which provides unity to our experiences is a material thing, a Cartesian material "I" composed of three distinct entities (sometimes more as Haitian metaphysics suggests that a fourth entity, *lwa met tet*, may constitute the nanm of serviteurs in order to guide them in their decision-making) that are also tied to the natural world and can be manipulated in life as well as death. On top of it's a priori forms of sensibility and Kantian categories are dream-states, trances, and extrasensory perceptions, which allows the nanm to have access to the world of

Vilokan/noumenal world where we can perceive the things that are phenomenal, relative to our a priori forms of experience, as they are in-themselves in order to achieve balance between the world as it appears to us and how it ought to be so that we can live abundantly as individual masters of our own destiny.

Hence Haitian epistemological transcendental idealism (Haitian Idealism, Vilokanism, Vodouism, or Vilokan Idealism) and realism is not only natural, but supernatural and paranormal to the extent that it supplements the synthetic a priori concepts Kant attributes to the categories of the mind with divinations, revelations, dream states, and extrasensory perceptions in order to ascertain the absolute (transcendentally real) concepts, ideals, ideas, etc., (lwa) of God as embedded in the noumenal (Vilokanic) world. Moreover, it posits that these absolute *lwa yo*, transcendentally real concepts, ideas, ideals, etc., are part of the noumenal world (sacred world of Vilokan), which is not a plural world as plurality, in keeping with the logic of Arthur Schopenhauer, belongs to the world of phenomenon, and can eventually be known by extrasensory perceptions, human reason, understanding, and experience. However, in the human sphere the world of phenomenon and its plurality is a result of interpretations and the different levels of development (reason, experience, capacity, and modality) of the consciousness of the human subjects (not all humans develop their form of sensibilities and understanding at the same rate or in the same life cycle) where the concepts of lwa yo are embedded and embodied and recursively organized and reproduced as the practical consciousness of the human actor. Albeit humanity is reincarnated until they have ascertained all of the true concepts of the unitary world, which can be done so through experience and a priori, and will seize to exist (will seize to experience reincarnation) once they do so.

Haitian/Vilokan Idealism and Realism as such indicates a condition of transcendentally real absolutes on the one hand as it pertains to the Vilokanic or noumenal world; and relativity in our notions of objects and reality on the other as it pertains to the transcendentally ideal phenomenal world. In terms of the latter, the phenomenal world, in other words, is simply the world of plurality constituted by imperfect beings, anti-dialectically (constantly fighting against the praxis of others for their own understanding and praxis), living through their aggregated material bodies and imperfections according to their interpretations of the concepts and level of learning, development, capacity for knowledge, and modality, i.e., the way they know more profoundly—kinesthetically, visually, etc.

This is why, epistemologically speaking, the phenomenal world in Haiti, resembles an epistemological anarchic world where everyone exists for their own liberty and existence according to their own developmental track, capacities, modalities, belief systems, and methods governed by an eye for an eye normative worldview, which prevents others from encroaching on an individual's (regardless of their level of development) method and right to exist.

The Phenomenology of Haitian/Vilokan Idealism

Hence Haitian/Vilokan Idealism is phenomenological, material, and antidialectical in the sense that the emphasis is on the things (concepts, ideas, ideals) of consciousness as revealed to, and interpreted by, human individuals (via the form of sensibility and understanding) from the noumenal world of Vilokan. These things (concepts, ideas, and ideals) of consciousness they in-turn recursively reorganize and reproduce as their practical consciousness in the material world antidialectically against the interpretive practical consciousnesses of others within a normative ethic of reciprocal justice of the socioeconomic/political structure of the Lakou as organized in a material resource framework. The human actor, in other words, encounter contents in their consciousness, which, with the aid of an elder, priest, or priestess, of a lakou, they must interpret in the material world as their practical consciousness, when things in their lives go awry, in order to have balance within themselves, nature, and their social interactions within the lakou system. The lakou is a community of people and houses organized and gathered around a common yard under the directions of a oungan (Vodou priest), manbo (Vodou priestess), or family elder that promoted and promotes an egalitarian existence rooted in the Vodou religion and ancestor worship, land ownership arrangements, and working the soil. Within the lakou system, each individual or nuclear family owned/own their own land, through which they provided/provide for basic necessities by growing food and raising livestock for their own consumption and for sale in local markets. They also grew and grow export crops, such as coffee, in order to buy imported consumer goods such as clothes and tools. The lakou thus divided power in a way that allowed rural residents to live and work as they wished (through land and garden ownership to provide for their own subsistence), while preventing the consolidation of wealth, and therefore control and inhibitor of equality, in the hands of any one person within the community through a set of customs and secret societies of the Vodou religion that regulate(d) land ownership, land transfers, family relationships, and community affairs. Communal assistance and exchange, via food sharing, harvesting, house building, religious life, and ancestral worship, under the leadership of women also characterized and characterizes lakou life. In essence, the purpose of lakou life is to promote total liberty and equality, via land ownership and self-sufficiency, for all without distinctions and economic differentiation. Hence the lakou system helps to institutionalize the antihumanism that would come to constitute Haitian rural life in that the emphasis is not on promoting the universality of the autonomous rational individual as the purpose of socialization. Instead, the emphasis is on allowing total liberty and equality so that the individual actor can experience Being or existence as they interpret the concepts of the noumenal/Vilokanic world as their practical consciousness. The autonomous rational self is simply one aspect (analytics) of being amongst a plethora of other forms and agential moments by which the individual social actor can choose (based on their analytics in consciousness) to recursively reorganize and reproduce their existence without facing marginalization from their community unless their choice harms other individuals. Hence, like Martin Heidegger's phenomenology, the phenomenology of Haitian/Vilokan Idealism highlights the things of consciousness as they are interpreted by a human actor as their practical consciousness vis-à-vis their analytics, i.e., their conscious awareness or not of these concepts, lwa yo, as they experience being-in-the-world with others who may inhibit their existence.

The Vodou Ideology and the Spirit of Communism

Hence the metaphysics of Vodou gave rise to its epistemology, Haitian/Vilokan idealism, which in-turn gave rise to its form of system and social integration, lakouism and the Vodou Ethic and the spirit of communism, respectively. As Milo Rigaud highlights,

> The Voodoo pantheon of gods is composed of *loas* (gods) that come from all parts of Africa. Tradition has it that the term *vo-du* is drawn from the language of the Fons. Other tribes that contributed Voodoo gods were the Nago people, the Ibos, Congos, Dahomeans, Senegalese, Haoussars, Caplaous, Mandinges, Mondongues, Angolese, Libyans, Ethiopians, and the Malgaches. Moreover, the names of these tribes generally serve to designate separate Voodoo rites themselves. For example, to serve the Mondongue gods, the Mondongue rite is followed, which, although it does not differ basically and fundamentally from the other rites, nevertheless appears superficially different. To serve the Ibo gods, the Ibo rite is celebrated. And this rite too is fundamentally related to the other rites although it may appear different... Each rite has its distinctive characteristics, although all rites generally speaking arise from the same source, have the same origin, and are completely integral (1985, pg. 8).

If we assume the African origins of civilization hypothesis of Cheik Anta Diop (1981, 1988, 1989), Vodou gave rise to all of the other traditional metaphysical systems found among the early inhabitants of this planet, the animism of the native people of the Americas, Hinduism, Shintoism, Santeria, etc., which encountered the earth in bountiful conditions, as well as Judaism (In Vodou, the understanding is that Moses, who would teach the Israelites about Vodou/Judaism, was raised in Egypt as an Egyptian and trained in the Egyptian mystery system by an oungan named Ra-Gu-El Pethro or Jethro. Moses would later bastardize the system giving rise to the perversities of Judaism) (Rigaud, 1985, pg. 14). Whereas slavery, racism, and the colonization of Africa interrupted the enchantment of the world around the Vodou religion and communal way of life among many people of African descent in Africa and the diaspora, the Africans of Haiti given their early freedom from slavery and the fact that the majority of them, almost sixty-seven percent of the population, were directly from Africa when the Haitian Revolution commenced were able to maintain, reorganize, and reproduce, the Vodou way of life, and its ethic, communism/lakouism, in its purest form for system and social integration (Genovese, 1979; Bellegarde-Smith and Michel, 2006; Du Bois, 2004, 2012).

According to Haitian oral history, at Bois Caiman or Bwa Kay-Imam (near the Imam Boukman Dutty's house), the birthplace of the Haitian Revolution in 1791, leaders of the "maroon republics," nineteen African tribes or nations and one tribe of the Taino nation, assembled and organized a Vodou ceremony led by the oungan, Boukman Dutty, manbo Cecile Fatiman, and Edaïse to create one new nation, the Empire of Ayiti, the twenty-first tribe or nation of the ceremony, in the Americas around the Vodou religion, its ethic of egalitarianism, democracy, communal living, and the Kreyol language. As highlighted by Boukman's prayer, the aims were to recursively reorganize and reproduce the Vodou religion and its way of life, practical consciousness, through the new Haitian empire against the European worldview or language game practiced by the Europeans and the *Affranchis*:

Bon Dje ki fè la tè. Ki fè soley ki klere nou enro. Bon Dje ki soulve lanmè. Ki fè gronde loray. Bon Dje nou ki gen zorey pou tande. Ou ki kache nan niaj. Kap gade nou kote ou ye la. Ou we tout sa blan fè nou sibi. Dje blan yo mande krim. Bon Dje ki nan nou an vle byen fè. Bon Dje nou an ki si bon, ki si jis, li ordone vanjans. Se li kap kondui branou pou nou ranpote la viktwa. Se li kap ba nou asistans. Nou tout fet pou nou jete potre dje Blan yo ki swaf dlo lan zye. Koute vwa la libète k ap chante lan kè nou.

The god who created the sun which gives us light, who rouses the waves and rules the storm, though hidden in the clouds, he watches us. He sees all that the white man does. The god of the white man inspires him with crime, but our god calls upon us to do good works. Our god who is good to us orders us to revenge our wrongs. He will direct our arms and aid us. Throw away the symbol of the god of the whites who has so often caused us to weep, and listen to the voice of liberty, which speaks in the hearts of us all.

Although the usurpation of the Revolution by the Affranchis leadership, curtailed the nationalization of Vodou via the nation-state of Haiti, the power elites of the Vodou worldview were able to institutionalize and constitute it in the provinces and mountains of the island as the form of social/system integration for the masses.

Within the Vodou worldview or language game and its communal organizations and practices, serviteurs, practitioners of Vodou, as previously highlighted, believe *Bon-dye*, the primeval pan-psychic field, created the multiverse and all of its objects out of itself. As such, the earth, its objects, and all life on it are a manifestation of *Bon-dye* through our *nanm* (soul), and as such are sacred. Bon-dye manifests itself in the material and spiritual, or energy world, through the spiritual and conceptual essences of the four hundred and one *lwa yo* and deceased ancestors (*lwa rasin* or *lwa eritaj*) (ancestor worship is huge in Haiti), who manifest themselves to the living in dreams, divinations, and bodily possessions so that they can maintain balance and harmony within the material world, which is the manifestation of Bon-dye. *Lwa yo*, in essence, are manifestations of Bon-dye who exist, without a material body, in a different dimension of spacetime from living human beings as energy. Because the energy force of Bon-dye is so vast and powerful, it manifests itself in the material world through the deceased ancestors and *Lwa yo*, who represent cosmic forces, concepts, values, and personalities for us to model in the material world in order to achieve balance, harmony, subsistence living, and perfection as we experience being-in-the-world. Although they do not possess corporeal bodies, *lwa yo* nonetheless have personalities and enjoy corporeal things such as drinking, eating, smoking, dancing, and talking.

Lwa yo, essentially, are cosmic forces, the spirits of the ancestors, and the major forces or concepts of the universe, i.e., beauty, good, evil, health, reproduction, death, and other aspects of daily life. Each *Lwa* is represented by a hieroglyphic symbol, a hieroglyphic *vévé*, and are predominantly divided into two nations or families, *Rada* and *Petwo Lwa yo*, representing *lwa yo* of the twenty-one nations of Bois Caiman. The

Rada *Lwa yo* are relatively peaceful, happy spirits, cosmic forces, and concepts, beauty, reproduction, etc., of daily life served by *oungan yo* and *manbo yo*. *Petwo Lwa yo* represent malevolent spirits of animals and other forces of nature, and are usually served by members, Bókós/Bokors, of secret societies to gain wealth, political power, do harm, kill, or cripple. Bokors (Bokor yo, plural form in Kreyol) are also the police force of the society or village life, and mitigate the harshest punishment, zombification, in Vodou.

The Rada traditions constitute ninety-five percent of Vodou practices, and Petwo five percent. Notwithstanding its sacerdotal hierarchy, Vodou is very democratic. Once initiated, everyone establishes their lakous and peristyles and serves their *lwa* or *lwa yo* according to the will and desires of *lwa yo* (this is similar to the Protestant faith, where pastors establish their own churches based on their readings and interpretations of the bible). However, recently, in January, 2008, all the lakous and peristyles organized themselves under one political organization *Konfederasyon Nasyonal Vodou Ayisyen* (KNVA) led by an *ATI-oungan* of Vodou.

Whereas in the Petwo tradition the human individual seeks assistance from *lwa yo* through a bokor for wealth, power, i.e., *pwen*, to do harm to someone, vindicate oneself, revenge, etc., in the Rada tradition, that is not normally the case. In the Rada tradition, the human individual does not seek *lwa yo*. (Albeit, they can seek certain *Lwa* to assist them in acquiring wealth, love, health, political power, revenge, etc. But this is done through Bokors (sorcerers), initiates of secret societies in Vodou). Each person has a spiritual court, meaning that particular spirits show interest in them and become intertwined in their lives. Everyone's spiritual court is different and people must learn to recognize their spirits so they can effectively work with them. Since it can be difficult to decipher exactly what a spirit wants and which spirit is affecting a person's life, religious professionals or the power elites of Vodou, i.e., *oungan yo, Manbo yo, Bokor yo, gangan yo,* and *granmoun yo* (elders) in the family are consulted to decipher the spiritual court of an individual and ensure that their life is being led in harmony with the desires and wills of *lwa yo* who constitute their spiritual court. Once an individual's spiritual court is determined through a card reading or Vodou ceremony, many people use this knowledge to create a home altar to strengthen their relationship between themselves and *lwa yo* of their spiritual court. For individuals who are called further, they may choose to have a head washing (*lave tét*), which connects them permanently to their *mét tét* (ruler of the head) who is the spirit most closely aligned with them. The next step, if one chooses, would be to initiate into the religion into one of three stages: *ounsi* (congregation member), *manbo* or *oungan* (priestess or priest), and *manbo asogwe* or *oungan asogwe* (high priestess or high priest). These levels of initiation (*kanzo*) are not decided by the individual but by the spirits and revealed through dreams, card readings, and other forms of communication. This is a permanent life-time commitment and each level requires different duties to spirit and community. Contact provides a way to mitigate relationships with *lwa yo* and ancestors who otherwise could impact lives without individuals having the ability to negotiate their situation. *Lwa yo* and ancestors have individual personalities and preconceived notions about proper behaviors that can cause them to help or hinder people as they see fit. Engaging with *lwa yo* allow humans to gain their aid and take control over their own luck. However, this usually requires a pledge of either a direct exchange of offerings for services or a lifelong commitment to serve and honor. Failure to uphold a person's end of the deal or to recognize when a spirit is making a demand can result in punishment that affects luck, health, personal relationships, and financial situations. *Lwa yo* also become part of an extended spiritual/material family, and as such individuals love them and provide offerings because they enjoy making the Lwa yo and ancestors happy. Home altars, as in Hinduism, dedicate a space to honoring and feeding *lwa yo* and ancestors, dreams bring messages, and daily experiences reinforce their presence. Hence humans and spirit beings exist in a symbiotic relationship on earth.

Within this symbiotic relationship on earth, the Petwo tradition dialectically balances and harmonizes nature, the community, and the individual by counterbalancing the relatively peaceful and happy spirits or concepts of the Rada traditions with the malevolent forces and concepts of nature. In the Petwo tradition, the individual seeks the aid of a Bokor for wealth, political power, protection, or to do harm to an adversary through the aid of the malevolent forces or concepts, i.e., revenge, greed, hate, violence, etc., of nature. Whereas the killing, harming, etc. of an individual is not allowed in the Rada tradition, they are sanctioned in the Petwo tradition. The Petwo tradition houses both the secret societies of Vodou, which are in place to protect the society from those who violate the norms of the *ounfo*, and the sorcerers, bokors, who use their knowledge of *les mystere* to kill, cripple, or do harm (financially, socially, politically, etc.) to an individual. According to Max Beauvoir (2006), the late *ATI-oungan* of Haitian Vodou, the Bokors stem from the Taino tradition, which paralleled the Congo elements of the Africans, of the island, and when serving in the capacity as the protector of social norms and social relations, practitioners, Bokors, of the Petwo tradition must obtain the consent of leaders, *oungan yo avek manbo yo*, of the Rada tradition, of the *ounfo*, which is not the case when serving as sorcerers to benefit themselves or those seeking power, wealth, or to do harm to an adversary. In the former instance, zombification is the ultimate punishment allowed by *oungan yo avek manbo yo* to be meted out by a bokor for violation of social norms and relations, which are deemed sacred. In the latter instance anything and everything goes, i.e., financial, social, and political ruin, zombification, or death. The Petwo tradition is consider the black magic of Vodou, and it is this tradition and its practice of zombification that is and has been portrayed by Hollywood and Wade Davis's (1985) work, *The Serpent and the Rainbow*. Conceptually, the Vodou tradition is not one or the other it is both. The two traditions predominantly represent the energy/material symbiotic (binary) world that is Bon-dye and within which all life is constituted and experiences existence.

As the late *ATI-oungan* of Vodou, Max Beauvoir (2006), highlights, within this energy/material symbiotic relationship, the human being is a sentient being, which is constituted as three distinct entities, the physical body, the *gwo bon anj* (*sé médo*), and the *ti bon anj* (*sé lido*). The latter two constitute our *nanm* (soul), and the physical body is aggregated matter that eventually dies and rots. It is animated by the energy force of *Bon-dye* or the universe, the *gwo bon anj*, which is not active in influencing personality or the choices that the human subject makes in life. Instead, it is simply the spark of life or the energy force that keeps the body living or activated. In other words, metaphorically speaking, imagine the body as an electrical cord, Bon-dye as the socket, and the spark of energy from the socket that animates the appliance as the *gwo bon anj*.

The animated body, the physical body and the *gwo bon anj*, gives rise to consciousness and the personality through the *ti bon anj*. The most important part of the body is the head, which is the seat of consciousness and the space where sight, hearing, smell, and taste all reside. The five senses of the head, and the brain's reflection on what is smelled, heard, seen, tasted, and touched gives rise to the *ti bon anj*, which is consciousness, intellect, reflection, memory, will, and the personality. That is to say, it is the *ti bon anj* that houses the ego, self, personality, and ethics of the person from experiences in life. So the *gwo bon anj* animates the physical body, which gives rise to the *ti bon anj*, i.e., the individual ego or I of a human subject as they experience being in the world with others.

The three aforementioned distinct (materialist) entities constitute the average individual and can be separated at various points throughout their life cycle and at the time of death. As previously mentioned, people who are called to work with *lwa yo* also have a fourth entity, personal lwa, *mét tét*, who permanently resides within their head, i.e., a sort of split personality that guides the individual in making important and daily decisions. For the average individual, at the time of death the physical body dies and rots, the *ti bon anj*, the ego, personality, etc., returns to *Ginen* (Africa), and the *gwo bon anj* lingers around seeking to animate a new body. Serviteurs, *oungan yo, Manbo yo*, and *Bokor yo*, can work to bring the *ti bon anj* of elders back across the waters from Africa so that they can be an active and honored ancestor. This latter process of ancestor retrieval is usually done a day and a year after the death of the person, and requires an animal sacrifice, i.e., the taking of a life to feed lwa yo in order to retrieve the deceased ancestor from Ginen. Upon retrieval, the *ti bon anj* of the ancestor is kept in a *govi*, a small clay bottle. Bokors, who are members of secret societies in Vodou, and stand apart from *oungan yo* and *Manbo yo* as sorcerers who serve Petwo *lwa yo*, can also capture the lingering *ti bon anj* to do spiritual work aimed at healing, ascertaining money, love relationships, work , political power, i.e., *pwen*, or other desires. This latter act is one form of zombification wherein the *ti bon anj* of a deceased person is captured in a bottle, *govi*, and directed to serve either the Bokor or an individual seeking wealth, love, political power, or to do harm to another person, etc.

Aside from separation in death, separation can also take place during a person's life cycle. During a person's life cycle, the *gwo bon anj* can be displaced by a *lwa* during possession or a Bokor for zombification. The *lwa* utilizes the animated body (the person possessed is called a *chawl* or horse for the lwa) to experience the world, heal, protect, etc. The *ti bon anj* can be displaced during a person's life cycle by a Bokor for the mitigation of punishment through zombification. This latter action is essentially the death penalty in Vodou when individuals morally violate nature, communal life, or an individual. *Bokor yo* are called upon by *oungan yo* and *manbo yo* to punish the transgressor through the removal of their *ti bon anj* from their bodies. During this process, the ego and personality, *ti bon anj*, is removed, and the person is left with the material body and the *gwo bon anj*. The purpose of this act is to render the transgressor without the desire and drive to commit any further acts, which arose from their *ti bon anj*. The person is not killed, but the desire and passion that caused them to commit the initial transgression that they committed is removed. Hence the person is left alive as a mindless zombie. Essentially, whereas oungan yo, manbo yo, and gangan/dokté fey are the readers, judges, and healers, Bokor yo are the sorcerers and police force of the village. They are practitioners of black magic, and are visited by people seeking to do harm to someone, wealth, power, luck, revenge, etc. There are three other, external, cosmic force and lwa yo that impact the individual. They are the *zetwal*, i.e., the star of a person, which determines their fate; the *lwa rasin*, or *lwa eritaj*, the spirit of the ancestors "who enter the path of the unconscious to talk to him or her in dreams, to warn of danger, and to intervene at the many levels of his [or her] life"; and the *wonsiyon*, "these are a series of spirits that accompany the *lwa mét tét* and modify somewhat the amplitude and the frequencies of its vibration or presence" (Beauvoir, 2006, pg. 128).

The Power Elites, Ideological apparatuses, and Mode of Production of Vodou

The arrangements of individual, social and familial obligations, relationships, and interactions move outwards from this central cosmic, geometric, spiritual, and communal worldview or language game of Vodou, also known as the mystery system, through its power elites, oungan yo, Manbo yo, Bokor yo, gangan yo/dokté fey, and granmoun yo (elders); the agricultural mode of production, husbandry, and commerce (*komes*), which provide food for sustenance and herbs for medicinal purposes; and their ideological apparatuses, lwa yo, lakous (lakou yo), peristyles, alters, secret societies, herbal medicines, vévés, Vodou ceremonies, magic and rituals, songs, dances, musical instruments, proverbs, and zombification, which serves as the form of system integration (Beauvoir, 2006). In Vodou, the emphasis is on balance and harmony with the laws of creation, cosmic forces, nature, the community, and within the individual all of which are interconnected. As such, agricultural production, i.e., the tilling, cultivation, and protection of the earth by men and women for food and medicinal purposes; husbandry, for food, clothing, and the making of musical instruments; and the trade (commonly referred to as commerce*, komes*, usually performed by women) of agricultural and animal products for other goods are emphasized as the proper form for human environmental, communal, and individual interactions with nature and each other. Hence initiates of Vodou are environmentally conscientious as village religious, medicinal, and agricultural life is depended on the environment, which is deemed sacred, an extension of the primeval pan-psychic field.

Village life in the majority of the provinces is constituted around the lakou, family compound, and its peristyle where everything is shared. All provinces, cities, communes in Haiti have Lakous and peristyles. The three dominant Lakous, Souvenans, Badjo, and Soukri, are located in Gonaives, Haiti and maintain the rites and traditions of Dahomey, Nago, and the

Congo, respectively. The social class structure of the lakous (lakou yo) and the villages or regions they influence are not based on the mode of production but on the spiritual relationship, which is tied to nature, i.e., the sun, earth, the cycle of birth, rebirth, and death in nature. That is religious leaders and elders of the community constitute the power elites of the society followed by the middle-aged, and the young. The elders are the intermediaries between the young and the religious leaders. The functions of the religious leaders, oungan yo, manbo yo, and gangan yo/dokté féy, are healing through herbal medicine, performing Vodou ceremonies to call or pacify the spirits and bring about harmony to village life, initiating new oungan and manbo, telling the future, reading dreams, casting spells, resolving village disputes, protecting the society, and creating protections. Conversely, Bokor yo are the sorcerers and police force of the society. They are responsible for black magic, patrolling village life, through Sanpwels, Bizangos, and lougawous, and meting out punishment through zombification.

As previously mentioned, Vodou morality is not a black and white understanding of right and wrong, but rather a contextual response that above all works to maintain balance, harmony, and perfection in the universe and community. As Leslie G. Desmangles (1992) highlights,

> [v]oduisants' concepts of good and evil correspond to their idea of the forces that operate within the universe. They distinguish between good as a higher force and evil as a lower one, and correlate both with the natural order of forces in the world. A good act is of a higher order because it increases Bondye's power in the world, while a bad act is of a lower order because it decreases that power. Hence, every act, every detail of human behavior that militates against Bondye's vital force or against the increase of his power in the maintenance of order in the universe, is bad. For instance, Vodouisants consider murder wrong because, by a person's death, Bondye's divine influence is decreased in the human community. Sorcery is not wrong, because it increases the power of Bondye, as the sorcerers "tap" it from one of the lwas. The willful eradication of life is thought to be a sacrilege since it is not only a departure from Bondye's will for orderliness in the world, but an actual destruction of that order as Bondye established it (pgs. 96-97).

The universe exists in harmony as a natural state, which communal and individual life replicates, and any action that creates discord is a moral transgression. Moral transgressions are not individual acts that permanently taint the soul and change the outcome of the afterlife as one finds in Islam, Christianity, Hinduism, Buddhism, etc. There is no defined concept of heaven in Haitian Vodou and reincarnation of the *nanm* is not affected by the sins of the past life. Rather, moral transgressions change the circumstances of the individual and community in the here and now but can be overcome and moved past through some form of retribution or punishment. Also important is that the moral violation of harmony by one individual can affect the morality of the group and cause repercussions from spirits and ancestors that affect the community. This places a huge focus upon the collective and tends to downplay the individual. Yet, it would be wrong to characterize the Haitian Vodou worldview as solely a collective one. That is to say, individual action is an important part of disrupting, maintaining, and repairing balance through the religious leaders and elders of the community who must decide the appropriate course of action to take against any transgressions in order to restore balance and harmony. As the taking of life is prohibited in the Rada Vodou family, the ultimate punishment in the Haitian worldview is the second form of zombification outlined above, which is usually performed by Bokor yo of the Petwo tradition. Vodou requires that some form of retribution or punishment is required for all forms of moral transgression in order to restore balance and harmony in nature, the community, and within each individual involved in the transgression. Understandably, this is why the Haitian Revolution commences with a Petwo Vodou ceremony at Bois Caiman on August 14th, 1791. The ceremony was called upon by oungan yo, Manbo yo, Bokor yo, gangan yo, and granmoun yo (elders) under the leadership of oungan Boukman Dutty, manbo Cecile Fatiman, and Edaïse to bring about retribution and punishment against whites for the institution of slavery, which was causing great disharmony and imbalance in nature and the African communities on the island. According to Seviteurs, manbo Fatiman was mounted by the Petwo lwa, Manbo Erzulie Danthor (the lunar Goddess of the Haitian nation who the Africans summoned through the sacrifice), who meted out the punishment for the whites, and laid out the hierarchy of the leadership of the revolution. In return, as highlighted by the aforementioned Boukman's prayer, the participants promised not to serve the white man's God or allow inequality on the island. In the Vodou structuring structure, Haiti's problems are a result of the fact that they have failed to implement the covenant they made with Bon-dye (the universe) for her assistance in the form of the lunar lwa Erzulie Danthor at Bois Caiman.

Following the revolution, it would be the struggle between the modes of production, ideology, ideological apparatuses, communicative discourse, and the agents of the two systems or structuring structures, the Vodou Ethic and the spirit of communism language game of the Africans of the provinces/mountains and the Catholic/Protestant Ethic and the spirit of capitalism language game of the *Affranchis*, mulatto elites and petit-bourgeois blacks, who were seeking to reproduce the French structuring structure in a national position of their own, which would bring about the great disharmony and imbalance that has plagued Haiti since the death of oungan Jean-Jacques Dessalines October 17th, 1806, the father of the Haitian nation, who, with his *lwa mét tét,* Ogou Feray, sought to protect the interests of those whose fathers were in Africa. Ostensibly, this struggle, contemporarily, is captured in the political discourses of political leaders and the masses as the ideas, social inclusion, democracy, equitable distribution of wealth, social wealth, social justice, etc., of the children of Dessalines vs. the ideas, i.e., capitalism, individual wealth, liberalism, etc., of the children of Pétion who assassinated him. I disagree, however, as for me, contemporarily, both the children of Dessalines and Pétion are subjects of the same form of system and social integration.

Perpetual Civil War in Haiti

Whereas Dessalines, unlike Toussaint, attempted to constitute the Haitian-nation by reconciling these two forms of system and social integrations via his nationalization project, the agents of the Affranchis class, since independence, have sought to integrate Haiti into the capitalist world-system while serving as a comprador political bourgeoisie for its hegemonic powers, i.e., Canada, France, and the United States. This attempt by the children of Pétion and Dessalines/Toussaint to integrate Haiti into the global Protestant capitalist world-system as a periphery state has undermined the revolutionary and independence movement of the Haitian Revolution as commenced by the African majority, the children of Sans Souci, and embroiled the country into a perpetual civil war.

The impending defeat of the French in Haiti is widely credited with contributing to Napoleon's decision to sell the Louisiana territory to the United States in 1803. Haiti is the world's oldest black republic and the second-oldest republic in the Western Hemisphere after the United States. Although Haiti actively assisted the independence movements of many Latin American countries, the independent nation of former slaves was excluded from the hemisphere's first regional meeting of independent nations in Panama in 1826, and did not receive U.S. diplomatic recognition until 1862 under Abraham Lincoln. In 1825, French officials arrived and informed the Haitian government that they were willing to recognize the country as a sovereign nation but it would do so on account that they pay compensation and reparation in exchange for the revolution. Whereas Dessalines and Henri Christophe rebuked this idea, the Haitians, following the death of Christophe, under the leadership of the Affranchis mulatto, Jean-Pierre Boyer, seeking equality of opportunity, recognition, and distribution with their white counterparts in France agreed. The French government sent a team of accountants and actuaries into Haiti in order to place a value on all lands, all physical assets, the 500,000 citizens who were formerly enslaved (including members of the Cabinet who were also valued because they had been enslaved people before independence), animals, and all other commercial properties and services. The sums amounted to 150 million gold francs. Haiti was requested to pay this reparation to France in return for national recognition. The Haitian government under Boyer's administration agreed; payments began immediately. Boyer shut down all of the Western ideological apparatuses, schools, etc., in the provinces so that the masses could return to the *corvée* system in order to pay the independence debt. He also attacked Vodou through his anti-superstition laws and campaigns (Ramsey, 2014; Du Bois, 2012; Mocombe, 2016).

Thus, began the systematic destruction of the Republic of Haiti and its dependent development within the Protestant capitalist world-system under the leadership of the Affranchis class at the expense of the Africans in the provinces and mountains (Pierre-Louis, 2000; Nicholls, 1979; Du Bois, 2012). The French government bled the nation and rendered it a failed state. It was a merciless exploitation that was designed and guaranteed to collapse the Haitian economy and society. Haiti was forced, on the backs of the Africans in the provinces and mountains whose crops, they used for *komes*, were taxed heavily, to pay this sum until 1947 when the last installment was made. During the long 19th century, the payment to France amounted to up to 70 percent of the country's foreign exchange earnings. In the years when the coffee crops failed, or the sugar yield was down, the Haitian government borrowed on the French money market at double the going interest rate in order to repay the French government. When the Americans invaded the country in the early twentieth century, 1915-1934, one of the reasons offered was to assist the French in collecting its reparations (Du Bois, 2012).

Thus, the collapse of the Haitian nation-state resides at the hands of France and America, especially, in alliance with the mulatto merchant and petit-bourgeois black landowning classes of the island serving as a Francophile neocolonial oligarchy seeking equality of opportunity, recognition, and distribution with whites against the African leadership of oungan yo, manbo yo, gangan yo, granmoun yo and the masses who sought to establish an independent nation-state for all blacks as envisioned by Dessalines, Macaya, Sans Souci, etc. What France did openly in the nineteenth and early twentieth-centuries, the United States, with the assistance of the landowning and merchant classes, continued clandestinely up to the twenty-first century.[3]

After the revolution, two separate regimes—north and south— emerged, but were unified in 1820 under Boyer's government. Two years later, Haiti occupied Santo Domingo, the eastern, Spanish-speaking part of Hispaniola. In 1844, however, Santo Domingo, with the assistance of the Americans and the Spanish, broke away from Haiti and became the Dominican Republic. With 22 changes of government from 1843 to 1915, Haiti experienced numerous periods of intense political and economic disorder between the mulatto merchant and petit-bourgeois black landowning classes fighting over control of the state apparatus, prompting, as previously mentioned, the United States' military intervention of 1915. It is under this occupation and America's southern brand of racism that the mulatto elites began to recognize their own racism towards the so-called black and African masses (Du Bois, 2012). Following the 19-year occupation, U.S. military forces were withdrawn in 1934, and Haiti regained sovereign rule under the leadership of the mulatto and merchant classes until 1957 when Francois "papa-doc" Duvalier assumed the presidency, declared himself president for life, and through his *noirisme* philosophy attempted to make the black landowning class the power elites of the society, undergirded by the *Tonton Macoutes* composed of members of the peasant class, against the mulatto elites and merchant classes. Duvalier, a former doctor in the provinces and mountains, also utilized elements from Vodou to buttress his power while continuing the integration of Haiti into the global Protestant capitalist world-system, which the United States of America with the aid of the landowning and merchant classes had established. As Francois Pierre-Louis further notes of this transition,

> The U.S. occupation restructured three major aspects of Haitian society: the army, public administration and class relationships.... The marines refashioned the army making it the sole authority in the country and they gave it additional roles previously filled by civilians. The army called Gendarmerie built roads, supervised travel, collected census information, enforced various health and sanitation codes, and also supervised the prisons.... By recruiting primarily light skinned Haitians, the marines further exacerbated the skin color conflict in the country. Even though the previous army was repressive, this was the first time a professional army in the country was created not to fight foreign enemies, but to oppress its own people. The new army created by the Americans did not only fight Haitian peasants, but it repressed urbanites, students, and all others who dared challenge the occupiers.... Another major aspect in the restructuring of the

army was centralization. Whereas under the national army there were different points of power, the marines centralized the command center of the army. Port-au-Prince once again became the center of power.... [Moreover, i]nstead of restructuring class relationship in Haiti as it has done elsewhere such as the Dominican Republic and several countries in Central America through massive investments in the agricultural sector, the United States practically left class relationships as it had found it. They made no land reforms or major attempts to integrate the peasant population into mainstream life. There were some investments in light manufacturing and processing plants, however, the bulk of the reform was in public administration. This reform eventually favored the merchant class as it had the technical and intellectual capacity to work in the reformed administration. Furthermore, the marines' racial prejudice exacerbated the color problem in the country.... From 1915 to 1947, all the Haitian Presidents were mulattoes.... From 1934 until the reign of Francois Duvalier, the army was the power broker in Haiti. No one was elected to rule the country without its prior approval. Whenever it did not like a President, it overthrew him. Francois Duvalier, who came to power with the acquiescence of the army, attempted to control it by introducing an alternative force called the Tonton Macoutes. The Tonton Macoutes were primarily peasants who were drafted as militia members by Duvalier to check the power of the Army. Using the *noiriste* propaganda, which advocated that black skinned Haitians should rule Haiti, Duvalier succeeded in allying a major sector of the middle class and large landowners to support him. To prevent the merchant class from using the army to stage a coup against him, he removed a number of mulatto generals in the military. He then replaced these generals with military personnel who supported his *noiriste* policies. Several attempts by the merchant class and its sympathizers in the military to overthrow Duvalier ended in catastrophe (2000, pgs., 7-9).

From February 7, 1986—when the 29-year dictatorship of the Duvalier family, backed by the CIA, ended—until 1991, Haiti was ruled by a series of provisional military governments trained and supported by the United States. In March 1987, with the fall of Duvalier, a constitution was ratified that provided for an elected, bicameral parliament; an elected president that served as head of state; and a prime minister, cabinet, ministers, and supreme court appointed by the president with parliament's consent. The Haitian Constitution (1987) also provides for political decentralization through the election of mayors and administrative bodies responsible for local government. Essentially, under the guise of the United States the attempt was to convert Haiti into an export-oriented Western neoliberal democratic capitalist state under the guise of what Robert Dahl refers to as a polyarchy, a democracy of rotating elites, the mulatto merchant/professional class and so-called black landowning professional and managerial class as their interests stood against the mode of production (subsistence agriculture, husbandry, and komes) and ideological apparatuses (Lakous, peristyles, etc.) of the Africans of the provinces and mountains.

In December 1990, in spite of US efforts to get Marc Bazin elected so as to facilitate their neoliberal agenda for incorporating Haiti into the global capitalist world-system via tourism, textile manufacturing, and export agriculture, the Haitian masses in Haiti's first democratic elections elected father Jean-Bertrand Aristide, a former Catholic priest, who won 67 percent of the vote in a presidential election that international observers deemed largely free and fair. Aristide took office on February 7, 1991, but was overthrown that September in a violent coup led by army elements supported by many of the country's economic elite, who were against Aristide's increase of the Haitian minimum wage and land and social policies for the peasant class who constituted over 65 percent of the population. The coup, given the political persecution that ensued, contributed to a large-scale exodus of Haitian peasants by boat to the United States. From October 1991 to September 1994 a de facto military regime governed Haiti. Various OAS (Organization of American States) and UN (United Nations) initiatives to end the political crisis through the peaceful restoration of the constitutionally elected government failed. On July 31, 1994, the UN Security Council adopted Resolution 940, which authorized member states to use all necessary means to facilitate the departure of Haiti's military leadership and to restore Haiti's constitutionally elected government to power. The United States took the lead in forming a multinational force (MNF) to carry out the UN's mandate by means of a military intervention. In mid-September, with U.S. troops prepared to enter Haiti by force, General Raoul Cedras, a mulatto, and other top leaders agreed to accept the intervention of the MNF. On September 19, 1994, the first contingents of what became a 21,000-member international force touched down in Haiti to oversee the end of military rule and the restoration of the constitutional government. President Aristide and other elected officials exiled in the US returned on October 15. Upon his return, Aristide disbanded the army, and served out the remainder of his five-year term. As the Haitian constitution of 1987 prevents back to back terms, Aristide was replaced by his former prime-minister Rene Préval in 1995. Following Préval's, a former Marxist, first term Aristide was reelected in 2000. Once again, however, Aristide, in a coup led by the merchant class, mulatto elites, and petit-bourgeois black classes, the United States, Canada, and France, who were against his liberation theology, leftist-leaning economic policies, Africanization of Haiti via his attempt to make Vodou and Kreyol the national religion and language of the island, and suit in the World Court to obtain the 150 million francs, with interest, from France, which Haiti had to pay following the Revolution, was eventually deposed in February 2004 and sent into Exile to South Africa. Following the brief stance of a provisional government, Aristide was subsequently replaced by Rene Préval who was governing the nation when the massive earthquake of January 12, 2010 that killed almost 200,000 to 230,000 citizens struck the island. Préval was subsequently replaced by Michel Martelly, a mulatto and former Konpa singer, who the US backed in flawed elections to implement their and the economic classes' neoliberal agenda, which they had started under Boyer, under the slogan, "Haiti is Open for Business." Under this mantra the emphasis is on high-end tourism for the economic elites, the merchant class, of the Protestant capitalist world-system, export-oriented agro-industry, athletics (soccer and basketball), and textile and manufacturing sweatshops. The grandon class is not necessarily against the aforementioned, they simply fight to gain control of the political apparatus of the nation-state so as to facilitate the neoliberal processes of the West and the Haitian oligarchy.

Conclusions

At the time of the writing of this work, Haiti, under a United Nations force (MINUSTAH), continues to be under occupation within the capitalist world-system under American hegemony. The continuous struggle between the mulatto merchant/professional class and the black landowning managerial classes for control of the state and its apparatuses, at the expense of the African masses in the provinces and mountains whose children they arm and use against each other as they migrate to Port-au-Prince amidst American neoliberal policies seeking to displace the masses off their land for tourism, agro and textile industries, and athletics (basketball and soccer) continues to be a hindrance for the constitution of a sovereign Haitian nation-state. The former two, interpellated and embourgeoised in Western ideological apparatuses, seek to constitute Haiti, with the aid of whites (France, Canada, and America), as an export-oriented periphery state within the capitalist world-system under American hegemony against the desires of the masses of Africans in the urban slums, provinces, and mountains seeking to maintain their *komes*, subsistence agriculture, and husbandry, which are deemed informal. The *grandon* class, composed of educated professionals, former drug dealers, entertainers, and police officers attack the former Affranchis class, which is now a comprador bourgeoisie (composed of Arab merchants) seeking to build, own, and manage hotels and assembly factories producing electronics and clothing for the US market, under the moniker the children of Dessalines against the children of Pétion in the name of the African masses of the island, the majority of whom are peasant farmers interpellated and ounganified by the Vodou Ethic and the spirit of communism. Instead of focusing on infrastructure (artificial lakes, potable water, food security, mache—modern market spaces for *komes*, universities, and state-owned companies for the peasant class to sell, etc.) to augment national agriculture and the productive forces of the latter group, who constitute eighty-five percent of the population, the mulatto elites and petit-bourgeois blacks emphasize job creation through foreign direct investment in tourism, agro and textile industries, privatization of public services, infrastructure for an export-oriented economy similar to the one they had under slavery, and the constitution of a political bourgeoisie in control of the state apparatuses. However, their inabilities—given the voting power of the majority—to constitute two dominant rotating political parties to implement the desires of their former colonial slavemasters, leaves Haiti in perpetual turmoil. As in slavery, the African masses continue to fight, against their interpellation, embourgeoisement, and differentiation as wage-earners (commodities) in the tourism trade and textile factories of the Catholic/Protestant Ethic and spirit of capitalism of these two power elites seeking equality of opportunity, recognition, and distribution with whites at their expense, for the Vodou Ethic and the spirit of communism of *oungan yo, manbo yo,* and *granmoun yo* of Bois Caiman. As the current historical conjuncture parallels the conjuncture of 1791 either a unifying national conference that parallels Bois Caiman or a second war of independence will determine the outcome of this perpetual economic and cultural civil war in Haiti. As for now, the masses of Port-au-Prince, galvanized by the grandon class, protest against the neoliberal capitalist world-system under American hegemony under the moniker, the children of Pétion v. the children of Dessalines.

Notes

[1] The term marronage fails to capture the practical consciousness by which the Africans of Haiti went about recursively reorganizing and reproducing their world. Eugene Genovese, in his usage of the term, is one scholar who does.

[2] By emphasizing Vodou over Islam, which also united many of the Africans from the Congo region, the intent is not to minimize it. Instead, my intent is to highlight the fact that in spite of the fact that many Africans adopted Islam they still held on to their original tribal faiths, which united them in the colonies.

[3] The Americans would be responsible for the centralization of all economic activities in the capital city, Port-au-Prince. Prior to their occupation, the country was decentralized under the ruling of different generals.

CHAPTER VI

CONCLUSIONS:
"THE MY NIGGA HAITIAN"

The constitution of African American and Haitian cultures or practical consciousnesses in the emerging Protestant capitalist world-system of the seventeenth and eighteenth centuries represent two divergent processes the understanding of which can shed light on the subtle differences between the Haitian Revolution and the black American civil rights movement, which many scholars have inadequately attempted to understand, both movements, via Hegel's master/slave dialectic, and the emergence of the "my nigga Haitian" practical consciousness in the Haitian US diaspora. Whereas, the application of Hegel's master/slave dialectic can be said to hold true in the case of the black American and the emergence of the "my Nigga Haitian" practical consciousnesses, it is not applicable for the purposive-rationality of the originating moments of the Haitian Revolution, which was an antidialectical response by the Africans to slavery.

In the case of the black American, many scholars of the pathological-pathogenic school conclude that the antagonistic practical interrelationship between the dualities of Africans and that of white European Protestants when they encountered each other eventually made the majority of black consciousness, within the American, white, Protestant bourgeois symbolic order, nothing more than a "poor" (pathological-pathogenic) or "absurd" form of American consciousness due to racial and class differentiation (Frazier, 1939, 1957; Stampp, 1956, 1971; Elkins, 1959; Genovese, 1974; Moynihan, 1965; Wilson, 1978, 1996).[1] The adaptive-vitality school, supplanting Du Bois's concepts of race and nation with culture, on the contrary, argues that blacks developed a Du Boisian double-consciousness, their African racial practical consciousness, and the American one characterized not solely by the Protestantism of the American capitalist symbolic order, but also by "an improvisational communal consciousness," emotionalism, musical style, and intuition rooted in a folk culture grounded in their Africanness or, what amounts to the same thing, their sense of blackness (Levine, 1977; Gutman, 1976; Blassingame, 1972;

Holloway, 1990; Karenga, 1993; Gilroy, 1993; Allen, 2001).

Mocombe's phenomenological structurationists understanding of the relationship refutes both of these positions. My application of Mocombe's phenomenological structuralism supposes that not all social actors or groups operate from a transcendental or (present-at-hand) objective standpoint. Instead, they constitute an historical structure of interpretative understanding, which is thus always already engaged in the activity of interpretation within the structures of signification of those who control the resources of the material resource framework within which the historical structure of interpretative understanding is ensconced. In fact, the historical structure of interpretative understanding of those in power position in a particular resource framework becomes the ideological superstructure for maintaining control of "other" interpretative understandings and the material resource framework.

This understanding of the constitution of society based on the "colonization of the life-world" by a systematized life-world structure of signification, social class language game, constituted via language, communicative discourse, mode of production, ideology, and ideological apparatuses, does not mean that social actors are unable to transcend the interpretative structures of signification of those in power position in a particular resource framework in order to access the ontological directly or create a new ideology. On the contrary, consciousness, and by logical association, agency or practical consciousness is contingent on either the integrative rules of conduct, recursively organized and reproduced in material practice, of those who control the resources of the material resource framework, or the reformulation, through the deferment of meaning in ego-centered communicative action and other processes, of these rules of conduct in material practices for "other" marginalized forms of being-in-the-world, "identities-in-differential," or structuring structures, which are in turn symbolically used by those in power positions to maintain their power position, and relationally delimit their historical structure of interpretative understandings and practices. Hence social structure is both a duality and a dualism: A duality, when structure is internalized and recursively organized and reproduced by some, constituted by discriminating against other marginalized dualities, which come to view and constitute the world as both a duality and a dualism, i.e., an "other" recursively reproducing their intermarginalized practical consciousness (a practical consciousness that is integrated in society to be marginalized so that power can constitute their structuring structure), against the purposive-rationality of the dominant order as reified via bodies, language, ideologies, and ideological apparatuses.

In this theoretical framework, which posits the constitution of society to be the result of two contradictory principles, marginality and integration, human society is seen as a Durkheimian "mechanical solidarity" or social structure constituted by social actors, with a distinct form of Being-in-the-world, (practical) consciousness, who marginalize and discriminate against "other" behaviors or forms of (practical) consciousnesses either structurally differentiated or arrived-at through the deferment of meaning in ego-centered communicative discourse, and other processes given their stance, in order to integrate the dominant social practices of the society.

It is within this solidarity or constitution of modern American Protestant society, as opposed to the liberal bourgeois "organic" or rational model proposed by Jürgen Habermas's (1987 [1981]) communicative action model, I outlined the constitution of African American practical consciousness, culture, and spiritualism as it relates to black, Haitian, diasporic practical consciousness, culture, and spiritualism that led to the divergent purposive-rationalities of the black American civil rights movement and the originating moments of the Haitian Revolution, respectively, and the emergence of the "my Nigga Haitian" identity in the Haitian US diaspora.

The premise that unfolds from this theoretical position is that black American consciousness became, as a result of blacks' social integration (as marginalized "non-beings") into the white, American protestant, bourgeois social structure, multiple and diverse (Patterson, 1982, pgs. 38-42).[2] They were differentially related to, and delimited by, the dominating purposive-rationality of the liberal black (male) heterosexual bourgeoisie and underclasses, who discriminated against structuring structures, homosexuality, transgenderism, pan-Africanism, Vodouism, feminism, bisexualism, etc. which emerged as a result of the deferment of meaning in ego-centered communicative discourse and other processes. The bourgeoisie which, as a structurally differentiated "racial-class-in-itself" serving as a reference group for other blacks in the society, became the bearers of ideological domination for black folk and led the black American struggle for freedom against slavery and marginalization by recursively organizing and reproducing the integrative Protestant "practical consciousness" of the American social structure against the pathologies of the black poor and other fully visible black "other" practical consciousnesses, i.e., black feminism, homosexuality, pan-Africanism, transgenderism, etc., for equality of opportunity, recognition, and distribution for themselves and the black poor. In other words, this need to recursively (re) organize and reproduce the integrative Protestant practical consciousness of the American social structure, the liberal black (male) heterosexual bourgeoisie did in order to obtain equality of opportunity, distribution, and recognition, against the contemptuous gaze of white agents and the agents of other black adaptive responses to enslavement.

Unlike the position of the pathological-pathogenic school, it is not my view that this *adaptive* response of many black Americans to recursively organize and reproduce the purposive rationality of the American Protestant social structure defined by the accumulation of capital to prove one's predestination in a "calling," against their original African practical consciousness, was a result of self-hatred or a lack of black agency under the patriarchal brutality and oppressiveness of "racial" slavery.[3] Quite the reverse, this was a self-directed phenomenon driven by the more liberal segment of the enslaved and discriminated against black population, the "best" of the house servants, mulattoes, artisans, and the educated free Negro from the North, who sought (by positioning themselves as a reference group for the black community), as a "racial" "class-for-itself," to define the black situation for all blacks, the black poor, etc., of the American social structure along its Protestant and capitalist ethos, which they took to be the nature of reality and existence as such.

Given this dialectical response amongst the more free and powerful majority of the descendants of African slaves, who were barred from organizing and reproducing their African institutions within the material resource framework of the American Protestant social and economic order, it is in terms of the structural variables (i.e., class and status, given the economic basis for the social relations of the society) of the society, not other factors, that black consciousness in America can be and has been assessed and determined. For all other forms of practical-consciousness amongst blacks within American society were defined and relationally delimited as "other" by these blacks, the "best" of the house servants, mulattoes, artisans, and the educated free Negro from the North, who, when they became institutional regulators within the American social structure, delimited or represented the "proper" and "pure" way of being-in-the-world for all blacks in terms of Protestant bourgeois practical consciousness, i.e., interest, ideals, habitus, etc.

Thus, "after the end of the [(slave)] trade in America in the latter half of the eighteenth and early part of the nineteenth centuries [Africanisms] importance as an explanation of slave personality declines: only about 400,000 native-born Africans had been brought to the United States before 1807 [(the slave trade, as sanctioned by the US Constitution, legally ended in 1808)]. Since an overwhelming percentage of nineteenth-century Southern slaves were native Americans" (Blassingame, 1972, pg. 39), they, about 3,953,760 of the black population at the outbreak of the Civil

War, had to construct their identity or consciousness as a deployable unit of the American social structure in relation to and led by "the best of the house servants, who were freed by their masters, [and] the educated free Negro from the North," who together numbered about 500, 000, twelve percent of the total black population, "at the outbreak of the Civil War"[4] (See Table 6.1).

So, as my reinterpretation of the black or African experience within the American Protestant structuring symbolic order demonstrated, it is not that black Americans have a "double consciousness" or are bicultural. The majority, according to my theoretical reading of the historical experiences of blacks in America, adopted a singular practical consciousness, the Protestant ethic of the society, which structured the developing slave community and culture, which they incorporate, or incorporated them, by warring (i.e., discriminating) against other (feminists, nationalists, Catholics, Muslims, etc.) fully visible alternative forms of being-in-the-world available to a minority of blacks and some whites, who became marginalized and discriminated against, within the social structure, by whites and the black bourgeoisie, who are only distinguishable from one another by skin color.[5]

Table 6.1: *Growth of the Slave and Free Negro Population in the United States 1790-1860*

	NEGRO POPULATION			
		Free		
CENSUS YEAR	**Total**	**Number**	**Per Cent**	**Slave**
1860	4,441,830	488,070	11	3,953,760
1850	3,638,808	134,495	11.9	3,204,313
1840	2,873,648	386,293	13.4	2,487,355
1830	2,328,642	319,599	13.7	2,009,043
1820	1,771,656	233,634	13.2	1,538,022
1810	1,377,808	186,446	13.5	1,191,362
1800	1,002,037	108,435	10.8	893,602
1790	757,181	59,557	7.9	697,624

Note. Adapted from *The American Negro: His History and Literature* (p. 5), by E. Franklin Frazier, 1968, New York: Arno Press and The New York Times. Copyright 1968 by Arno Press, Inc.

For the Africans of Haiti, the contrary held true. The initial response of the Africans in Haiti to enslavement was an anti-dialectical response, which emerges out of their Vodou metaphysics and its transcendental epistemology. Constituting the majority of persons on the island of Haiti, the five hundred thousand Africans of Haiti, when the Haitian Revolution ignites in 1791, were almost all born in Africa. Given the brutality of the French slavery system, *Code Noir*, many of the Africans escaped into the mountains of the island where they established maroon communities. By the late eighteenth century Haiti or Sainte-Domingue had many large communities of maroons, who maintained and recursively reorganized and reproduced their African practical-consciousness, vodou, kreyol, polygamy, etc. in the mountains of the island against the liberal bourgeois practical consciousness of the whites or *blancs* and the *Affranchis* or *gens de couleur*, who either worked as artisans in the island's towns, or farmed small plots of land with the aid of slaves imported from Africa.

Be that as it may, Haiti by 1791 was constituted by the practical consciousness of the thirty thousand *Affranchis* or *gens de couleur*, free people of color, including mulattoes as well as freed slaves, who adopted the practical consciousness of the forty thousand liberal white, predominantly Catholic, French who prevented them from fully participating in the life of the colony (see Table 6.2). This liberal bourgeois practical consciousness of the whites or *blancs* and the *Affranchis* or *gens de couleur* would be integrated by marginalizing the practical consciousness of the Africans on the island. Hence what developed on the island by 1791 was an immutable four tier caste-system (which differed from America's two-tier caste-system, in the US a third caste was drawn among the slaves between house and field slaves) in which the *blancs* or white planter class represented the power elite of the society who discriminated against the *Affranchis* or *gens de couleur*, who wanted to be like the whites; the maroon communities of enslaved Africans, who reproduced their West African Vodou practical-consciousness in the mountains of the island; and newly arrived or imported Africans, who replaced the runaways of the maroon communities (see Table 6.3). It would be the practical consciousness of the maroon communities, their desire to institute their African practical consciousness on the island as a class-for-itself against all things white and *Affranchis* or *gens de couleur* that would ignite the Haitian Revolution on August 14th, 1791 at Bois Caïman. With the assassination of Jean-Jacques Dessalines in 1806, the Affranchis or *gens de couleur* would subsequently usurp the movement to push forth their claim, like their black American liberal bourgeois Protestant counterparts in North America, for equality of opportunity, distribution, and recognition in the white Protestant dominated Capitalist world-system. Consequently, with the defeat and expulsion of the whites from the island following the Revolution, it would be the continuing struggle between the Affranchis or *gens de couleur*, dialectically, seeking equality of opportunity, distribution, and recognition, with whites in the global capitalist Protestant world-system at the expense of the practical consciousness of the masses of African-Haitians on the island seeking to recursively organize and reproduce their African way of life in a national position of their own that would plague Haiti's socio-political development from 1804 to the present.

Table 6.2: *Haiti's Population by 1790*

Haiti's Population by 1790				
	Total	Whites or blancs	Affranchis or *gens de couleur*	Slaves
1790	570,000	40,000	30,000	500,000

Table 6.3: *Race and Class in Haiti and US 1790*

Race and Class in Haiti and US 1790	
Haiti	US
Whites or blancs	Whites
Affranchis or *gens de couleur*	Blacks
	Free Blacks (House Slaves)
Slaves	Slaves (Field Slaves and Newly Arrived Africans)
Maroon Community of Africans	Maroon Community of Africans

Hence, the purposive-rationality of the originating moments of the Haitian Revolution at Bois Caïman diametrically opposed the purposive-rationality of the liberal agents of the Affranchis and the black American civil rights movement in that the latter two sought to dialectically recursively (re) organize and reproduce the practical consciousness of their former white slavemasters for equality of opportunity, distribution and recognition, while the agents of the former did not. Instead, at Bois Caïman, the originating moment of the Haitian Revolution, Boukman and Faitman, anti-dialectically, through the deferment of meaning in ego-centered communicative discourse and other processes, sought to recursively organize and reproduce their African practical consciousness, synthesized with the Taino, against the purposive-rationality of their former slavemasters. It is the usurpation of the Revolution by the Affranchis that would give the Revolution its dialectical liberal bourgeois orientation, which makes Hegel's master/slave dialectic an appropriate heuristic tool for understanding the subsequent developments of the Haitian Revolution following Bois Caïman. This liberal bourgeois orientation is the basis for both the emergence of the "my Nigga Haitian" practical consciousness, and the subsequent exploitation and oppression of the African masses on the island by the Affranchis seeking, like their black American counterparts, continual equality of opportunity, recognition, and distribution with their former white masters through the re-enslavement of the African masses who grow poor and sick so that a few of their fellow citizens can live lavishly within the capitalist world-system.

This traditional liberal bourgeois interpretation of the Haitian revolution attempts to understand its denouement through the sociopolitical effects of the French Revolution when the National Constituent Assembly (*Assemblée Nationale Constituante*) of France passed la Déclaration des droits de l'homme et du citoyen or the Declaration of the Rights of Man and Citizen in August of 1789. The understanding from this perspective is that the slaves, many of whom could not read or write French, understood the principles, philosophical and political principles of the Age of Enlightenment, set forth in the declaration and therefore yearned to be like their white masters, i.e., freemen seeking liberty, equality, and fraternity, the rallying cry of the French Revolution. Although, historically this understanding holds true for the mulattoes and free blacks or Affranchis who used the language of the declaration to push forth their efforts to gain liberty, equality, fraternity with their white counterparts, this position is not an accurate representation for the slaves who met at Bois Caïman.

The Affranchis, Toussaint, for example, pushed for liberty, equality, and fraternity with their white counterparts at the expense of the enslaved

Africans who were not only discriminated against by whites but by the mulattoes and free blacks as well. Toussaint believed that the technical and governing skills of the *blancs* and Affranchis would be sorely needed to rebuild the country after the revolution and the end of white rule on the island. Dessalines to some extent would adopt the same position. This purposive-rationality of the Affranchis is, however, a Western liberal dialectical understanding of the events and their desire to be like their white counterparts, which stands against the purposive rationality of Boukman, Fatiman, and the rest of the maroon Africans who congregated for the Vodou ceremony at Bois Caïman/ Bwa Kayiman. Following the Haitian Revolution, the desire of the Affranchis for equality of opportunity, recognition, and distribution with their white counterparts would re-enslave the African masses on the island as they were forced to return to the sugar plantations to pay reparations to France for the recognition of the island as an independent nation-state.

Hence, for me, the events at Bois Caïman do not fit well within the attempt by many Western scholars to conceptualize the social agency of the African participants of Bois Caïman within the Hegelian master/slave dialectical thinking. Instead, the events at Bois Caïman, represent, through the deferment of meaning in ego-centered communicative discourse, a rejection by the African participants of white culture and god for the actualization of an African ethos as a "class-for-itself," a group of people with their own gods and culture, who rejected the inhumanity of the whites and their gods. It is this postmodern attempt to constitute an African/Taino ethos into the eighteenth-century world, while rejecting the inhumanity of whites, their culture, and god that Pat Robertson and many other fundamentalist Christians refer to, after the devastating earthquake that hit Haiti on January 12, 2010, as a "pact to the devil." The difference between what the Africans at Bois Caïman wanted and the aspirations of the mulattoes or Affranchis can be summed up through a parallel or complimentary analysis of the dialectical master/slave relationship of the black American experience with their white masters in America and the emergence of the "my Nigga Haitian" practical consciousness.

Susan Buck Morss (2009) in her work, *Hegel, Haiti, and Universal History* attempts to understand the originating moments of the Haitian Revolution metaphorically through Hegel's master/slave dialectic. Suggesting, in fact, that it is the case of Haiti that Hegel utilized to constitute the metaphor:

> Given the facility with which this dialectic of lordship and bondage lends itself to such a reading, one wonders why the topic Hegel and Haiti has for so long been ignored. Not only have Hegel scholars failed to answer this

question; they have failed, for the past two hundred years, even to ask it (2009, p. 56).

My position here is that neither Morss's nor Hegel's conclusions hold true for the Africans who met at Bois Caïman, and only holds true for the case of the Affranchis of Haiti—who usurped the originating moments of the Revolution from the Africans who met at Bois Caïman—and the black Americans who, in choosing to rebel against their former masters, were not risking death to avoid subjugation, but in rebelling were choosing life in order to be like the master and subjugate.

In Hegel's master/slave dialectic as Morss explains,

Hegel understands the position of the master in both political and economic terms. In the *System der Sittlichkeit* (1803): "The master is in possession of an overabundance of physical necessities generally, and the other [the slave] in the lack thereof." At first consideration the master's situation is "independent, and its essential nature is to be for itself"; whereas "the other," the slave's position, "is dependent, and its essence is life or existence for another." The slave is characterized by the lack of recognition he receives. He is viewed as "a thing"; "thinghood" is the essence of slave consciousness—as it was the essence of his legal status under the *Code Noir*. But as the dialectic develops, the apparent dominance of the master reverses itself with his awareness that he is in fact totally dependent on the slave. One has only to collectivize the figure of the master in order to see the descriptive pertinence of Hegel's analysis: the slaveholding class is indeed totally dependent on the institution of slavery for the "overabundance" that constitutes its wealth. This class is thus incapable of being the agent of historical progress without annihilating its own existence. But then the slaves (again, collectivizing the figure) achieve self-consciousness by demonstrating that they are not things, not objects, but subjects who transform material nature. Hegel's text becomes obscure and falls silent at this point of realization. But given the historical events that provided the context for *The Phenomenology of Mind*, the inference is clear. Those who once acquiesced to slavery demonstrate their humanity when they are willing to risk death rather than remain subjugated. The law (the *Code Noir*!) that acknowledges them merely as "a thing" can no longer be considered binding, although before, according to Hegel, it was the slave himself who was responsible for his lack of freedom by initially choosing life over liberty, mere self-preservation. In *The Phenomenology of mind*, Hegel insists that freedom cannot be granted to slaves from above. The self-liberation of the slave is required through a "trial by death": "And it is solely by risking life that freedom is obtained…The individual, who has not staked his life, may, no doubt, be recognized as a Person [the agenda of the abolitionists!]; but he has not attained the truth of his recognition as an independent self-consciousness." The goal of this liberation, out of slavery, cannot be subjugation of the master in turn, which would be merely to repeat the master's "existential impasse," but, rather, elimination of the institution of slavery altogether (53-56).

The Africans at Bois Caïman, given that they were already recursively reproducing their African practical consciousness in the maroon community of Bois Caïman away from the master/slave dialectic of whites neither cared for the master, nor his structuring metaphysics, but instead wanted to be free to exercise their African practical consciousness, which would be precarious, given the possibility of their re-enslavement if captured, if whites and the Affranchis, who also practiced slavery, remained on the island. In essence, the events at Bois Caïman represented an attempt by the Africans to exercise their already determining independent African self-consciousness against the whites and Affranchis's dependent self-consciousness. On the contrary, the liberal Affranchis and the black Americans who would lead the civil rights movement, wanted, given that their very practical consciousness was determined by their relations to, and yearning to be like, their masters, rebelled in order to themselves be "free" masters and not an "independent self-consciousness." In essence, the Affranchis, like their black American counterparts, merely rebelled in order to be like their masters, and sought neither to subjugate the master nor eliminate "the institution of slavery altogether," since their consciousness as slaves was from the onset revealed to them only through the eyes of the master. Hence, the only other consciousness they had, outside of their slave consciousness, "thinghood," was that of the master, whose position they desired, and that of the African masses whose practical consciousness they abhorred. But Boukman, Fatiman, and the other maroon Africans of Bois Caïman had their abhorred African Consciousness, which to revert to. The Affranchis, like their black American counterparts did not. Be that as it may, whereas the former sought to institute a new historical/universal order onto the material resource framework of Haiti by invoking the aid of their loas/lwaes to assist them in rooting out the whites and their gods, the latter, like their black American counterparts, wanted to maintain the status quo, the master/slave relationship by which their practical consciousness was constituted, in a national position of their own.

In other words, black Americans subjectified/objectified in the "Protestant Ethic and the spirit of capitalism" of American society were completely subjectified and subjugated on account of race and class position (Mocombe, 2004). They were subjectified objects, i.e., slaves, things, whose initial practical consciousness prior to their enslavement was used by the master, by presenting the practical consciousness of the slave as backwards and damned within the metaphysics of the master's practical consciousness, against the slave to objectify them as a thing. W.E.B Du Bois, for example, relying on the racial and national ideology of the late nineteenth and early twentieth century theoretically, enframed by Hegel's master/slave dialectic, conceived of the ambivalence that arose in him as a self-conscious thing, as a result of the "class racism" (Étienne Balibar's term) of American society, as a double consciousness: "two souls," "two thoughts," in the Negro whose aim is to merge these two thoughts into one distinct way of being, i.e., to be whole again.

> After the Egyptian and Indian, the Greek and Roman, the Teuton and Mongolian, the Negro is a sort of seventh son, born with a veil, and gifted with second-sight in this American world, —a world which yields him no true self-consciousness, but only lets him see himself through the revelation of the other world. It is a peculiar sensation, this double-consciousness, this sense of always looking at one's self through the eyes of others, of measuring one's soul by the tape of a world that looks on in amused contempt and pity. One ever feels his twoness, —an American, a Negro; two souls, two thoughts, two unreconciled strivings; two warring ideals in one dark body, whose dogged strength alone keeps it from being torn asunder.
>
> The history of the American Negro is the history of this strife, —this longing to attain self conscious manhood, to merge his double self into a better and truer self. In this merging he wishes neither of the older selves to be lost. He would not Africanize America, for America has too much to teach the world and Africa. He would not bleach his Negro soul in a flood of white Americanism, for he knows that Negro blood has a message for the world. He simply wishes to make it possible for a man to be both a Negro and an American, without being cursed and spit upon by his fellows, without having the doors of Opportunity closed roughly in his face. This, then, is the end of his striving: to be a coworker in the kingdom of culture, to escape both death and isolation, to husband and use his best powers and his latent genius (Du Bois, 1995 [1903]: 45-47).

This double-consciousness resulting from his thingness in relation to the master's consciousness, Du Bois alludes to, in this famous passage of his work *The Souls of Black Folk*, is not a metaphor for the racial duality of black American life in America (Mocombe, 2009). Instead, it speaks to Du Bois's, as a black liberal bourgeois Protestant man, ambivalence about the society because it prevents him from exercising, not his initial African practical consciousness which is "looked on in amused contempt and pity," but his true (master) American consciousness because of the society's anti-liberal and discriminatory practices, which made him a thing, i.e., slave. Although over time his "thinghood" forced Du Bois to adopt "pan-African communism" against his early beliefs in liberal bourgeois Protestantism, i.e., his desire to be like the masters, whites (Mocombe, 2009). Du Bois, in this passage, like the many black Americans who would share his class position and liberal bourgeois Protestant worldview, does not want an independent self-consciousness that is not the masters' since the only other consciousness he is familiar with is that of the slaves, but simply wants to be like the collective dependent masters, whites, "without being cursed and spit upon by his fellows, without having the doors of Opportunity closed roughly in his face." His later pan-African communist message simply turns this desire, the attempt to be a master, into a desire to constitute the master/slave dialectic in a national position of his own. But contrary to this later "pan-African communist" message against assimilation for a nationalist position of his own, however, to make themselves whole the majority of black Americans of the civil rights movement, especially, did not yearn for or establish (by averting their gaze away from the eye of power or their white masters) a new independent object formation or totality, based on the initial "message" of their people prior to their encounter with the master, which spoke against racial and class stratification and would have produced heterogeneity into the American capitalist bourgeois world-system; instead, since there was no other "message" but that of the society which turned and represented the "original" African message of their people into inarticulate, animalistic backward gibberish, they (blacks) turned their gaze back upon the eye of power (through protest and success in their endeavors) for recognition as "speaking subjects" of the society seeking not to subjugate the master in a national position of their own but for equality of opportunity, distribution, and recognition with their white counterparts. Power hesitantly responded by allowing some of them (the hybrid modern "other" liberal bourgeois Protestant) to partake in the order of things, which gave rise to the black American identity, the liberal black bourgeoisie or hybrids, which delimits the desired agential moments of the social structure for all blacks (Frazier, 1957; Hare, 1965 [1991]; Woodson, 1933 [1969]; Kardiner, 1962 [1951]).

Thus black American protest as a structurally differentiated "class-in-itself" (subjectified/objectified thing) led by this liberal black bourgeoisie within the American protestant bourgeois master/slave order did not reconstitute American society, but integrated the black subjects, whose ideals and practices (acquired in ideological apparatuses, i.e., schools, law, churches (black and white)), as speaking subjects, were that of the larger society, i.e., the protestant ethic, into its exploitative and oppressive order—an order which promotes a debilitating performance principle actualized through calculating rationality, which may result in economic gain for its own sake for a few predestined individuals. The black American, like the early Du Bois of *the Souls* prior to his conversion to pan-African communism, in a word, became like their masters within the master/slave dialectic, which constituted their historical experiences.

The same can be said for the Affranchis of Haiti, who sought for equality of opportunity, distribution, and recognition with their blanc counterparts at the expense of the agential initiatives of the Bois Caïman African participants, Macaya, Sans Souci, and other Africans of the maroon communities. The Affranchis, like Toussaint, for example, who owned African slaves, rebelled not to eliminate slavery or subjugate the master, but to be a master, like their liberal black American counterparts, through their claim for equality of opportunity, distribution, and recognition. Their slave status only revealed to them the "other" consciousness in the dialectic, i.e., the master consciousness. Therefore, their desire was not to be slaves, who had no other consciousness to look to but that of the newly arrived Africans and the maroon Africans, but masters who enslaved the other slaves, i.e., the newly arrived Africans and the marooned Africans, who were not like themselves. This desire of Toussaint, for example, to be like the master, however, was not the aim of Boukman, Fatiman, and the other participants at Bois Caïman. The former, Affranchis, like their black American counterpart, wanted equality of opportunity and recognition from, and with, their former white masters by recursively organizing and reproducing their (the slave masters) liberal agential moments; the latter, Boukman, Fatiman, and the Africans of Bois Caïman did not. Instead they sought to practice their traditional African ways of life against the purposive-rationality of their former white masters. The slaves at Bois Caïman were already an independent self-consciousness in their maroon communities. The originating Vodou moments of the Revolution was an attempt to get rid of the whites and Affranchis, who desired to be whites, in order that they may recursively organize and reproduce their practical consciousness, not to be like their white masters as Toussaint and the rest of the Affranchis desired. That the Affranchis would come to direct the Revolution after the death of Boukman would give rise to their purposive-rationality, their desire for equality of opportunity, distribution, and recognition within the global capitalist social structure, at the expense of the agential moments of Boukman, Fatiman, and the other participants of Bois Caïman who sought to manifest their self-consciousness onto the stage of history by evoking the aid of their own Gods to fight against the Gods and metaphysics of the whites and Affranchis who had adopted the purposive-rationality of their white masters, which has led to the rise of the "my Nigga Haitian" personality.

Essentially, the Frankfurt school's "Negative Dialectics" represents the means by which the Du Bois of *The Souls*, the majority of liberal bourgeois black Americans, and the Affranchis of Haiti confronted their historical situation. The difference between the "negative dialectics" of Du Bois of *The Souls*, the majority of liberal bourgeois black Americans, the Affranchis, and the discourse or purposive-rationality of the enslaved Africans of Bois Caïman is subtle, but the consequences are enormously obvious. For the Frankfurt school, "[t]o proceed dialectically means to think in contradictions, for the sake of the contradiction once experienced in the thing, and against that contradiction. A contradiction in reality, it is a contradiction against reality" (Adorno, 1973 [1966]: 145). This is the ongoing dialectic they call "Negative Dialectics:"

> Totality is to be opposed by convicting it of nonidentity with itself—of the nonidentity it denies, according to its own concept. Negative dialectics is thus tied to the supreme categories of identitarian philosophy as its point of departure. Thus, too, it remains false according to identitarian logic: it remains the thing against which it is conceived. It must correct itself in its critical course—a course affecting concepts which in negative dialectics are formally treated as if they came "first" for it, too (Adorno, 1973 [1966], pg.147).

This position, as Adorno points out, is problematic in that the identitarian class convicting the totality of which it is apart remains the thing against which it is conceived. As in the case of black Americans and the Affranchis, their "negative dialectics," their awareness of the contradictions of the heteronomous racial capitalist order did not foster a reconstitution of that order but a request that the order rid itself of a particular contradiction and allow their participation in the order, devoid of that particular contradiction, which prevented them from identifying with the totality, i.e., that all men are created equal except the enslaved black American or the mulatto. The end result of this particular protest was in the reconfiguration of society (or the totality) in which those who exercised its reified consciousness, irrespective of skin-color, could partake in its order. In essence, the contradiction, as interpreted by the black Americans, and just the same the Affranchis, was not in the "pure" identity of the heteronomous order, which is reified as reality and existence as such, but in the praxis (as though praxis and structure are distinct) of the individuals, i.e., institutional regulators or power elites, who only allowed the participation of blacks within the order of things because they were "speaking subjects" (i.e., hybrids, who recursively organized and reproduced the agential moments of the social structure) as opposed to "silent natives" (i.e., the enslaved Africans of **Bois Caïman**). And herein rests the problem with attempting to reestablish an order simply based on what appears to be the contradictory practices of a reified consciousness. For in essence the totality is not "opposed by convicting it of nonidentity with itself—of the nonidentity it denies, according to its own concept," but on the contrary, the particular is opposed by the constitutive subjects for not exercising its total identity. In the case of liberal black bourgeois America, the totality, American racial capitalist society, was opposed through a particularity, i.e., racism, which stood against their bourgeois identification with the whole. In such a case, the whole remains superior to its particularity, and it functions as such. The same holds true for the Affranchis of Haiti, but not for Boukman and the other participants of Bois Caïman who went beyond the master/slave dialectic.

In order to go beyond this "mechanical" dichotomy, i.e., whole/part, subject/object, master/slave, universal/particular, society/individual, etc., by which society or more specifically the object formation of modernity up till this point in the human archaeological record has been constituted, so that society can be reconstituted wherein "Being" (Dasein) is nonsubjective and nonobjective, "organic" in the Habermasian sense, it is necessary, as Adorno points out, that the totality (which is not a "thing in itself") be opposed, not however, as he sees it, "by convicting it of nonidentity with itself" as in the case of black America and the Affranchis or mulattoes, but by identifying it as a nonidentity identity that does not have the "natural right" to dictate identity in an absurd world with no inherent meaning or purpose except those which are constructed by social actors operating within a sacred metaphysic. This is not what happened in black America or with the Affranchis or mulattoes of Haiti, but I am suggesting that this is what took place with the participants of Bois Caïman within the eighteenth-century Enlightenment discourse of the whites and Affranchis.

The liberal black American and the Affranchis by identifying with the totality, which Adorno rightly argues is a result of the "universal rule of forms," the idea that "a consciousness that feels impotent, that has lost confidence in its ability to change the institutions and their mental images, will reverse the conflict into identification with the aggressor" (Adorno, 1973 [1966]: 94), reconciled their double consciousness, i.e., the ambivalence that arises as a result of the conflict between subjectivity and forms (objectivity), by becoming "hybrid" Americans or mulattoes desiring to exercise the "pure" identity of the American and French totality and reject the contempt to which they were and are subject. The contradiction of slavery in the face of equality—the totality not identifying with itself—was seen as a manifestation of individual practices, since subjectively they were part of the totality, and not an absurd way of life inherent in the logic of the totality. Hence, their protest was against the practices of the totality, not the totality itself, since that would mean denouncing the consciousness that made them whole. On the contrary, Boukman and the participants at Bois Caïman decentered or "convicted" the totality of French modernity not for not identifying with itself, but as an adverse "sacred-profaned" cultural possibility against their own "God-ordained" possibility (alternative object formation), which they were attempting to exercise in the world. This was the pact the participants of Bois Caïman made with their loas/lwa, Ezili Danto, when they swore to neither allow inequality on the island, nor worship the god's of the whites "who has so often caused us to weep." In fact, according to Haitian folklore, the lwa, Ezili Danto, who embodied Faitman, or Mambo Marinette, joined the participants of Bois Caïman when they initially set-off to burn the plantations, but her tongue was subsequently removed by the other participants so that she would not reveal their secrets should she be captured by the whites. Haiti has never been able to live out this pact the participants of Bois Caïman made to Ezili Danto, given the liberal bourgeois Affranchis's, backed by their former colonizers, America, Canada, and France, claims to positions of economic and political power positions, which have resulted in the passage of modern rules and laws that have caused the majority of the people to weep in dire poverty as wage-laborers in an American dominated Protestant postindustrial capitalist world-system wherein the African masses are constantly being forced via ideological apparatuses such as Protestant missionary churches, for example, to adopt the liberal bourgeois Protestant ethos of the Affranchis and the black Americans.

According to Vodouisants, given Mambo Danto's dual nature (she is both a vengeful fearsome warrior and a faithful mother protector), she punishes the Haitian people with one calamity after another for their failure to fulfill their pact given the inequality that plagues the nation within the contemporary American dominated postindustrial capitalist world-system. Haiti has "been cursed by one thing after the other" not because they "swore a pact to the devil," but because the former enslaved Africans have not instituted the pact they swore to their Gods, loas, at Bois Caïman. The hybrid usurpation of the agential initiative of the originating moments of the Haitian Revolution converted the aims of the revolution to that of the initiative of a small group of mulatto elites and petit-bourgeois blacks, looking to France and America for recognition, who sought, and are seeking, since the constitution of the Haitian Republic, to reconstitute Haiti as a liberal periphery capitalist state by enslaving the African masses as cheap wage-laborers for the corporate elite of the American dominated Protestant capitalist world-system. Hence, in an ironic twist of fate the reinstitution of slavery, wage-labor slavery, on the island following the covenant the participants of Bois Caïman made with Ezili Danto has seen Haiti go from the richest colony under mercantile slave capitalism to the poorest in the Western Hemisphere under slave wage-labor industrial and postindustrial capitalism. The latter processes would give rise to the "my Nigga Haitian" practical consciousness in the Haitian US diaspora.

Following the Haitian Revolution, it would be the struggle between the modes of production, language, ideology, ideological apparatuses, communicative discourse, and the agents of the two systems or structuring structures, the Vodou Ethic and the spirit of communism language game of the Africans of the provinces/mountains and the Catholic/Protestant Ethic and the spirit of capitalism language game of the *Affranchis*, mulatto elites and petit-bourgeois blacks, who were seeking to reproduce the French structuring structure in a national position of their own, which would bring about the great disharmony and imbalance that has plagued Haiti since the death of oungan Jean-Jacques Dessalines October 17th, 1806. Amidst this struggle of system and social integration, a new structurally determined Haitian identity, the my nigga Haitian, which is tied to the black American underclass, would emerge amongst Haitian youth in the US and Haiti. As a result of the displacement of the African/Haitians from their lands in the mountains and provinces of the country and their migration to the capital city, Port-au-Prince, and abroad for capitalist development and a labor supply source for global capital, a new Haitian identity, "the my nigga Haitian," has emerged in Haiti and the Haitian diaspora in America, which is tied to the black practical consciousness of the black American underclass.

As we have seen, interpellated and embourgeoised by the language, ideology, ideological apparatuses, and communicative discourse of the West, i.e., the Protestant Ethic and the spirit of capitalism, the black American in the postindustrial capitalist world-system of America are no longer Africans. Instead, their practical consciousnesses are the product of two identities, the negro, i.e., black bourgeoisie, or African Americans, on the one hand, under the leadership of educated professionals and preachers; and the "my nigga," i.e., the black underclass, on the other hand, under the leadership of street and prison personalities, athletes, and entertainers vying for ideological and linguistic domination of black

America. These two structurally determined social class language games as highlighted in this work were historically constituted by different ideological apparatuses, the church and education on the one hand and the streets, prisons, and the athletic and entertainment industries on the other, of the global capitalist racial-class structure of inequality under American hegemony, which replaced the African ideological apparatuses of Vodou, peristyles, lakous, and agricultural production as found in Haiti. Among Haitian youth in the US diaspora, post-1986 following the topple of Jean-Claude "baby doc" Duvalier, the latter would come to serve as the bearers of ideological and linguistic domination, forming the "my nigga Haitian" identity emerging today in the Haitian-American diaspora and Haiti.

Contemporarily, the continuous struggle between the mulatto merchant/professional class and the black landowning managerial classes for control of the state and its apparatuses, at the expense of the African masses in the provinces and mountains whose children they arm and use against each other as they migrate to Port-au-Prince amidst American neoliberal policies seeking to displace and dislocate the masses off their land for tourism, agro and textile industries, and athletics (basketball and soccer), continues to be a hindrance for the constitution of a sovereign Haitian nation-state. The former two, interpellated and embourgeoised in Western ideological apparatuses, seek to constitute Haiti, with the aid of whites (France, Canada, and America), as an export-oriented periphery state within the capitalist world-system under American hegemony against the desires of the masses of Africans in the provinces and mountains seeking to maintain their *komes*, subsistence agriculture, and husbandry, stemming from the Vodou Ethic and the spirit of communism and the lakou system, which are deemed informal. The *grandon* class, composed of educated professionals, former drug dealers, entertainers, and police officers attack the former Affranchis class, which is now a comprador bourgeoisie (composed of mulattoes, blacks, and Arab merchants) seeking to build, own, and manage hotels and assembly factories producing electronics and clothing for the US market, under the moniker the children of Dessalines against the children of Pétion in the name of the African masses of the island, the majority of whom are peasant farmers interpellated and ounganified by the Vodou Ethic and the spirit of communism. Instead of focusing on vertically integrating the lakou system and infrastructure (artificial lakes, potable water, food security, mache—modern market spaces for *komes*, universities, and state-owned companies for the peasant class to sell, etc.) to augment national agriculture and the productive forces of the latter group, who constitute eighty-five percent of the population, the mulatto elites and petit-bourgeois blacks emphasize job creation through foreign direct investment in tourism, agro and textile industries, unbridled individualism, privatization of public services, infrastructure for an export-oriented economy similar to the one they had under slavery, and the constitution of a political bourgeoisie in control of the state apparatuses. However, their inabilities—given the voting power of the majority—to constitute two dominant rotating political parties to implement the desires of their former colonial slavemasters, leaves Haiti in perpetual turmoil. As in slavery, the African masses continue to fight, against their interpellation, embourgeoisement, and differentiation as wage-earners (commodities) in the tourism trade and textile factories of the Catholic/Protestant Ethic and spirit of capitalism of these two power elites seeking to displace them off their lands and into urban centers of Haiti and elsewhere to facilitate capitalist development. This displacement and dislocation of the African masses of Haiti to urban centers at home and abroad have led to the emergence of new identities amongst them as they scatter throughout the world in search of better opportunities in the face of neoliberal policies on the island. For example, Haitian immigration to the United States most recently has seen the rise of what is more appropriately labeled the "my nigga" Haitian identity, which is tied to the "my nigga" black American underclass consciousness of the inner-cities previously mentioned.

Black American social agency was constituted by and within the dialectic of the American Protestant capitalist social structure of racial-class inequality. Unlike the African Haitians, the children of Sans Souci, no African ideological apparatuses were put in place to reorganize and reproduce an African worldview on the American landscape. The African body, which embodied its initial African practical consciousnesses that were reified in Africa, were thrown in, interpellated by, and socialized (embourgeoised) in new "white" capitalist ideological apparatuses that they would subsequently adopt and reproduce, i.e., the black church, nuclear family, etc., in regards to the politics of their black bodies not an African worldview. That is, their social agency centered on their identification as members of the society who recursively reproduced its ideas and ideals as people with black skin not as Africans with a distinct worldview, social class language game (language, communicative discourse, ideology, ideological apparatuses, and modes of production), from that of their former slavemasters and colonizers. As such, American blacks, as interpellated (workers) and embourgeoised agents of the American dominated global capitalist social structure of inequality, represent the most modern (i.e. embourgeoised) people of color, in terms of their "practical consciousness," in this process of homogenizing social actors as agents of the protestant ethic or disciplined workers working for owners of production in order to obtain economic gain, status, and upward mobility in the larger American society and the world. Whereas, they once occupied the social space as agricultural and industrial workers, the former less educated than the latter, which were much wealthier because of their education and industrial work and therefore made education and industry the means to economic gain and upward economic mobility. Today, they continue to constitute the social space and their practical consciousness in terms of their relation to the means of production in post-industrial capitalist America. This relation, as previously highlighted, differentiates black America for the most part into two status groups, a dwindling middle and upper class (living in suburbia) that numbers about 25 percent of their population (13 percent) and obtain their status as preachers, doctors, athletes, entertainers, lawyers, teachers, and other high-end professional service occupations; and a growing segregated "black underclass" of criminals, unemployed, and under-employed wage-earners occupying poor inner-city communities and schools focused solely on technical skills, multicultural education, athletics, and test-taking for social promotion given the relocation of industrial and manufacturing jobs to poor periphery and semi-periphery countries and the introduction of low-end post-industrial service jobs and a growing informal economy in American urban-cities (Wilson, 1978, 1998; Sennett, 1998). Whereas street and prison personalities, rappers, athletes, and entertainers, many of whom refer to themselves and their compatriots as "my niggas," are the bearers of ideological and linguistic domination for the latter; the former, once called negroes, the black bourgeoisie (E. Franklin Frazier's term), and now African-Americans, is predominantly influenced by preachers and educated professionals as the bearers of ideological and linguistic domination. Both groups share the same ideals and goals, i.e., economic gain, status, and upward social mobility, within the class division and social relations of production of the Protestant capitalist world-system under American hegemony. Therefore, their practical consciousness is neither progressive, nor counter-hegemonic. It is reproductive and structurally differentiated.

However, America's transition to a postindustrial, financialized service, economy beginning in the 1970s, decentered the negro (black bourgeoisie/African American) practical consciousness, and reified and positioned black American "my nigga" underclass ideology and language, hip-hop culture, as a viable means for black American youth to identify with and achieve economic gain, status, and upward economic mobility in the society over education and succeeding academically as emphasized by black bourgeois discourse. Finance capital in the US beginning in the 1970s began investing in entertainment and other service industries where the inner-city language, street, prison, entertainment, and athletic youth culture of black America became both a commodity and the means to economic gain, status, and upward mobility for the black poor in America's postindustrial economy, which subsequently outsourced its industrial work to semi-periphery nations thereby blighting the inner-city communities. Blacks, many of whom migrated to the northern cities from the agricultural south looking for industrial work in the north following the Civil War (1861-1865), became concentrated in blighted communities where work began to disappear, schools were underfunded, and poverty increased. The black migrants, which migrated North with their Black/African-American English Vernacular (BEV/AAEV) from the agricultural South, became segregated sociolinguistic underclass communities, ghettoes, of unemployed laborers looking to illegal, athletic, and entertainment activities (running numbers, pimping, prostitution, drug dealing, robbing, participating in sports, music, etc.) for economic success, status, and upward mobility. Educated in the poorly funded schools of the urban ghettoes, given the process of deindustrialization and the flight of capital to the suburbs, with no work prospects, many black Americans became part of a permanent, BEV/AAEV speaking and poorly educated underclass looking to other activities for economic gain, status, and upward economic mobility. Those who were educated became a part of the social class language game of the Standard-English-speaking black middle class of professionals, i.e., preachers, teachers, doctors, lawyers, etc. (the black bourgeoisie), living in the suburbs, while the uneducated or poorly educated constituted the social class language game of the black underclass of the urban ghettoes where the streets, prisons, athletics, and the entertainment industries became the ideological apparatuses for their socialization. Beginning in the late 1980s, finance capital began commodifying and distributing (via the media industrial complex) the social class language game of the underclass black culture for entertainment in the emerging postindustrial economy of the US over the ideology and language, social class language game, of the black bourgeoisie. Be that as it may, efforts to succeed academically among black Americans, which constituted the ideology and language of the black bourgeoisie, paled in comparison to their efforts to succeed as speakers of Black English, athletes, "gangstas", "playas", and entertainers, which became the ideology and language of the black underclass living in the inner-cities of America. Authentic black American identity became synonymous with black underclass hip-hop ideology and language represented by young athletes and entertainers, LeBron James, Derek Rose, Lil ' Wayne, Jay-Z, Kanye West, Tupac Shakur, Biggie Smalls, etc., over the social class language game of the educated black professional class under the ideological and linguistic domination of black preachers, TD Jakes, Creflo Dollar, Jamal Bryant, Juanita Bynum, etc., and other educated black professionals.

The black underclass in America's ghettoes has slowly become, since the 1980s, with the financialization of hip-hop culture as an art form and entertainment by record labels such as Sony and others, athletics, and the entertainment industry, the bearers of ideological and linguistic domination for the black youth community in America. Their language and worldview as constituted through the streets, prisons, hip-hop culture, athletics and the entertainment industry financed by finance capital, has become the means by which black youth (and youth throughout the world) attempt to recursively reorganize and reproduce their material resource framework against the purposive-rationality of educated black bourgeois or middle-class America. The upper-class of owners and high-level executives of the American dominated capitalist world-system have capitalized on this through the commodification of black "my nigga" underclass culture, which mainstreamed it. This is further supported by an American media and popular culture that glorifies the streets, athletes, entertainers, and the "Bling bling," wealth, diamonds, cars, jewelry, and money. Hence the aim of many young blacks in the society is no longer to seek status, economic gain, and upward mobility through a Protestant Ethic that stresses hard work, diligence, differed gratification, and education; on the contrary, the Protestant ethic in sports, music, instant gratification, illegal activities (drug dealing), and skimming are the dominant means portrayed for their efforts through the entertainment industry financed by post-industrial capital. Schools throughout urban inner cities are no longer seen as means to a professional end in order to obtain economic gain, status, and upward mobility, but obstacles to that end because it delays gratification and is not correlative with the means associated with economic success and upward mobility in black urban America. More black American youth (especially the black male) want to become, football and basketball players, rappers and entertainers, like many of their role models, LeBron James, Derek Rose, Lil ' Wayne, Jay-Z, Kanye West, Tupac Shakur, Biggie Smalls, etc., who were raised in their urban underclass environments and obtained economic gain and upward mobility that way, over doctors, lawyers, engineers, etc., the social functions associated with the status symbol of the black and white middle class (negroes) of the civil rights generation. Hence the end and social action of the larger society remains the same, economic success, status, and upward economic mobility (embourgeoisiement), only the means to that end have shifted with the rise, financed by finance capital, of the black underclass as the bearers of ideological and linguistic domination in black America given the commodification of hip-hop culture and their high visibility in the media and charitable works through basketball and football camps and rap concerts, which reinforce the aforementioned activities as viable professions (means) to wealth and status in the society's postindustrial economy, which focuses on services and entertainment for the world's transnational bourgeois class as the mode of producing surplus-value.

This linguistic and ideological domination and the ends of the power elites (rappers, athletes, gangsters) of the black underclass are juxtaposed against the Protestant Ethic and spirit of capitalism of the educated black middle and upper middles classes represented in the discourse and discursive practices of black American prosperity preachers in the likes of TD Jakes, Creflo Dollar, Jamal Bryant, Juanita Bynum, Eddie Long, etc. who push forth, via the black American church, education and professional jobs as the more viable means to economic gain, status, and upward economic mobility in the society over the street life of the urban ghettoes. Hence, whereas, for agents of the Protestant Ethic in the likes of Jakes, Dollar, Bryant, Bynum, and Long the means to "Bling bling," or the American Dream, is through education, obtaining a professional job, and material wealth as a sign of God's grace, salvation, and blessings. Rapping, hustling, sports, etc., for younger black Americans growing up in inner-cities throughout the US, where industrial work has disappeared, represent the means (not education) to the status position of "Bling bling."

Beginning in the late 1950s Haitians immigrated to the US differentiated within the racial-class socio-culture of Haiti previously highlighted. The first wave of Haitian immigrants to arrive in the US were predominantly your upper-class mulatto elites and members of the black grandon class escaping the Francois "papa-doc" Duvalier regime. They deemed the regime racist as it emphasized Duvalier's noirisme ideology, which highlighted Haiti as a black country that should be ruled by blacks against the mulatto elites who for so long dominated the nation's politics via what is referred to as *politique de doublure* (the politics of having a dark-skinned Haitian as the face of the government while the mulatto elites directed its politics and their racial-class interest) (Du Bois, 2012). Highly educated, upon their arrival to the US, however, they became segregated from the larger mainstream society because of race, language, and culture, and the black American class structure because of language and embourgeoised French culture. Hence, Haitian practical consciousness early on evolved, segregated, by emphasizing the embourgeoised praxis of the mulatto elites and petit-bourgeois black grandon class of the island seeking to reproduce French culture and ideas among their children. In public, they established small businesses catering to the segregated Haitian population, emphasized upward economic mobility, the French language, the Catholic religion, playing a musical instrument, i.e., the piano, and professional education, i.e., law, medicine, and engineering, over the Kreyol language and Vodou religion of the African masses on the island.

Following the fall of the Duvalier regime in 1986, more Haitian immigrants from the provinces and mountains began emigrating from the island to the US escaping the political repression of anti-Jean Bertrand Aristide forces and the American embargo, which sought to get the latter to adopt neoliberal policies, which displaced and dislocated the masses to the capital city, Port-au-Prince, and abroad as laborers for the tourist industry, textile industry, Vodou entertainers for tourists, and athletes. Proselytized by American Protestant missionary forces allowed on the island under the Duvalier regime to provide social welfare to the masses in place of government institutions, many of these recent immigrants to the US were anti-Vodou (given their Protestant indoctrination) and its form of system and social integration, poorer, less educated, Protestant, and Kreyol speaking. Upon their arrival to the US they became segregated in poorer Haitian communities in proximity to the black inner-city communities of the black American underclass as wealthier Haitians had, following the black American bourgeoisie, relocated to the suburbs. In facing the discriminatory effects of the black underclass the practical consciousness of their children became divided between the embourgeoised aspirations of their parents seeking to follow the practical consciousness of the previous immigrant generation and the shifting American postindustrial economy, which began to valorize the practical consciousness of the black underclass as enframed by the athletics industry and "Hip-Hop" culture as means to economic gain, status, and upward mobility in the larger society. As such with the rise of the Haitian rapper Wyclef Jean to prominence in the early 90s, the "my nigga" practical consciousness of the black underclass took hold among young Haitian immigrants who integrated and reproduced elements of it amongst themselves in their own segregated poor communities. Against the embourgeoisement of their parents, they sought economic gain, status, and upward mobility via athletics, hustling, and the entertainment (cultural) industry. Becoming Haitian flag waving, Jesus loving, tattoo-wearing, Vodou hating, and Ebonics speaking Haitians whose only connections to Haiti were and are a broken form of Kreyol synthesized with English, Wyclef, Kodak black (another rapper), zo pound (a Haitian gang that developed in the inner-cities of Miami to protect Haitians who were discriminated against by African Americans), soup joumou (the independence day soup eaten by Haitians on January 1st), griot (fried pork prepared by Haitians), and the annual Haitian flag day festival in Miami held annually on May 18th.

Like many black Americans of the late 1980s and 90s who turned to roots and an Afrocentric culture to combat both the capitalist and materialist pathologies of the black bourgeoisie and underclasses, in response to both the "my nigga" Haitian identity and the French embourgeoisement of earlier generations, the middle-age children of the first generation of Haitian immigrants have begun to return to their Vodou and Kreyol roots in search of an authentic Haitian identity by which to recursively reorganize and reproduce their being-in-the-world. For now, in the age of globalization and post-industrialism, "the my nigga" Haitian identity dominates in the US and is starting to take hold on the island over the latter two.

Notes

1. The debate among historians of slavery has been the extent to which the nature (benevolent and patriarchal or oppressive and cruel) of the slave system, gave rise to black consciousness or identity. On the one hand, you have U.B. Philips, and to a less racist extent Eugene Genovese, Robert Fogel and Stanley Engerman, who argue that the slave system was benevolent and patriarchal, and blacks, given their childlike nature, accommodated to the system, where they were "civilized." On the other hand, E. Franklin Frazier, Kenneth Stampp, John Hope Franklin, Stanley Elkins, among many others, although they bear witness to blacks' accommodation to the system, nonetheless highlight the oppressiveness and brutality of the system and blacks' different forms of resistance to the system. I rather agree with August Meier (1966) that the system was both, and what accounts for the different perspectives are the time frames the historians are studying, the geographical locations, the origins of the Africans, and the plantation owners.
2. Joseph E. Holloway (1990) argues in his essay "The Origins of African-American Culture" that the West African ancestors of African Americans were culturally heterogeneous, which contradicts the cultural homogeneous assumption of many scholars such as Carter G. Woodson (1936), W.E.B. Du Bois (1939), and Lorenzo Turner (1949).
3. Stanley Elkin's *Slavery: a Problem in American Institutional and Intellectual Life* (1959), although somewhat flawed in its understanding of the slave institution through the eyes of the slaves, nonetheless, brilliantly captures the ambivalence between patriarchy and brutality.
4. See E. Franklin Frazier's *Black Bourgeoisie* (1957), Pp. 15.

5. Using a multivariate, locational-attainment approach in place of a segregation-index one, Alba et al (2000) found that "middle-income, suburban African Americans live in neighborhoods with many more whites than do poor, inner-city blacks" (545). Thus, corroborating the widely held position that differences (structural variables—class and status) in education, income and wealth, or property ownership, explain a substantial part of black-white segregation and identity formation (Clark, 1986; Galster, 1988; Wilson, 1987; Allen, 2000).

REFERENCES CITED

Adorno, Theodor W. (2000). *Negative Dialectics*. New York: Continuum.

Allen, Ernest Jr. (2002). "Du Boisian Double Consciousness: The Unsustainable Argument." *The Massachusetts Review*, 43 (2): 217-253.

Allen, Ernest Jr. (1992). "Ever Feeling One's Twoness: 'Double Ideals and 'Double Consciousness' in the Souls of Black Folk." *Critique of Anthropology*, 12 (3): 261-275.

Allen, Richard L. (2001). *The Concept of Self: A Study of Black Identity and Self Esteem*. Detroit: Wayne State University Press.

Alleyne, M. (1980). *Comparative Afro-American*. Ann Arbor: Karoman Press.

—. (1989) *The Roots of Jamaican Culture*. London: Pluto Press.

Althusser, Louis (2001). *Lenin and Philosophy and Other Essays*. New York: Monthly Review Press.

Althusser, Louis and Étienne Balibar (1970). *Reading Capital* (Ben Brewster, Trans.). London: NLB.

Altschuler, Richard (ed.) (1998). *The living Legacy of Marx, Durkheim, and Weber: Applications and Analyses of Classical Sociological Theory by Modern Social Scientists*. New York: Gordian Knot Books.

Appiah, Anthony (1985). "The Uncompleted Argument: Du Bois and the Illusion of Race." *Critical Inquiry*, 12: 21-37.

Aptheker, Herbert (ed.) (1985). *W.E.B. Du Bois Against Racism: Unpublished Essays, Papers, Addresses, 1887-1961*. Amherst: The University of Massachusetts Press.

Archer, Kevin et al (2007). "Locating Globalizations and Cultures." *Globalizations*, 4, 1: 1-14.

Archer, L. (2009) The 'Black' Middle classes and Education: Parents and Young People's Constructions of Identity, Values and Educational Practices. Paper Presented to British Education Research Association (BERA) September. University of Manchester.

Archer, L. (2011) Constructing Minority Ethnic Middle-class identity: An Exploratory Study with Parents, Pupils and Young Professionals. *Sociology* 45 (1): 134-151.

Archer, L. & Francis, B. (2007) *Understanding Minority Ethnic Achievement: Race, Gender, Class and 'Success'*. London: Routledge.

Archer, Margaret S. (1985). "Structuration versus Morphogenesis." In H.J. Helle and S.N. Eisenstadt (Eds.), *Macro-Sociological Theory: Perspectives on Sociological Theory* (Volume 1) (pp. 58-88). United Kingdom: J.W. Arrowsmith Ltd.

Asante, Molefi Kete (1988). *Afrocentricity*. New Jersey: Africa World.

Asante, Molefi K. (1990a). *Kemet, Afrocentricity and Knowledge*. New Jersey: Africa World.

Austin, J.L. (1997). *How to do Things With Words* (Second edition, J.O. Urmson and Marina Sbisà, editors). Cambridge, Massachusetts: Harvard University Press.

Bailey, B.L. (1966). *Jamaican Creole Syntax*. Cambridge: Cambridge University Press.

Baker, Houston A., Jr. (1985). "The Black Man of Culture: W.E.B. Du Bois and The Souls of Black Folk." In William L. Andrews (Ed.), *Critical Essays on W.E.B. Du Bois* (pp.129-139). Boston: G.K. Hall & Co.

Balibar, Etienne & Immanuel Wallerstein (1991 [1988]). *Race, Nation, Class: Ambiguous Identities*. London: Verso.

Ballantine, Jeanne, H. (1993). *The Sociology of Education: A systematic Analysis* (3rd Edition). New Jersey: Prentice Hall.

Barone, C. (2006). Cultural Capital, Ambition and the Explanation of Inequalities in Learning Outcomes: A Comparative Analysis. *Sociology*, 40 (6): 1039–1058.

Barrs, M. and Cork, V. (2001). *The Reader in the Writer: The Links between the Study of Literature and Writing Development at Key Stage 2*. London: Centre for Language in Primary Education.

Barthes, Roland (1972). *Mythologies* (Annette Lavers, Trans.). New York: Hill and Wang.

Bashi, V and Hughes, M. (1997). Globalization and Residential Segregation by 'Race.' *Annuls of the American Academy of Social and Political Science*, 551: 105-20.

Beauvoir, Max (2006). "Herbs and Energy: The Holistic Medical System of the Haitian People." In Bellegarde-Smith, Patrick and Claudine Michel (eds.) *Haitian Vodou: Spirit, Myth, & Reality* (pgs. 112-133). Bloomington, IN: Indiana University Press.

Bellegarde-Smith, Patrick and Claudine Michel (2006). *Haitian Vodou: Spirit, Myth, & Reality*. Bloomington, IN: Indiana University Press.

Bell, Daniel (1985). *The Social Sciences Since the Second World War*. New Brunswick (USA): Transaction Books.

Bell, Bernard W. et al (editors) (1996). *W. E. B. Du Bois on Race and Culture: Philosophy, Politics, and Poetics*. New York and London: Routledge.

Bell, Bernard W. (1996). "Genealogical Shifts in Du Bois's Discourse on Double Consciousness as the Sign of African American Difference." In Bernard W. Bell et al (Eds.), *W.E.B. Du Bois on Race and Culture: Philosophy, Politics, and Poetics* (pp. 87-108). New York and London: Routledge.

Bell, Bernard W. (1985). "W.E.B. Du Bois's Struggle to Reconcile Folk and High Art." In William L. Andrews (Ed.), *Critical Essays on W.E.B. Du Bois* (pp.106-122). Andrews. Boston: G.K. Hall & Co.

Bennett, Lerone (1982). *Before the Mayflower*. Chicago: Johnson Publishing Company.

Bernstein, B. (1971) *Class, Codes and Control*. New York: Schocken Books.

Berthoud, R. (2000) Ethnic Employment Penalties in Britain. *Journal of Ethnic and Migration Studies*. 26 (3): pp. 389-416.

Bhabha, Homi (1995a). "Cultural Diversity and Cultural Differences." In Bill Ashcroft et al (Eds.), *The Post-colonial Studies Reader* (pp. 206-209). London and New York: Routledge.

Bhabha, Homi (1995b). "Signs Taken for Wonders." In Bill Ashcroft et al (Eds.), *The Post-colonial Studies Reader* (pp. 29-35). London and New York: Routledge.

Bhabha, Homi (1994). "Remembering Fanon: Self, Psyche and the Colonial Condition." In Patrick Williams and Laura Chrisman (Eds.), *Colonial Discourse and Post-Colonial Theory A Reader* (pp. 112-123). New York: Columbia University Press.

Bickerton, D. (1975). *Dynamics of a Creole System*. Cambridge: Cambridge University Press.

Billingsley, Andrew (1968). *Black Families in White America*. New Jersey: Prentice Hall.

Billingsley, Andrew (1970). "Black Families and White Social Science." *Journal of Social Issues*, 26, 127-142.

Billingsley, Andrew (1993). *Climbing Jacob's Ladder: The Enduring Legacy of African American Families*. New York: Simon & Schuster.

Bizzell, Patricia and Bruce Herzberg (2001). *The Rhetorical Tradition: Readings from Classical Times to the Present*. Boston: Bedford/St. Martin's.

Blackaby, D.H, Leslie, D.G.& Murphy, :D. (2005) N. C. O'Leary Born in Britain: How Are Native Ethnic Minorities faring in the British Labor Market? *Economic Letters* 88 (3): 370-375.

Blassingame, John W. (1972). *The Slave Community: Plantation Life in the Antebellum South*. New York: Oxford University Press.

Bleich, E. (2003) *Race and Politics in Britain and France: Ideas and Policy-making since the 1960s*. Cambridge: Cambridge University Press.

Boskin, Joseph (1965). "Race Relations in Seventeenth-Century America: The Problem of the Origins of Negro Slavery." In Donald Noel (Ed.), *The Origins of American Slavery and Racism* (pp. 95-105). Ohio: Charles E. Merrill Publishing Co.

Boswell, Terry (1989). "Colonial Empires and the Capitalist World-Economy: A Time Series Analysis of Colonization, 1640-1960." *American Sociological Review*, 54, 180-196.

Bourdieu, Pierre (1984). *Distinction: A Social Critique of the Judgement of Taste* (Richard Nice, Trans.). Cambridge MA: Harvard University Press.

Bourdieu, P. (1986). The Forms of Capital. In J.E. Richardson (Ed.), *Handbook of Theory and Research for the Sociology of Education* (pp. 241–258). Westport: Greenwood Press.

Bourdieu, Pierre (1990). *The Logic of Practice* (Richard Nice, Trans.). Stanford, California: Stanford University Press.

Boxill, Bernard R. (1996). "Du Bois on Cultural Pluralism." In Bell W. Bernard et al (Eds.), *W.E.B. Du Bois on Race and Culture: Philosophy, Politics, and Poetics* (pp. 57-86). New York and London: Routledge.

Brathwaite, E. (1984). *History of the Voice.* London: New Beacon Books

Brecher, Jeremy and Tim Costello (1998). *Global Village or Global Pillage: Economic Reconstruction from the bottom up* (second ed.). Cambridge, Mass.: South End Press.

Brennan, Teresa (1997). "The Two Forms of Consciousness." *Theory Culture & Society*, 14 (4): 89-96.

Broderick, Francis L. (1959). *W.E.B. Du Bois, Negro Leader in a Time of Crisis*. Stanford, California: Stanford University Press.

Brown, C. (1985) *Black and White Britain*. London: Policy Studies Institute.

Bruce, Dickinson D., Jr. (1992). "W.E.B. Du Bois and the Idea of Double Consciousness." *American Literature*, 64: 299-309.

Bryne, D. (2001) *Understanding the Urban*. London: Palgrave.

Buck-Morss, Susan (2009). *Hegel, Haiti, and Universal History*. Pittsburgh: University of Pittsburgh Press.

Bullock Report (1975). *A Language for Life.* London. HMSO.

Byron, M. (1994) Post-war Caribbean Migration to Britain. The Unfinished Cycle. Aldershot: Avebury

Carrington, L.D. (2001). The status of Creole in the Caribbean. In P. Christie (Ed.), *Due Respect: Papers on English and English-Related Creoles in the Caribbean in Honor of Professor Robert Le Page* (pp. 24-36). Mona, Kingston: University of the West Indies Press.

Caws, Peter (1997). *Structuralism: A Philosophy for the Human Sciences.* New York: Humanity Books.

Chanda-Goo, S. (2006) *South Asian Communities; Catalysts for Educational Change.* Stoke-on-Trent: Trentham.

Chase-Dunn, Christopher and Peter Grimes (1995). "World-Systems Analysis." *Annual Review of Sociology*, 21, 387-417.

Chase-Dunn, Christopher and Richard Rubinson (1977). "Toward a Structural Perspective on the World-System." *Politics & Society*, 7: 4, 453-476.

Chase-Dunn, Christopher (1975). "The effects of international economic dependence on development and inequality: A cross-national study." *American Sociological Review*, 40, 720-738.

Chiswick, B. (1978) The effect of Americanization on the Earnings of Foreign Born Men. *Journal of Political Economy*, 86 (5), pp.897-922.

Christie, P. (2003). *Language in Jamaica.* Kingston, Jamaica: Arawak.

Clark, K and Drinkwater, S. (2007) *Ethnic Minorities in the Labor Market: Dynamics and Diversity.* Abingdon: Joseph Rowntree Foundation. Policy Press.

Clark, Robert P. (1997). *The Global Imperative: An Interpretive History of the Spread of Humankind.* Boulder, Colorado: Westview Press.

Clarke, John Henrik, et. al. (eds.) (1970). *Black Titan: W.E.B. Du Bois.* Boston: Beacon Press.

Clark, P. (1988) *Prejudice and Your Child.* Middletown, Connecticut: Wesleyan University Press.

Coard, B. (1971) *How the Education West Indian Child is Made Educationally Subnormal in the British School System: The Scandal of the Black Child in School.* London: New Beacon Books.

Cohen, J. (2002). *Protestantism and Capitalism: The Mechanisms of Influence.* New York: Aldine de Gruyter.

Cole, M. (2011) Racism and Education in the UK and US. Palgrave Macmillan. New York.

Collinson, Diane (1987). *Fifty Major Philosophers: A Reference Guide.* London: Routledge.

Coser, Lewis (1956). *The functions of social conflict.* New York: The Free Press.

Covino, William A. and David A. Jolliffe (1995). *Rhetoric: concepts, definitions, boundaries.* Needham Heights, Massachusetts: Allyn and Bacon.

Cox, C.B. and Boyson, R. (1977) *Black Paper 1977.* London: Temple-Smith.

Craig, D.R. (1976). Bidialectal education: Creole and Standard in the West Indies. *IJSL* 8: 93–134.

Crosley, Reginald O. (2006). "Shadow-Matter Universes in Haitian and Dagara Ontologies: A Comparative Study." In Bellegarde-Smith, Patrick and Claudine Michel (eds.) *Haitian Vodou: Spirit, Myth, & Reality* (pgs. 7-18). Bloomington, IN: Indiana University Press.

Crothers, Charles (2003). "Technical Advances in General Sociological Theory: The Potential Contribution of Post-Structurationist Sociology." *Perspectives*, 26: (3), 3-6.

Crouch, Stanley (1993). "Who are We? Where Did We Come From? Where Are We Going?" In Gerald Early (Ed.), *Lure and Loathing: Essays on Race, Identity, and the Ambivalence of Assimilation* (pp. 80-94). New York: The Penguin Press.

Culler, Jonathan (1976). *Saussure.* Great Britain: Fontana/Collins.

Curtin, Philip D. (1969). *The Atlantic Slave Trade: A Census.* Madison, Wisconsin: The University of Wisconsin Press.

Dahrendorf, Ralf (1959). *Class and Class Conflict in Industrial Society.* Stanford, California: Stanford University Press.

Dayan, Joan (1998). Haiti, History, and the Gods. Berkeley and Los Angeles: University of California Press.

Degler, Carl N. (1972). "Slavery and the Genesis of American Race Prejudice." In Donald Noel (Ed.), *The Origins of American Slavery and Racism* (pp. 59-80). Ohio: Charles E. Merrill Publishing Co.

DeMarco, Joseph P. (1983). *The Social Thought of W.E.B. Du Bois.* Lanham, MD: University Press of America.

Deren, Maya (1972). *The Divine Horsemen: The Voodoo Gods of Haiti.* New York: Delta Publishing Co.

Desmangles, Leslie G. (1992). *The Faces of the Gods: Vodou and Roman Catholicism in Haiti.* Chapel Hill: The University of North Carolina Press.

Devonish, H. (1986). *Language and Liberation: Creole Language Politics in the Caribbean.* London: Karia Press.

Diop, Cheikh A. (1981). *Civilization or Barbarism: An Authentic Anthropology.* New York: Lawrence Hill Books.

Diop, Cheikh A. (1988). *Precolonial Black Africa.* Chicago: Chicago Review Press.

Diop, Cheikh A. (1989). *The African Origin of Civilization: Myth or Reality*. Chicago: Chicago Review Press.

Dogson, E. (1986) *Motherland: West Indian Women to Britain in the 1950s*. London: Heinemann Education Books.

Douglas, M. (1986). *How Institutions Think.* New York: Syracuse University Press.

Drake, St. Claire (1965). "The Social and Economic Status of the Negro in the United States." In Talcott Parsons and Kenneth B. Clark (Eds.), *The Negro American* (pp. 3-46). Boston: Houghton Mifflin Company.

Du Bois, Laurent (2004). *Avengers of the New World: The Story of the Haitian Revolution*. Cambridge, Massachusetts: Harvard University Press.

Du Bois, Laurent (2012). Haiti: The Afterschocks of History. New York: Metropolitan Books.

Du Bois, W.E.B. (1995 [1903]). *The Souls of Black Folk*. New York: Penguin Putnam Inc.

Du Bois, W.E.B. (1984 [1940]). *Dusk of Dawn: An Essay toward an Autobiography of a Race Concept*. New Brunswick and London: Transaction Books.

Du Bois, W.E.B. (1971a [1897]). "The Conservation of Races." In Julius Lester (Ed.), *The Seventh Son: The Thought and Writings of W.E.B. Du Bois* (Volume I) (pp. 176-187). New York: Random House.

Du Bois, W.E.B. (1971b [1935]). "A Negro Nation Within The Nation." In Julius Lester (Ed.), *The Seventh Son: The Thought and Writings of W.E.B. Du Bois* (Volume II) (pp. 399-407). New York: Random House.

Du Bois, W.E.B. (1970 [1939]). *Black Folk, Then and Now: An Essay in the History and Sociology of the Negro Race*. New York: Octagon Books.

Du Bois, W. E. B. (1968). *The Autobiography of W.E.B. Du Bois: A Soliloquy on Viewing My Life from the Last Decade of its First Century*. US: International Publishers Co., Inc.

Du Bois, W.E.B. (1967 [1899]). *The Philadelphia Negro: A Social Study*. New York: Schocken Books.

Dupuy, Alex (1989). *Haiti in the World Economy: Class, Race, and Underdevelopment Since 1700.* Boulder, CO: Westview Press.

Durkheim, Emile (1984 [1893]). *The Division of Labor in Society* (W.D. Halls, Trans.).New York: The Free Press.

Eagleton, Terry (1999). *Marx*. New York: Routledge.

Eagleton, Terry (1991). *Ideology: An Introduction*. London: Verso.

Early, Gerald (ed.) (1993). *Lure and Loathing: Essays on Race, Identity, and the Ambivalence of Assimilation*. New York: The Penguin Press.

Edgar, Andrew and Peter Sedgwick (Eds.) (1999). *Key Concepts in Cultural Theory*. London: Routledge.

Economic and Social Survey (2001). Jamaica: Planning Institute of Jamaica.

Elkins, Stanley (1959). *Slavery: A Problem in American Institutional and Intellectual Life*. Chicago: University of Chicago Press.

Elkins, Stanley M. (1972). "The Dynamics of Unopposed Capitalism." In Donald Noel (Ed.), *The Origins of American Slavery and Racism* (pp. 45-58). Ohio: Charles E. Merrill Publishing Co.

Engels, Frederick (2000 [1884]. *The Origin of the Family, Private Property, and the State*. New York: Pathfinder Press.

Fanon, Frantz (1967). *Black Skin, White Masks* (Charles Lam Markmann, Trans.). New York: Grove Press.

Fanon, Frantz (1963). *The Wretched of the Earth* (Constance Farrington, Trans). New York: Grove Press.

Fick, Carolyn E. (1990). *The Making of Haiti: The Saint Domingue Revolution from Below.* Knoxville, Tennessee: The University of Tennessee Press.

Fleurant, Gerdés (2006). "Vodun, Music, and Society in Haiti: Affirmation and Identity." In Bellegarde-Smith, Patrick and Claudine Michel (eds.) *Haitian Vodou: Spirit, Myth, & Reality* (pgs. 45-57). Bloomington, IN: Indiana University Press.

Fogel, Robert W. (2003). *The Slavery Debates, 1952-1990: A Retrospective*. Baton Rouge: Louisiana State University Press.

Foner, Eric (1988). *Reconstruction: America's Unfinished Revolution 1863-1877.* New York: Harper&Row Publishers.

Foner, Eric (1990). *A Short History of Reconstruction 1863-1877.* New York: Harper & Row Publishers.

Foner, P. (1979) *Jamaica Farewell.* Jamaican Migrants in London: London: Routledge Kegan & Paul.

Foucault, Michel (1977). *Discipline and Punish: The Birth of the Prison* (Alan Sheridan, Trans.). London: Penguin Books.

Franklin, John Hope and Alfred A. Moss Jr. (2000). *From Slavery to Freedom: A History of African Americans* (Eighth Edition). New York: Alfred A. Knopf.

Fraser, Nancy (1997). *Justice Interruptus: Critical Reflections on the "Postsocialist" Condition*. New York & London: Routledge.

Frazier, Franklin E. (1939). *The Negro Family in America*. Chicago: University of Chicago Press.

Frazier, Franklin E. (1957). *Black Bourgeoisie: The Rise of a New Middle Class*. New York: The Free Press.

Frazier, Franklin E. (1968). *The Free Negro Family*. New York: Arno Press and The New York Times.

Freud, Sigmund (1989 [1940]. *An Outline of Psycho-Analysis* (James Strachey, Trans. and Editor). New York: W.W. Norton & Company.

Freud, Sigmund (1989 [1921]. *Group Psychology and the Analysis of the Ego* (James Strachey, Trans. and Editor). New York: W.W. Norton & Company.

Freud, Sigmund (1989 [1917]. *Introductory Lectures on Psycho-Analysis* (James Strachey, Trans. and Editor). New York: W.W. Norton & Company.

Fryer, P. (1984) *Staying Power: The History of Black People in Britain*. London: Pluto Press.

Gadamer, Hans-Georg (2002). *Truth and Method* (Second, Revised Edition, Joel Weinsheimer and Donald G. Marshall, Trans.). New York: Continuum.

Gartman, David (2002). "Bourdieu's Theory of Cultural Change: Explication, Application, Critique." *Sociological Theory* 20 (2): 255-277.

Gates, Henry L. et al. (Eds.) (1997). *The Norton Anthology: African American Literature*. New York: W.W. Norton & Company Inc.

Gates, Henry Louis, Jr. and Cornel West (1996). *The Future of the Race*. New York: Vintage Books.

Gilroy, P. (1990) 'The end of Anti-Racism.' *New Community*. 17 (1): pp. 71-83.

Geertz, Clifford (1973). *The Interpretation of Cultures*. New York: Basic Books.

Geertz, Clifford (2000). *Local Knowledge: Further Essays in Interpretive Anthropology*. New York: Basic Books.

Genovese, Eugene (1974). *Roll, Jordan, Roll*. New York: Pantheon Books.

Geronimus, Arline T. and F. Phillip Thompson. "To Denigrate, Ignore, or Disrupt: Racial Inequality in Health and the Impact of a Policy-induced Breakdown of African American Communities." *Du Bois Review* 1; 2: 247-279.

Giddens, Anthony (1984). *The Constitution of Society: Outline of the Theory of Structuration*. Cambridge: Polity Press.

Gilroy, Paul (1987) *There Ain't no Blacks in the Union Jack: The Cultural Politics of Race and Nation*. London: Routledge

Gilroy, Paul (1993). *The Black Atlantic: Modernity and Double Consciousness*. Cambridge, Massachusetts: Harvard.

Glazer, Nathan and Daniel P. Moynihan (1963). *Beyond the Melting Pot*. Cambridge: Harvard University Press.

Gooding-Williams, Robert (1996). "Outlaw, Appiah, and Du Bois's "The Conservation of Races."" In Bell W. Bernard et al. (Eds.), *W.E.B. Du Bois on Race and Culture: Philosophy, Politics, and Poetics* (pp. 39-56). New York and London: Routledge.

Gramsci, Antonio (1959). *The Modern Prince, and Other Writings*. New York: International Publishers.

Greene, Joshua (2013). *Moral Tribes: Emotion, Reason, and the Gap Between Us and Them*. New York: The Penguin Press.

Greene, M. & Way, N. (2005) Self-Esteem Trajectories among Ethnic Minority Adolescents: A Growth Curve Analysis of the Patterns and Predictors of Change. *Journal of Research on Adolescence*, (15), 151-178.

Grutter v. Bollinger et al, 539 U.S. 02-241 (2003); 13 (Slip Opinion).

Gutiérrez, Ramón A. (2004). "Internal Colonialism: An American Theory of Race." *Du Bois Review*, 1; 2: 281-295.

Gutman, Herbert (1976). *The Black Family in Slavery and Freedom 1750-1925*. New York: Pantheon Books.

Habermas, Jürgen (1987). *The Theory of Communicative Action: Lifeworld and System: A Critique of Functionalist Reason* (Volume 2, Thomas McCarthy, Trans.). Boston: Beacon Press.

Habermas, Jürgen (1984). *The Theory of Communicative Action: Reason and the Rationalization of Society* (Volume 1, Thomas McCarthy, Trans.). Boston: Beacon Press.

Handlin, Oscar and Mary F. Handlin (1972). "The Origins of Negro Slavery." In Donald Noel (Ed.), *The Origins of American Slavery and Racism* (pp. 21-44). Ohio: Charles E. Merrill Publishing Co.

Harding, Vincent (1981). *There is a River: The Black Struggle for Freedom in America*. New York: Harcourt Brace & Company.

Hare, Nathan (1991). *The Black Anglo-Saxons*. Chicago: Third World Press.

Harris, Marvin. (1999). *Theories of culture in postmodern times*. Walnut Creek, California: AltaMira Press.

Harris, David R. and Jeremiah Joseph Sim (2002). "Who is Multiracial? Assessing the Complexity of Lived Race." *American Sociological Review* 67; 4: 614-627.

Heath, A. and Cheung, S. (2006) *Ethnic Penalties in the Labor Market: Employers and Discrimination*. Research report No 341. London: Department of Work and Pensions.

Heath, A. and Yu, S. (2005) *Explaining Ethnic Minority Disadvantage* (pp.187-224). In: Heath, A., Ermisch, J. and Gallie, D. *Understanding social change*. Oxford, Oxford University Press

Hegel, G.W.F. (1977 [1807]). *Phenomenology of Spirit* (A.V. Miller, Trans.). Oxford: Oxford University Press.

Heidegger, Martin (1962 [1927]). *Being and Time*. New York: HarperSanFrancisco.

Helle, H.J. and S.N. Eisenstadt (ed.) (1985). *Macro-Sociological Theory: Perspectives on Sociological Theory* (Volume 1). United Kingdom: J.W. Arrowsmith Ltd.

Helle, H.J. and S.N. Eisenstadt (ed.) (1985). *Micro-Sociological Theory: Perspectives on Sociological Theory* (Volume 2). United Kingdom: J.W. Arrowsmith Ltd.

Herskovits, Melville J. (1958 [1941]). *The Myth of the Negro Past*. Boston: Beacon Press.

Hewitt, R. (1986) *White Talk Black Talk: Inter-Racial Friendship and Communication amongst Adolescents*. Cambridge: Cambridge University Press.

Hiro, D. (1973*) Black British, White British*. Harmondsworth: Penguin.

HMSO (1991) *Aspects of Britain's Ethnic Minorities*. London: H.M.S.O.

Hochschild, Jennifer L. (1984). *The New American Dilemma: Liberal Democracy and School Desegregation*. New Haven: Yale University Press.

Hogue, Lawrence W. (1996). *Race, Modernity, Postmodernity: A look at the History and the Literatures of People of Color Since the 1960s*. Albany: State University of New York Press.

Holloway, Joseph E. (ed.) (1990a). *Africanisms in American Culture*. Bloomington and Indianapolis: Indiana University Press.

Holloway, Joseph E. (1990b). "The Origins of African-American Culture." In Joseph Holloway (Ed.), *Africanisms in American Culture* (19-33). Bloomington and Indianapolis: Indiana University Press.

Holt, Thomas (1990). "The Political Uses of Alienation: W.E.B. Du Bois on Politics, Race, and Culture, 1903-1940." *American Quarterly* 42 (2): 301-323.

Horkheimer, Max and Theodor W. Adorno (2000 [1944]. *Dialectic of Enlightenment* (John Cumming, Trans.). New York: Continuum.

Horne, Gerald (1986). *Black and Red: W.E.B. Du Bois and the Afro-American Response to the Cold War, 1944-1963*. New York: State University of New York Press.

House, James S. (1977). "The Three Faces of Social Psychology." *Sociometry* 40: 161-177.

House, James S. (1981). "Social Structure and Personality." In Morris Rosenberg and Ralph Turner (Eds.), *Sociological Perspectives on Social Psychology* (pp. 525-561). New York: Basic Books.

Hudson, Kenneth and Andrea Coukos (2005). "The Dark Side of the Protestant Ethic: A Comparative Analysis of Welfare Reform." *Sociological Theory* 23 (1): 1-24.

Hunton, Alphaeus w. (1970). "W.E.B. Du Bois: the meaning of his life." In John Henrik Clarke et al (Eds.), *Black Titan: W.E.B. Du Bois* (pp. 131-137). Boston: Beacon Press.

Inkeles, Alex (1959). "Personality and Social Structure." In Robert K. Merton, Leonard Broom, and Leonard S. Cottrell, Jr. (eds.), *Sociology Today* (pp. 249-276). New York: Basic Books.

Inkeles, Alex (1960). "Industrial man: The Relation of Status, Experience, and Value." *American Journal of Sociology* 66: 1-31.

Inkeles, Alex (1969). "Making Men Modern: On the causes and consequences of individual change in six developing countries." *American Journal of Sociology* 75: 208-225.

James, C.L.R., Breitman, G. & Keemer, E. (1980) Fighting Racism in World War 1. New York: Monad Press.

James, CLR (1986). *The Black Jacobins: Toussaint L' Ouverture and the San Domingo* Revolution. Vintage

Jameson, Fredric and Masao Miyoshi (ed.). (1998). *The Cultures of Globalization.* Durham: Duke University Press.

Jones, G.S. (1971). *Outcast London: A Study in the Relationship Between Classes in Victorian Society.* Oxford: Clarendon Press.

Jordan, Winthrop D. (1972). "Modern Tensions and the Origins of American Slavery." In Donald Noel (Ed.), *The Origins of American Slavery and Racism* (pp. 81-94). Ohio: Charles E. Merrill Publishing Co.

Kardiner, Abram and Lionel Ovesey (1962 [1951]. *The Mark of Oppression: Explorations in the Personality of the American Negro.* Meridian Ed. Karenga, Maulana (1993). *Introduction to Black Studies.* California: The University of Sankore Press.

Kellner, Douglas (2002). "Theorizing Globalization." *Sociological Theory*, 20: (3), 285-305.

Kneller, George F. (1964). *Introduction to the Philosophy of Education.* New York: John Wiley & Sons, Inc.

Kuhn, Thomas S. (1996). *The Structure of Scientific Revolutions* (Third Edition). Chicago: The University of Chicago Press.

Laclau, Ernesto and Chantal Mouffe (1985). *Hegemony & Socialist Strategy: Towards a Radical Democratic Politics*. New York and London: Verso.

Layton-Henry, Z. (1984) *The Politics of Race in Britain*. London: Allen & Unwin

Lester, Julius (ed.) (1971). *The Seventh Son: The Thought and Writings of W.E.B. Du Bois* (Volume I). New York: Random House.

Lester, Julius (ed.) (1971). *The Seventh Son: The Thought and Writings of W.E.B. Du Bois* (Volume II). New York: Random House.

Lewis, David Levering (1993). *W.E.B. Du Bois: Biography of a Race 1868-1919*. New York: Henry Holt and Company.

Levine, Lawrence W. (1977). *Black Culture and Black Consciousness: Afro-American Folk Thought from Slavery to Freedom*. New York: Oxford University Press.

Lévi-Strauss, Claude (1963). *Structural Anthropology* (Claire Jacobson and Brooke Schoepf, Trans.). New York: Basic Books.

Lincoln, Eric C. and Lawrence H. Mamiya (1990). *The Black Church in the African American Experience*. Durham and London: Duke University Press.

Lowenthal, D. (1972) *West Indian Societies*. Oxford: Oxford University Press.

Luckmann, Thomas (Ed.) (1978). *Phenomenology and Sociology: Selected Readings*. New York: Penguin Books.

Lukács, Georg (1971). *History and Class Consciousness: Studies in Marxist Dialectics* (Rodney Livingstone, Trans.). Cambridge, Massachusetts: The MIT Press.

Lukács, Georg (2000). *A Defence of History and Class Consciousness: Tailism and the Dialectic* (Esther Leslie, Trans.). London and New York: Verso.

Luscombe, David (1997). *A History of Western Philosophy: Medieval Thought*. Oxford: Oxford University Press.

Lyman, Stanford M. (1997). *Postmodernism and a Sociology of the Absurd and Other Essays on the "Nouvelle Vague" in American Social Science*. Fayetteville: The University of Arkansas Press.

Lyman, Stanford M. and Arthur J. Vidich (1985). *American Sociology: Worldly Rejections of Religion and Their Directions*. New Haven and London: Yale University Press.

Lyman, Stanford M. (1972). *The Black American in Sociological Thought*. New York.

Mageo, Jeannette Marie (1998). *Theorizing Self in Samoa: Emotions, Genders, and Sexualities.* Ann Arbor: The University of Michigan Press.

Massey, D.S., and Denton, N.A. (1993). *American Apartheid: Segregation and the Making of the Underclass.* Cambridge, MA: Harvard University Press.

Marable, Manning (1986). *W.E.B. Du Bois: Black Radical Democrat.* Boston: Twayne Publishers.

Marcuse, Herbert (1964). *One-Dimensional Man.* Boston: Beacon Press.

Marcuse, Herbert (1974). *Eros and Civilization: A Philosophical Inquiry into Freud.* Boston: Beacon Press.

Marshall, Gordon (Ed.) (1998). *A Dictionary of Sociology* (Second edition). Oxford: Oxford University Press.

Martin, R. and Rowthorn, R, (Eds.) (1986) The Geography of Deindustrialization, London: Macmillan.

Marx, Karl and Friedrich Engels (1964). *The Communist Manifesto.* London, England: Penguin Books.

Marx, Karl (1992 [1867]). *Capital: A Critique of Political Economy* (Volume 1, Samuel Moore and Edward Aveling, Trans.). New York: International Publishers.

Marx, Karl (1998 [1845]). *The German Ideology.* New York: Prometheus Books.

Mason, Patrick L. (1996). "Race, Culture, and the Market." *Journal of Black Studies*, 26: 6, 782-808.

Mead, George Herbert (1978 [1910]). "What Social Objects Must Psychology Presuppose." In Thomas Luckmann (Ed.), *Phenomenology and Sociology: Selected Readings* (17-24). New York: Penguin Books.

Meier, August (1963). *Negro Thought in America, 1880-1915: Racial Ideologies in the Age of Booker T. Washington.* Ann Arbor: The University of Michigan Press.

Meier, August and Elliott M. Rudwick (1976 [1966]). *From Plantation to Ghetto; an Interpretive History of American Negroes.* New York: Hill and Wang.

Métraux, Alfred (1958 [1989]). *Voodoo in Haiti.* New York: Pantheon Books.

Michel, Claudine (2006). Of Worlds Seen and Unseen: The Educational Character of Haitian Vodou." In Bellegarde-Smith, Patrick and Claudine Michel (eds.) *Haitian Vodou: Spirit, Myth, & Reality* (pgs. 32-44). Bloomington, IN: Indiana University Press.

McMichael, Philip (2008). *Development and Social Change: A Global Perspective.* Los Angeles, California: Sage Publications.

Milner, D. (1975) *Children and Race*. Harmondsworth: Penguin.

Mirza, H. (2005) The more things change, the more they stay the same: Assessing Black Underachievement 35 years on. In B Richardson. (Ed.) *Tell it like it is. How our School fail Black Children* (pp.111-119). Stoke-on-Trent: Trentham Books.

Mocombe, Paul (2019). *The Theory of Phenomenological Structuralism*. Newcastle upon Tyne, United Kingdom: Cambridge Scholars Publishing.

Mocombe, Paul (2016). *The Vodou Ethic and the Spirit of Communism: The Practical Consciousness of the African People of Haiti*. Maryland: University Press of America.

Mocombe, Paul C. (2017). "Phenomenological Structuralism: A Structurationist Theory of Human Action." *Sociology International Journal*, 1(1): 0005. DOI: 10.15406/sij.2017.01.00005.

Mocombe, Paul C., Carol Tomlin, Cecile Wright (2014). *Race and Class Distinctions Within Black Communities: A Racial Caste in Class*. Routledge Research in Race and Ethnicity (Vol. 9). New York and London: Routledge.

Mocombe, Paul C., Carol Tomlin, and Cecile Wright (2014). "A Racial Caste in Class: Race and Class Distinctions within Black Communities in the United States and United Kingdom." *Race, Gender, & Class*, 21, 3-4: 101-121.

Mocombe, Paul C., Carol Tomlin, and Cecile Wright (2014). "Race and Class Distinctions within Black Communities in the United States and United Kingdom: A Reading in Phenomenological Structuralism." *African and Black Diaspora: An International Journal*,

Mocombe, Paul C., Carol Tomlin, and Victoria Showunmi (2014). "Jesus and the Streets: A Hermeneutical Framework for Understanding the Intraracial Gender Academic Achievement Gap in Black Urban America and the United Kingdom." *Language and Sociocultural Theory*, 1, 2: 125-152.

Mocombe, Paul C., Carol Tomlin, and Cecile Wright (2014). "A Structural Approach to Understanding Black British Caribbean Academic Underachievement in the United Kingdom." *Journal of Social Science for Policy Implications*, 2, 2: 37-58.

Mocombe, Paul C., Carol Tomlin, and Cecile Wright (2013). "Karl Marx, Ludwig Wittgenstein, and Black Underachievement in the United States and United Kingdom." *Diaspora, Indigenous, and Minority Education*, 7, 4: 214-228.

Mocombe, Paul C., Carol Tomlin, and Cecile Wright (2013). "Postindustrial Capitalism, Social Class Language Games, and Black Underachievement in the United States and United Kingdom." *Mind, Culture, and Activity*, 20, 4: 358-371.

Mocombe, Paul C. and Carol Tomlin (2013). *Language, Literacy, and Pedagogy in Postindustrial Societies: The Case of Black Academic Underachievement*. Routledge Research in Education (Vol. 97). New York and London: Routledge.

Mocombe, Paul C. (2012). *Liberal Bourgeois Protestantism: The Metaphysics of Globalization*. Studies in Critical Social Sciences (Vol. 41). Leiden, Netherlands: Brill Publications.

Mocombe, Paul C. and Carol Tomlin (2010). *Oppositional Culture Theory*. Maryland: University Press of America.

Mocombe, Paul C. (2009). *The Liberal Black Protestant Heterosexual Bourgeois Male: From W.E.B. Du Bois to Barack Obama*. Maryland: University Press of America. Mocombe, Paul C. (2008). *The Soulless Souls of Black Folk: A Sociological Reconsideration of Black Consciousness as Du Boisian Double Consciousness*. Maryland: University Press of America.

Model, S. and Fisher, G. (2002) Unions between Blacks and Whites: England and the US Compared. *Ethnic and Racial Studies* 25 (5) pp 728-754.

Modood, T., Berthoud, R., Lakey, J., Nazroo, J., Smith, P., Virdee, S. and Beishon, S. (1997) *Ethnic Minorities in Britain: Diversity and Disadvantage*. Policy Studies Institute, London.

Moore, Jerry D. (1997). *Visions of Culture: An Introduction to Anthropological Theories and Theorists*. Walnut Creek, California: AltaMira Press.

Moynihan, Daniel P. (1965). *The Negro Family*. Washington, D.C.: Office of Planning and Research, US Department of Labor.

Mullard, C. (1982) 'Multiracial Education in Britain: from Assimilation to Cultural Pluralism' in J. (Ed.) (1982) Race, Migration and Schooling. pp.120-33. London: Holt, Rinehart and Winston.

Murray, Charles (1984). *Losing Ground: American Social Policy 1950-1980*. New York: Basic Books.

Murray, R.N. & Gbedemah, G.L (1983) *Foundations of Education in the Caribbean*. London: Hodder & Stoughton.

Myrdal, Gunnar (1944). *An American Dilemma: The Negro Problem and Modern Democracy*. New York: Harper & Row Publishers.

Nash, Gary B. (1972). "Red, White and Black: The Origins of Racism in Colonial America." In Donald Noel (Ed.), *The Origins of American*

Slavery and Racism (pp. 131-152). Ohio: Charles E. Merrill Publishing Co.

Nicholls, David (1979). *From Dessalines to Duvalier: Race, Colour, and National Independence in Haiti*. New Jersey: Rutgers University Press.

Nietzsche, Friedrich (1956). *The Birth of Tragedy* and *The Genealogy of Morals* (Francis Golffing, Trans.). New York: Anchor Books.

Nobles, Wade (1987). *African American Families: Issues, Ideas, and Insights*. Oakland: Black Family Institute.

Noel, Donald L. (Ed.) (1972). *The Origins of American Slavery and Racism*. Columbus, Ohio: Charles E. Merrill Publishing Co.

Noel, Donald L. (1972). "A Theory of the Origins of Ethnic Stratification." In Donald Noel (Ed.), *The Origins of American Slavery and Racism* (pp. 106-127). Ohio: Charles E. Merrill Publishing Co.

Noel, Donald L. (1972). "Slavery and the Rise of Racism." In Donald Noel (Ed.), *The Origins of American Slavery and Racism* (pp. 153-174). Ohio: Charles E. Merrill Publishing Co.

Obeyesekere, Gananath (1997 [1992]). *The Apotheosis of Captain Cook: European Mythmaking in the Pacific*. Hawaii: Bishop Museum Press.

Ortner, Sherry (1984). "Theory in Anthropology Since the Sixties," *Comparative Studies in Society and History* 26: 126-66.

Outlaw, Lucius (1996). "Conserve" Races?: In Defense of W.E.B. Du Bois." In Bernard W. Bell et al (Eds.), *W.E.B. Du Bois on Race and Culture: Philosophy, Politics, and Poetics* (pp. 15-38). New York and London: Routledge.

Parsons, Talcott (1951). *The Social System*. Glencoe, Illinois: Free Press.

Parsons, Talcott (1954). *Essays in Sociological Theory*. Glencoe, Illinois: Free Press.

Parsons, Talcott (1977). *Social Systems and the Evolutions of Action Theory*. New York: Free Press.

Patterson, Orlando (1982). *Slavery and Social Death: A Comparative Study*. Cambridge, Massachusetts: Harvard University Press.

Peach, C. (1968) *West Indian Migration to Britain*: A Social Geography. London: Oxford University Press.

Peach, C. (Ed.) (1996a) *The Ethnic Minority Populations of Great Britain*: Volume 2 of the Ethnicity in the 1991 Census. Office for National Statistics. London: HMSO.

Phillips, U.B. (1918). *American Negro Slavery: A survey of the Supply, Employment, and Control of Negro Labor as Determined by the Plantation Regime*. New York: D. Appleton and Company.

Phillips, U.B. (1963). *Life and Labor in the Old South*. Boston: Little Brown.

Pierre-Louis, Francois (2000). "Decentralization and Democracy in Haiti," paper presented at the International Conference on Democratic Decentralization May 23ʳᵈ-29ᵗʰ, 2000 Kerala, India.

Polanyi, Karl (2001 [1944]). *The Great Transformation: The Political and Economic Origins of Our Time*. Boston: Beacon Press.

Pollard, V. (1994). *Dread Talk: The Language of Rastafari*. Barbados, Jamaica, Trindad and Tobago: Canoe Press.

Power, S., Edwards, T., Whitty, G. & Wigfall, V. (2003) *Education and the Middle Class* Buckingham, Milton Keynes: Open University Press.

Price-Mars, Jean (1928). Ainsi Parla L' Oncle. Port-au-Prince: Imprimeria de Compiégne.

Psathas, George (1989). *Phenomenology and Sociology: Theory and Research*. Washington, D.C.: University Press of America.

Ramsey, Kate (2014). *The Spirits and the Law: Vodou and Power in Haiti*. Chicago: University of Chicago Press.

Rao, Hayagreeva et al (2005). "Border Crossing: Bricolage and the Erosion of Categorical Boundaries in French Gastronomy," *American Sociological Review* 70: 968-991.

Reed, Adolph L. (1997). *W.E.B. Du Bois and American Political Thought: Fabianism and the Color Line*. New York and Oxford: Oxford University Press.

Reyna, Stephen P. (1997). "Theory in Anthropology in the Nineties," *Cultural Dynamics* 9 (3): 325-350

Rex, J. & Moore, R. (1967) *Race, Community & Conflict*. London: Oxford University Press.

Rigaud, Milo (1985). *Secrets of Voodoo*. San Francisco, CA: City Lights Books.

Roediger, David R. (1999). *The Wages of Whiteness: Race and the Making of the American Working Class*. London and New York: Verso.

Rose, Sonya O. (1997). "Class Formation and the Quintessential Worker." In John R. Hall (Ed.), *Reworking Class* (pp. 133-166). Ithaca and London: Cornell University Press.

Rosen, H., and Burgess T. (1980). *Language and Dialects of London School Children*. London: Ward, Lock Educational.

Rosenau, Pauline Marie (1992). *Post-Modernism and the Social Sciences: Insights, Inroads, and Intrusions*. Princeton, New Jersey: Princeton University Press.

Roumain, Jacques S. (1940). "The Southeast and the West Indies." *In Prehistoric Patterns in the New World*, edited by Gordon R. Wiley, 165-72. New York: Viking Fund Publications in Anthropology.

Rubin, Vera (Ed.) (1960). *Caribbean Studies: A Symposium.* Seattle: University of Washington Press.

Sahlins, Marshall (1995a). *How "Natives" Think: About Captain Cook, For Example.* Chicago: University of Chicago Press.

Sahlins, Marshall (1995b). *Historical Metaphors and Mythical Realities.* Ann Arbor: University of Michigan Press.

Sahlins, Marshall (1990). "The Political Economy of Grandeur in Hawaii from 1810-1830." In Emiko Ohnuki-Tierney (Ed.), *Culture through Time: Anthropological Approaches* (pp. 26-56). California: Stanford University Press.

Sahlins, Marshall (1989). "Captain Cook at Hawaii," *The Journal of the Polynesian Society* 98; 4: 371-423.

Sahlins, Marshall (1985). *Islands of History.* Chicago: University of Chicago Press.

Sahlins, Marshall (1982). "The Apotheosis of Captain Cook." In Michel Izard and Pierre Smith (Eds.), *Between Belief and Transgression* (pp. 73-102). Chicago: University of Chicago Press.

Sahlins, Marshall (1976). *Culture and Practical Reason.* Chicago, IL: University of Chicago Press.

Said, Edward (1979). *Orientalism.* New York: Vintage Books.

Sarup, Madan (1993). *An Introductory Guide to Post-Structuralism and Postmodernism* (second edition). Athens: The University of Georgia Press.

Saussure de, Ferdinand (1972 [1916]. *Course in General Linguistics*, Edited by Charles Bally et al. Illinois: Open Court.

Sertima, Ivan V. ([1979] 1989). *They Came Before Columbus.* New York: Random House.

Schutz, Alfred (1978). "Phenomenology and the Social Sciences." In Thomas Luckmann (Ed.), *Phenomenology and Sociology: Selected Readings* (pp. 119-141). New York: Penguin Books.

Schutz, Alfred (1978). "Some Structures of the Life-World." In Thomas Luckmann (Ed.), *Phenomenology and Sociology: Selected Readings* (pp. 257-274). New York: Penguin Books.

Schwalbe, Michael L. (1993). "Goffman Against Postmodernism: Emotion and the Reality of the Self." *Symbolic Interaction* 16(4): 333-350.

Searle, John R. (1997). *The Mystery of Consciousness.* New York: The New York Review of Books.

Sebba, M. (1993). *London Jamaican.* London: Longman.

Sebba, M. (2007) *Caribbean Creoles and Black English*. In D. Britain (Ed.) *Languages in the British Isles: Language in the British Isles*. (pp. 276-292). Cambridge: Cambridge University Press.

Sennett, Richard (1998). *The Corrosion of Character*. New York: W.W. Norton & Company.

Slemon, Stephen (1995). "The Scramble for Post-colonialism." In Bill Ashcroft et al. (Eds.), *The Post-colonial Studies Reader* (pp. 45-52). London and New York: Routledge.

Smedley, Audrey (1999). *Race in North America: Origin and Evolution of a Worldview* (Second edition). Boulder, Colorado: Westview Press.

Smiley Group, Inc. (2006). *The Covenant with Black America*. Chicago: Third World Press.

Smith M.G. (1960). "The African Heritage in the Caribbean." In Vera Rubin (Ed.), *Caribbean Studies: A Symposium* (pp. 34-46). Seattle: University of Washington Press.

Solomon, Robert C. (1988). *A History of Western Philosophy: Continental Philosophy Since 1750, The Rise and Fall of the Self*. Oxford: Oxford University Press.

Sowell, Thomas (1975). *Race and Economics*. New York: David McKay.

Sowell, Thomas (1981). *Ethnic America*. New York: Basic Books.

Spivak, Chakravorty Gayatri (1994 [1988]). "Can the Subaltern Speak?" In Patrick Williams and Laura Chrisma (Eds.), *Colonial Discourse and Post-Colonial Theory A Reader* (pp. 66-111). New York: Columbia University Press.

Stack, Carol B. (1974). *All Our Kin: Strategies for Survival in a Black Community*. New York: Harper & Row Publishers.

Stampp, Kenneth (1967). *The Peculiar Institution*. New York: Alfred Knopf, Inc.

Strand, S. (2012) The White British-Black Caribbean Achievement Gap: Tests, Tiers and Teacher Expectations. *British Educational Research Journal* 28 (1): pp. 75-101.

Staples, Robert (ed.) (1978). *The Black Family: Essays and Studies*. California: Wadsworth Publishing Company.

Stewart, David and Algis Mickunas (1990). *Exploring Phenomenology: A Guide to the Field and its Literature* (Second edition). Athens: Ohio University Press.

Strauss, Claudia and Naomi Quinn (1997). *A Cognitive Theory of Cultural Meaning*. United Kingdom: Cambridge University Press.

Stone, M. (1981) *Education and the Black Child: the Myth of Multicultural Education*. London: Fontana

Stuckey, Sterling (1987). *Slave Culture: Nationalist Theory and the Foundations of Black America*. New York and Oxford: Oxford University Press.

Sturrock, John (ed.) (1979). *Structuralism and Since: From Lévi-Strauss to Derrida*. Oxford: Oxford University Press.

Sudarkasa, Niara (1980). "African and Afro-American Family Structure: A Comparison," The *Black Scholar*, 11: 37-60.

Sudarkasa, Niara (1981). "Interpreting the African Heritage in Afro-American Family Organization." In Harriette P. McAdoo (Ed.), *Black Families*. California: Sage Publications.

Sundquist, Eric J. (ed.) (1996). *The Oxford W.E.B. Du Bois Reader*. New York and Oxford: Oxford University Press.

Sutcliffe, D. (1992). *Systems in Black Language*. Avon, Clevedon: Multilingual Matters.

Swann Report (1985) *Education for all: Report of the Committee of Inquiry into the Education of children from Minority Ethnic Groups*. London: HMSO.

Thomas, Nicholas (1982). "A Cultural Appropriation of History? Sahlins Among the Hawaiians," *Canberra Anthropology* 5; 1: 60-65.

Thompson, E.P. (1964). *The Making of the English Working Class*. New York: Pantheon Books.

Thompson, E.P. (1978). *The Poverty of Theory and Other Essays*. New York: Monthly Review Press.

Tomlin, C. (1988). "Black Preaching Style". MPhil thesis. University of Birmingham, Birmingham.

Tomlin, C. (1999). *Black Language Style in Sacred and Secular Contexts*. Medgar Evers College (CUNY): Caribbean Diaspora Press.

Tomlinson, S. (1984) *Home and School in Multicultural Britain*. London: Batsford.

Tomlinson, S. (2001) Education in a Post-welfare Society. Buckingham: Open University Press.

Tomlinson, S. (2008) *Race & Education: Policy & Politics in Britain*. Maidenhead, Berkshire: Open University Press.

Tomlinson, S. (2011) More Radical Reform (but don't mention race) Gaps and Silences in the Government's Discourse. *Race Equality Teaching* 29 (2): 25-29.

Townsend, H.E.R. (1971) Immigrants in England: The LEA Response: Slough: National Foundation for Educational Research.

Trouillot, Michel-Rolph (1995). *Silencing the Past: Power and the Production of History*. Boston, Massachusetts: Beacon Press.

Troyna, B. (1979) Differential Commitment to Ethnic Identity by Black Youths in Britain. *New Community* (7): 406-414.

Troyna, B. (1993) *Racism and Education: Research Perspectives*. Buckingham: Open University Press.

Troyna, B. Smith, D.I. (Eds.) (1983) *Racism, School and the Labor Market*. Leicester: National Youth Bureau.

Troyna, B. and Carrington, B. (1990) *Education, Racism and Reform*: London: Routledge.

Trudgill, P. (1990). *Sociolinguistics: An Introduction*. Harmondsworth: Penguin.

Tulloch, Hugh (1999). *The Debate on the American Civil War Era*. Manchester: Manchester University Press.

Turner, Ralph H. (1976). "The Real Self: From Institution to Impulse." *American Journal of Sociology* 81: 989-1016.

Turner, Ralph H. (1988). "Personality in Society: Social Psychology's Contribution to Sociology." *Social Psychology Quarterly* 51; 1: 1-10.

Tussman, Joseph and Jacobus TenBroek (1949). "The Equal Protection of the Laws." *California Law Review* 37;3:341-381.

Wallerstein, Immanuel (1982). "The Rise and Future Demise of the World Capitalist System: Concepts for Comparative Analysis." In Hamza Alavi and Teodor Shanin (Eds.), *Introduction to the Sociology of "Developing Societies"* (pp. 29-53). New York: Monthly Review Press.

Walvin, J. (1984) Passage to Britain. Harmondsworth: Penguin.

Walvin, J. (1982) Black Ivory: A History of British Slavery. London: Harper Collins.

Ward, Glenn (1997). *Postmodernism*. London: Hodder & Stoughton Ltd.

Warren, S. and Gillborn, D. (2003). *Race Equality and Education in Birmingham*. London: Education Policy Research Unit, Institute of Education.

Watkins, S. Craig (1998). *Representing: Hip-Hop Culture and the Production of Black Cinema*. Chicago: The University of Chicago Press.

Weber, Max (1958 [1904-1905]). *The Protestant Ethic and the Spirit of Capitalism* (Talcott Parsons, Trans.). New York: Charles Scribner's Sons.

Weinreich, U. (1968). *Language in Contact*. The Hague: Mouton

West, Cornel (1993). *Race Matters*. New York: Vintage Books.

West, David (1996). *An Introduction to Continental Philosophy*. Cambridge: Polity Press.

Williams, Raymond (1977). *Marxism and Literature*. Oxford: Oxford University Press.

Wilson, Kirt H. (1999). "Towards a Discursive Theory of Racial Identity: The Souls of Black Folk as a Response to Nineteenth-Century Biological Determinism." *Western Journal of Communication*, 63 (2): 193-215.

Wilson, William J. (1978). *The Declining Significance of Race: Blacks and Changing American Institutions*. Chicago and London: The University of Chicago Press.

Wilson, William J. (1987). *The Truly Disadvantaged*. Chicago and London: University of Chicago Press.

Winant, Howard (2001). *The World is a Ghetto: Race and Democracy since World War II*. New York: Basic Books.

Winford, D. (1993). *Predication in Caribbean Creoles*. Amsterdam: John Benjamins.

Wittgenstein, Ludwig (2001 [1953]). *Philosophical Investigations* (G.E.M. Anscombe Trans.). Malden, Massachusetts: Blackwell Publishers Ltd.

Wright, Kai (Ed.) (2001). *The African-American Archive: The History of the Black Experience in Documents*. New York: Black Dog & Leventhal Publishers.

Woodson, Carter G. (1969 [1933]). *The Mis-Education of the Negro*. Washington: Associated Publishers Inc.

Youdell, D. (2003) Identity Traps or How Black Students Fail: The Interaction Between Biographical, Sub-cultural and Learner Identities. *British Journal of Sociology of Education* 24 (1): 3-20.

Young, Iris Marion (1994). "Gender as Seriality: Thinking about Women as a Social Collective," *Signs* 19: 713-738.

Zamir, Shamoon (1995). *Dark Voices: W.E.B. Du Bois and American Thought, 1888-1903*. Chicago & London: The University of Chicago Press.

Zeitlin, Irving M. (1990). *Ideology and the development of sociological theory* (4th ed.). Englewood Cliffs, New Jersey: Prentice-Hall.

INDEX